Football and European Iden

Shifting European identities, cultural loyalties and divisions are often expressed more directly through attitudes to our most popular game than in any other arena.

Building on detailed research into original language sources from across Western Europe, from the early twentieth century to the present day, *Football and European Identity* traces the fascinating evolution of football writing in the daily press.

The resulting cross-cultural analysis of national identity in Europe provides the basis for a unique study of the interplay between football, society, politics and the print media, in three parts:

Part I: Old Europe analyses the portrayal of national identity in football writing on England, France, Germany, Italy and Spain.
Part II: Nations within States examines the status of Corsican, Catalonian and Basque identities within French and Spanish football.
Part III: New (Football) Worlds explores the response of Europe's presses to the emergence of Africa, North East Asia and the USA as major forces in world football.

Providing valuable insights into the complex and fluid nature of identity, issues relating to Europeanization, the process of globalization and the rôle of the media in European sport and society, this text should be read by all those with an interest in sport studies, media and communications studies, and Europe.

Liz Crolley is Lecturer in the Business of Football and Communications in the Football Industry Group at the University of Liverpool, UK.

David Hand is Senior Lecturer in French at Manchester Metropolitan University, UK.

Football and European Identity

Historical narratives through the press

Liz Crolley and David Hand

Routledge
Taylor & Francis Group

LONDON AND NEW YORK

First published 2006
by Routledge
2 Park Square, Milton Park, Abingdon, Oxon OX14 4RN

Simultaneously published in the USA and Canada
by Routledge
270 Madison Ave, New York, NY 10016

Routledge is an imprint of the Taylor & Francis Group, an informa business
© 2006 Liz Crolley and David Hand

Typeset in Goudy by Prepress Projects Ltd, Perth, UK

Printed and bound in Great Britain by TJ International Ltd, Padstow, Cornwall

British Library Cataloguing in Publication Data
A catalogue record for this book is available from the British Library

Library of Congress Cataloging in Publication Data
A catalog record has been requested for this book

ISBN10: 0–415–32186–7 (hbk)
ISBN10: 0–415–32187–5 (pbk)
ISBN10: 0–203–29953–1 (ebk)

ISBN13: 978-0-415-32186-0 (hbk)
ISBN13: 978-0-415-32187-7 (pbk)
ISBN13: 978–0-203–29953–1 (ebk)

Dedications

Liz:
For my godson, Mark Cheminais, Becky and Beth

David:
For Edna and Harry

Contents

Acknowledgements

We would like to express our thanks to many people for their help and support offered in a variety of ways: to all at Routledge; to Samantha Grant, for her enthusiasm for the project when it was in its early stages, and Kate Manson, for her patience and sensitive management style while we were in the final stages of writing; to the Department of Languages at Manchester Metropolitan University, the Manchester European Research Institute and the Management School at the University of Liverpool, in particular colleagues from the Football Industry Group, for supporting our work as researchers; to CPEDERF, especially Julia McLaren for research assistance swiftly and efficiently performed; to Ralf Jeutter and Anika Luft for contributing material on Germany; to Elena Teso for perceptive comments on Spain; to all the journalists and newspapers whose contributions in their field have made this project possible; to the British Newspaper Library at Colindale and the John Rylands University Library of Manchester, for research assistance. Finally, we owe a special thanks to John, Hannah and Kathryn for their patience while Mum monopolized the computer.

The authors undertake to have the Woodland Trust (UK) plant new trees to help replenish the stock depleted in the production of this book.

Chapter 1

Introduction

Football and the European press: historical narratives

Football's conquest of Europe was already well under way as the twentieth century dawned. Born in England, the modern game first became professional there in the 1880s. Other countries saw the emergence of professional football somewhat later but precise dates are unreliable since professionalism was generally preceded by a period of unregulated amateurism and semi-professionalism. There was no national organization of football in France, for instance, until 1919, where professionalism was eventually openly recognized in 1932. In Spain, a national league was established in 1927–28 as professionalism became officially accepted. In Italy football turned professional in 1929. In Germany, political changes curtailed the nascent professionalism in the early 1930s and the national professional *Bundesliga* was not established until 1962, despite the foundation of the German FA back in 1900 (Hesse-Lichtenberger 2002: 62). Football, then, was professionalized across Europe at different stages in its development, often reflecting the social, historical and political contexts within which it was played (Wagg 1995) and meeting varying degrees of resistance or indigenization. As the socio-economic value of football (and sport more generally) to Europe increased, so did its coverage in the media. Indeed, such is the attention paid to all aspects of football today (from the coverage of matches on television, radio and newspapers, to pre- and post-match analyses, endless radio phone-ins, text alerts on mobile phones, fans' fora on the Internet and tabloid gossip about footballers' private lives) in the ever-multiplying media available to consumers that commentators talk now of over-saturation. This has not always been the case, however, and in our analysis of the print media in major European football nations over the last century, which is the subject of the present study, we have been able to track the development in terms of the burgeoning attention paid to football in the newspapers in our sample and, more interestingly, its rôle in the construction of national identities.

National identity

Football writing in Europe's daily press cannot be read, understood or interpreted within a cultural vacuum. Each media text is contextualized within its own contemporaneous social, political, economic and ideological environment. Thus, media sport communicates information not only about a given football event but also about its cultural milieu. A snapshot of media sport coverage today, for example, might reveal social attitudes towards racism, fair play, the family, religion, money, drugs or even child abuse, and the values mediated might well differ from one national source of data to another. In November 2004, for example, the reactions to racist chanting in a match between Spain and England in Madrid illustrated the differing attitudes towards racism in those two countries. Part of the information communicated by media sport texts over the last century involves national identities. It has long been recognized that sport can offer an insight into a nation's beliefs and attitudes towards other nations (Blain and Boyle 1998) and a historical exploration of the coverage of football in the print media can enlighten us to how different nations viewed themselves (autotypification) and others (heterotypification) throughout the twentieth century (Blain et al. 1993).

The press takes on the responsibility of transforming a complex and multifaceted reality (the football match and, often, its context) into a readily comprehensible and structurally simple written text (the match report or related article). In doing so, print media discourse employs what Nicholson and Stewart (2003) term 'interpretive frames'. Frames are the principles upon which selection, emphasis and presentation of media material are based. In other words, frames determine what is significant about the reality that is the object of the print media discourse and, crucially, how it is presented. For the purposes of the present study, one of the most important frames to be identified and analysed in print media discourse on football is that of national identity which, in a variety of ways, supplies meanings already familiar to newspaper readers through which they then make sense of the sporting events depicted in football match reports. The events on the football field are interpreted through existing cultural knowledge. It is the contention here that part of this cultural knowledge involves an awareness of the concept of national identity in general and of the specificities of any given nation's identity at a particular point in time. Print media discourse on football satisfies expectations in this respect because it is itself part of the interpretive framework for the communication of ideas around national identity. In short, much can be learned about notions of national identity by examining how this interface between football, society and the print media operates.

We have usually taken the nation-state as our unit of analysis. The national daily newspapers sampled are drawn from England, France and Spain (and, to a much lesser extent, Germany). Most of the territories analysed are also nation-states (e.g. Italy, Germany, Japan), with the obvious exception of the focus of Part II: Nations within States. Keating's definition of the nation-state is useful here and worth quoting extensively:

> [The nation-state] represents the coincidence in space of a number of principles of social and economic organization. It is the primary force of collective identity, reinforced and transmitted through culture and socialization. This collective identity in turn provides the basis for social solidarity. The state

is the framework for internal and external security. It frames an economic system, allowing us to talk of national economies, with definable, if not impermeable boundaries. It is a set of institutions and a mechanism for policy-making. Where the state as an institutional form coincides with the national as a cultural or felt reality, then we can speak of a nation-state.

(Keating 2000: 29)

Though the relationship between nation and state might change (as has clearly happened in Europe over the last century, particularly in multinational or federal states such as the United Kingdom, Spain and Germany), the underlying principle remains intact. Certainly, it is true that the nation-state has evolved significantly as a political and administrative unit since the establishment of football in Europe and has arguably become more sophisticated than ever before. The creation of a devolved parliament in Scotland and assemblies in Wales and Northern Ireland, the elaborate autonomy of the Spanish *Comunidades Autónomas* and recent proposals for a degree of autonomy for the French island of Corsica, for instance, mean that our definitions of nationalism, nation, state and, indeed, national identity need to be flexible and explained carefully. Generally speaking, we can regard the state as involving institutional organization and the nation as cultural belonging. The two concepts do not necessarily overlap. Recent transformations of the state involve the increasing importance of supra-national organizational structures, notably the European Union.

However, taking the nation-state as the basic currency poses challenges. It is increasingly accepted within cross-cultural studies that it is an inadequate unit of comparison as it clearly involves multiple cultures and co-cultures (Livingstone 2003). Since we are examining data over a period of a century, we have chosen it as a relatively 'stable' unit which is convenient, whilst acknowledging that it incorporates a range of cultures, histories and socio-political environments. We have endeavoured to explain some of these complexities where appropriate. Despite trends towards globalization, particularly in the rise of communications that do not rely on national boundaries (such as satellite television and Internet broadcasting), many national phenomena are still explained within the media within national boundaries.

National identity is, above all, a shared identity, an imagined community (Anderson 1983) but also a cultural product. Processes of national identity are 'both unifying and divisive' (Pickering 2001: 89) in that they establish common features that overcome differences within a nation (inclusivity) but also then seek to differentiate that nation from others (exclusivity). As among the strongest producers and consumers of culture, the powerful influence of the media in the communication of national identities cannot be understated. The media form part of a nation's recorded history and act as a conduit for concepts of national identity to be driven becoming 'powerful, heritage-laden collective notions offering shared points of reference that help to bind individuals into a national community' (Crolley and Hand 2002: 8). The long-standing tradition of reading sport as a code for broader national characterization is never more apparent than in football. In this context, the abstract, subjective perception of the nation that lies in the imagination of readers is brought into sharp focus and is articulated as a coherent, almost tangible, homogeneous concept. The print media play a large part in this process. As Hare notes (2003: 120), 'National consciousness and identity is not a once-and-for-all acquisition within a society.' National cultural identity is constructed and reproduced by narratives, notably including images and symbols, which portray shared meanings and values within nationhood. Collective identities of this nature are always provisional, in need of continual reinforcement, and it is in this reinforcement that the press is so often implicated. Football, as mediated – in part – by the press, becomes 'a purveyor of narratives and images of national significance' (ibid. 121).

Though the focus of the present study concerns the definition and transmission of shared national identities, broader issues regarding the concept of nation-state and nationalism also have a bearing on our research. 'It is commonly held in the social sciences that nationalism is a movement aimed at the establishment of a nation-state and that the nation-state is the fundamental unit of the world political order' (Keating 2000: 29). This is also the view of Kedourie (1960) and Hobsbawm (1990), both of whom acknowledge the nineteenth century as the start of the rise in nationalism and recognize its roots as European; hence the huge significance of the conceptual development of the nation to our research as football emerged in Europe and, in particular, international football, which pitted one nation(-state) against another. The vast amount of literature that relates to the creation of nation-states, notions of national identity and nationalism is almost impossible to consume. However, there is a general 'consensus over interpreting the nation as an instrument of historical and political consciousness' (Pérez Garzón 2003) while Hobsbawm (1990) demonstrates the rôle of the national football teams emerging prior to the Great War in helping to consolidate awareness of different national identities, thereby linking football studies with wider cultural issues in European history.

The growth of football journalism

Though the rôle of the press in the social fabric of each country and its development in coverage of football might vary slightly, its continual expansion throughout the period is consistent, and English, French and Spanish newspapers in particular share similar patterns in terms of subject content, which developed from briefing the reader with raw facts in the early parts of the twentieth century to more speculative debate over team selection (but still directly match-related debate), then engaging in increasingly creative prose moving from description-based to interpretative journalism, with interests in all aspects of football from serious business, financial or social perspectives to trivia and tittle-tattle. Inevitably, and across our entire sample, there is more material available in later years than earlier. Coverage of football in the newspapers in our sample at the start of the century was much thinner than that of a hundred years later. By way of example, the entirety of the report of France's first ever home international is provided below to be contrasted with the extensive football writing that now exists in 'quality' daily newspapers across the European continent:

> Yesterday's match between France and Switzerland was highly entertaining and the large crowd at the Parc des Princes saw a good game. The French won by one goal to nil thanks to a fine shot by Cyprès and the good game played by the keeper, Guichard. It can be said, though, that the two teams were equally matched and both played admirably.
>
> (*Le Matin*, 13 February 1905)

In England, sport was at the margins of the 'quality' press in the early nineteenth century when editors for *The Times*, for instance, were highly selective over which sporting events were deemed to be appropriate to their readership and it was left to a separate sporting press to emerge. Horse-racing set the pace for other sports and the interests of gamblers provided the commercial impetus for the publication of *Sporting Life* (1859 onwards). From the 1870s onwards, a wave of 'middle-class' enthusiasm for sport was responsible for the materialization of other sporting publications designed to address the interest in sport of the 'middle classes', emphasizing the physical and spiritual virtues of sport (Boyle and Haynes 2000: 26). During this period, the pressure was increasing for the general daily press to include sport in their editions as well. Coverage of football at the start of the twentieth century (still under its more formal title of 'Association Football' in order to distinguish it from 'Rugby Football') became the norm rather than an oddity in the sports pages of the 'quality' press. It generally consisted of short paragraphs, relating factual information or the condition of the pitch and in early reports where there was more lengthy prose (such as on an FA Cup final) the reader had to plough through the entire article to find out the result (it was not until the late 1950s that results were actually displayed prominently in the lead to the article). Photographs were an important step for football coverage and *The Times* comments enviously on Spain's impressive array of photographs accompanying their match reports in the mid-1950s (*The Times*, 9 May 1955). The advent of competing media coverage of football (radio in the 1930s and television as a serious force by the mid-1950s) stimulated a thrust in the extent and quality of football coverage in the print media. This was accompanied by a new era of specialized football correspondents who came onto the scene in the 1950s and 1960s (for example, Geoffrey Green and Brian Glanville) and helped raise the standard of sports journalism as well as broaden its remit to offer fresh perspectives beyond the purely sporting into the realms of the political, financial and social aspects of the game. By the time England hosted the 1966 World Cup, coverage of football in the English print media was already extensive and has flourished ever since.

In France in the early 1900s, writers in *Le Vélo*, *L'Auto* and *L'Echo des sports* maintained an elitist conception of sport and largely ignored football (Wahl 1989:

57). Before the Great War, the press favoured rugby as this was the game played by editors and journalists: *L'Auto*, for example, often gave over its front page to rugby but, prior to 1914, never once to football (ibid. 129), despite the fact that even in the 1900s there were over 350 registered football clubs in France and only about 140 rugby clubs (Hare 2003: 17). It was during the inter-war years that 'football and sport in general appear en masse in the pages of general newspapers' (Berthou 1999: 9), although football still generally played second fiddle to cycling, rugby and even motor sports (ibid. 11). The growing importance of football in France is demonstrated via the appearance of its own specialist press: *Football* (a weekly publication, founded in 1910), *Football et Sports athlétiques* (1909, bi-weekly) and *France Football*, which was founded in 1923 and still exists today as a bi-weekly (Berthou 1999: 9; Wahl 1989: 352). The much renowned sports daily, *L'Equipe*, is a relatively late arrival on the scene, first appearing in 1946.

Following the advent of professionalism in 1932, the French press devotes increasingly more column space to football (Wahl 1989: 314) but *L'Auto*, for instance, did not cover the first ever matches played in the professional league, preferring instead to cover the Italian Grand Prix (Berthou 1999: 11). Albert (1990: 163) notes how the French press of the inter-war years had to respond to new imperatives driving their content, which had to be adapted to the developing interests of the readers: interests in travel, cinema, radio and, of course, sport. One way of responding to the changing economic environment was to increase the typical pagination of a daily, well into double figures by the late 1930s. Another innovation was to increase the use of photo journalism. *Le Matin* had pioneered the use of the action shot to accompany match reports in the 1920s and this feature of football writing became even more prevalent after the Second World War (as it did in England and Spain). This early twentieth-century period is regarded by Charle (2004) as the golden age of the French press. At that time, France led the world in terms of circulation figures and the quality of its journalism. The economic difficulties of the inter-war years, coupled with the rise of competitor media (radio, cinema newsreel and, eventually, television) led to a decline in the fortunes of the national daily press from which it has never really recovered. However, the diffusion of the sports press was still significant and by the late 1950s and early 1960s, according to Seidler (1964: 10), 'France is one of the countries in which the importance of the sports press is greatest.'

The 1980s mark something of a sea change in attitudes to football in France as attention paid to the sport continued to grow in the 'quality' daily press. True, one journalist in *Le Monde* may lament the 'obsession' with the game, 'the tyranny of the high mass that is football' and the 'curious' nature of 'a planet where anything not to do with football is so readily forgotten [and] relegated to the background' during major tournaments (3 July 1982). Another, however, may equally well draw attention to football's qualities and its capacity to generate good copy. Football is like good theatre and outstrips in its importance other cultural phenomena such as music. It might exalt aggressive 'male, warlike values' but it does so 'in an acceptable way' in which 'players become symbolic warriors . . . patriots of their club, town or country'. Crucially from the perspective of the present volume, football's success, the article continues, is due to the fact that it has gradually taken over the rôle of representing the collective that used to be the domain of religion and the military to the extent that the heroes of the day are now footballers. Both the process and the end product are more than worthy of attention in the press and it is right that football commands the space it does in newspapers (*Le Monde*, 4 July 1982). By the 1980s, even the somewhat staid *Le Monde* was also, occasionally, using photographs to illustrate its football match reports and its coverage of the 1986 World Cup finals in Mexico stretched to at least one full page a day, signifying a significant step up in coverage from previous tournaments.

In Spain, the first coverage of sport was published in the generalist press towards the end of the nineteenth century. However, specialist sport publications were already in circulation. Altabella (1987) claims that *El Cazador*, edited in Barcelona in 1856/57, was the first such publication in Spain. *El Mundo Deportivo* is the oldest surviving sports paper, also printed in Barcelona. Founded in 1906 as a weekly, it became a daily paper in 1929. In actual fact, the first daily publication was *Excelsior*, edited in Bilbao between 1924 and 1931. For those Spaniards with an interest in sport, four main sources of information existed at this time: generalist dailies, specialist dailies, the *Hojas del lunes* (special Monday editions) and magazines dedicated usually to individual sports (Jones and Baró i Queralt 1996: 28). Indeed, though there were still few newspapers with a national circulation, the period between 1910 and 1920 – a period of increased leisure time and development of mass media – was something of a boom period for the sports press in Catalunya, when some 30 specialized titles were founded covering a range of sports. Jones and Baró i Queralt (1996: 42) note the strong Catalan nationalist leanings of some of these publications. Many were short-lived and few survived the Civil War (1936–39) when little sport was played and paper was a scarce commodity anyway.

The amount of sport coverage in the Spanish national press expanded slowly during the first half of the twentieth century and, as a market for football was identified, the space devoted to football increased. By 1925, football was the main sport covered in the generalist press with the exception of bullfighting, which still enjoyed a relatively high level of publicity. Unless it was the bullfighting season, main features and articles on the sports pages were by the 1930s usually football related. It had become '*el deporte rey*' (literally, 'the king of sports'). Nevertheless, coverage was still sparse and was frequently limited to dry factual data regarding team selections.

Today, *Marca* leads the market in Spain's daily print media as the best-selling daily sports publication, accounting for over 60 per cent of sales among the sports press (followed by *As*, *Sport* and *El Mundo Deportivo*). Established in 1938 in San Sebastián, *Marca* transferred its activities to Madrid in 1942 and generally vies with *El País* as the most widely read daily publication in Spain. Today, daily newspapers devote around 7–10 per cent of the total column inches to sport and, as in England and, latterly, France, often include extra supplements during the FIFA

World Cup and UEFA European Championship tournaments. Of their sports coverage, 70–80 per cent is dedicated to football.

In all the countries studied here, writing styles and language employed have evolved and, while we will inevitably encounter lazy, clichéd short-cuts to present many a stereotyped image in the chapters that follow, we have also enjoyed the pleasure of wallowing in pages and pages of rich, thought-provoking, ludic, entertaining prose and, at times, perceptive journalism.

Media sport is a product created for consumers who, when offered a growing variety of sources for their diversion, are increasingly discerning in their choices. There is no place in today's 'quality' print media for a poor product. For this reason, we should beware in the course of our research. Primary consideration rests with remembering the ultimate goal of football writing: to sell newspapers. Papers must sell by entertaining and informing and, therefore, offer the readers what they want, or what the editors believe they want. This should be borne in mind throughout the following presentation of our findings.

Methodology

Our methodology has involved the structural analysis of print media texts (which relates to their surface meaning but also requires an understanding of the underlying meaning of, for example, the lexis and imagery employed) as well as a contextual analysis of the social, political and historical environment in which the newspaper texts were produced, consumed and decoded. We understand that the media are not simply passive reproducers of existing social attitudes but are rather co-producers as they play a part in the creation and recycling of societal beliefs. The media create images anew with each textual (re)presentation but necessarily build upon an already existing framework. Their rôle in the production of identity is, therefore, semi-autonomous.

England, France, Italy, Germany, Spain, Africa, the USA and North East Asia form the focus of our study and, for professional and research expertise reasons, we have examined in considerable depth football writing in three of these countries in particular: England, France and Spain. Our broad aim is to explore the notions of national identities in major European football nations during the twentieth century. Within this synoptic aim, we seek to provide an understanding of both the country in which the report was written and the nation scrutinized by the writer.

Many methodological challenges face researchers of cross-national and cross-cultural media consumption. Which countries to compare? Which newspapers to examine and which to exclude? How to choose our sample? How can we identify culture-specific assumptions? Or distinctive aspects of national culture? Theoretical challenges, methodological concerns and practical difficulties in gathering data should not, however, prohibit our attempting to achieve certain aims. Perhaps foolishly, we were not deterred by the apparently impossible task of undertaking extensive cross-cultural research in a dataset one hundred years in the making. Our approach needed to be innovative.

Ideally, we would be able to examine national newspapers from each country with similar profiles in terms of readership, political leanings, geographic distribution throughout the nation-state and longevity. In reality, not only does our sample provide uneven distribution of football coverage, with publications coming and going, but we are faced with countries where the print media occupy different places in the national psyche (and even change their social function during the course of the twentieth century) and where professional football also developed at different times and in diverse social and political contexts. We have, therefore, drawn our data from a number of 'quality' daily newspapers that act as representative samples of the European press. The principal newspapers exploited in our sample were *The Times* and *The Guardian* in England, *Le Monde*, *Libération*, *Le Figaro*, *Le Temps* and *Le Matin* in France, and *ABC* and *El País* in Spain. Since relevant dates were not always available (for example, there are missing editions of *ABC* in Spain in the 1920s), we have occasionally drawn from sources not included in our original proposal.

Daily newspapers form an integral part of society in the United Kingdom, where sales reach around 12 million (though the popular and middle markets – the tabloids, *The Sun*, *The Daily Mail* and *The Daily Express* – account for around 75–80 per cent of this total [ABC Figures 2006]). Our main source of data for England was *The Times*. This is the UK's oldest national newspaper still printed today, with a daily circulation of around 670,000, representing a market share of 5.6 per cent. It is generally sympathetic to right-wing ideology and politics. We also drew some examples from *The Guardian*. *The Guardian* is a left-of-centre publication which has a circulation of just under 400,000, a market share of around 3.2 per cent. We avoided the alluring temptation to draw on the 'tabloid' or popular press. Though this would undoubtedly have proven a rich source of data for our English sample, it would have presented insurmountable obstacles in terms of cross-cultural comparisons as neither France nor Spain enjoy tabloids in the same way or to the same extent as their English neighbours. A research opportunity awaits, therefore, for a thorough study to be undertaken of the tabloids in England.

In France, *Le Monde*, founded in 1944, is 'The newspaper of reference, read by French political, economic and intellectual elites' (Hare 2003: 7) and by the end of the twentieth century it had established itself as the best-read daily in France (occasionally toppled in this respect by the sports daily *L'Equipe*). It is a serious publication with a staid reputation, not averse, for example, to using footnotes in football match reports right into the late twentieth century. *Le Figaro* is France's oldest daily. Founded in 1866 (and still in existence today), it is right-wing and highly influential. Its circulation increased from around 100,000 in the mid-1930s (Albert 1979: 65–7), peaking at 400,000 copies in the mid-1980s (Michaud and Kimmel 1996: 219). *Libération* is a relative newcomer to the French market, having been in circulation since 1971. Originally, a left-wing protest daily, it now holds a place in the top five French dailies and has retained a circulation of about 140,000 copies since the mid-1980s (Michaud and Kimmel 1996: 219; OJD 2005). *Le Matin* was one of the five main daily publications in France in the pre-Second

World War years. This right-wing publication was printed between 1884 and 1944. Its circulation slipped to about 300,000 copies by 1939 from its peak of around 600,000 in its heyday in the mid-1920s (Albert 1974: 96–7). Finally, *Le Temps* was a centre-right publication, in circulation between 1862 and 1942. It was regarded as a worthy quality daily with about 90,000 copies sold in the mid-1920s, dropping to around 60,000 by the eve of the Second World War (Albert 1979: 62, 67).

Over 100 daily publications are now printed in Spain (where there is no equivalent to the British tabloid press) but few have a circulation of more than 100,000. Daily sales total just 4.2 million but this hides the much higher estimated readership of around 12 million, according to the Spanish Association of Daily Newspaper Editors (AEDE), (quoted in *El País*, 14 December 2005; readership figures are, of course, higher than circulation figures). Spain's total readership is fairly low compared to many of its European neighbours. Founded in 1903, *ABC* became a daily publication in 1905. It has a right-wing leaning, enjoys a circulation of around 277,000 and sees itself as the old boys of Madrid journalism. Traditionally, it was a staunch supporter of the monarchy and then of General Franco's regime. Now, it claims to be independent, though it has been a consistent supporter of the right-wing Popular Party, advocating the politics of a modern, reformist and European centre-right. *El País* is the Spanish newspaper with the highest circulation, of around 470,000, and is influential with an estimated readership of over 2 million. The first publication was in 1976 as Spain was setting off on its journey towards democracy. It advocates social and political change and claims to symbolize the modern Spain within a European vocation.

Of course, we have not been able to consult every word of every football-related article in each country analysed. Selecting samples was a challenge, and here we acknowledge a level of subjectivism in our judgement, which is, therefore, open to debate. There are many ways in which we might have chosen to go about this phase of our work. However, the task was simplified somewhat by the availability (or unavailability) of material. We were inevitably controlled to some extent by the data – and that included the football fixtures themselves. Particularly in the first half of the century, we were much more likely to find a Spanish match report about England, for example, when the two countries actually played each other. Additionally, we would expect to find coverage of a team in other countries when that team is involved in – or better still wins – a major tournament.

Inevitably, the amount of data we have to work with varies enormously from one era to another and, though to a lesser extent, from one country to another. Prior to the 1930s, many match reports were short and comments were brief. It was not unusual for just the results of matches to be reported, perhaps with team selections. In Spain, it was not unusual for just the results of matches played in Madrid to be noted (hence the propensity for some to accuse the Spanish press of Madrid bias). Our task was not, then, simply to compare isolated bits of data in several countries. Rather, it involved understanding how 'systematic context' (Blumler *et al.* 1992) might have shaped the production of the football writing. Consequently, a newspaper report of an international football match might take the form of an article on the world of sport but its content is inextricably linked with wider psychological, cultural and ideological processes that provide information about the nations whose representatives are participating in the match. Football is in this way frequently appropriated to communicate information about national and cultural identities. It is said to be indexical in that it is used to represent perceived national characteristics about which it apparently presents direct evidence. This evidence, the media text itself, for all its passage through the prism of the press, is usually grounded in objective realities and it will, therefore, be useful to highlight its origins in political, cultural and economic developments outside football in society as a whole.

The authors are responsible for all translations from primary foreign sources. We have adhered as closely as possible to the nuances of the original text but, on occasions, these need to be paraphrased and explained. In terms of style, we have not modernized the expression or punctuation; hence, at times, quotations might sound odd to the modern-day ear in terms of vocabulary and syntax. Similarly, we have also kept the original use of capitalization within quotations, which, again, might not always be consistent with common practice today.

From there, we take a leap as we analyse football writing and attempt to interpret its contribution to international understanding. Our achievement is less a cross-national comparison of the ways in which national identities are mediated than an exploration of how and why identities are mediated in each context. Identification of similarities and differences in portrayals of national identities – generally considered a principle objective of cross-cultural research – was, therefore, not a primary objective of the research, though certain features clearly emerged in our analysis.

We cannot, of course, claim that our interpretations are the only possible understanding of the print media texts in question. Hall's model of encoding–decoding audiences theorized the range of possibilities for text interpretation, though emphasizing the determining influences of the discourse itself (1980). In an era in which the globalization of communications is under the spotlight, researchers with an interest in language are encouraged to address the cross-cultural dimension to products and audiences (Tomlinson 1999). We can only hypothesize, in an educated way, about both the writer's intent and the reader's understanding of the text, taking into consideration the context of the discourse.

Styles of play

Considering the development of national styles of play in football during the first half of the twentieth century, El País notes, 'If style makes the man, then style also makes the team. Years go by, generations of players, but the teams play the same, true to a style that was established, no one knows why, dozens of years ago and inevitably repeats itself. . . . It is difficult to explain why this happens, but the fact is that it does happen, as though there were some genetic reason for players from each of the great football nations of the world to interpret the game in the same way throughout their history' (18 June 1986). We are going to analyse the extent to which this is true and look at the rôle of the print media in the process. In this respect, Lanfranchi provides a starting point for the analysis: 'the observation of national styles in football is itself interesting. A national side is much more than a team of 11 players, it is the symbolic representation of one nation against another nation for 90 minutes. And each of the two teams owes it to itself to represent the qualities that the population recognizes in them. . . . Italians and Spaniards will be very skilful but deceitful and not strong enough while African teams demonstrate a natural talent branded with a childlike naïvety. The Germans on the other hand are tough, efficient, calculating and unspectacular but are rarely absent when it matters, while the English are stoic, phlegmatic but also predictable' (2002: 20). In terms of the styles of play, Dietschy (2005) claims that international styles were discovered at the 1934 World Cup and summarized by the French artist Ben in a series of drawings. Of Italy, for example, he claimed that 'Italian football was assimilated to a political style. It is true that *Calcio* played the fascist way won the World Championship in 1934 in front of Mussolini himself.' As well as commenting on Latin American and Eastern European national styles, he recognized the 'fighting spirit' of the English and that it was the 'strong and powerful game' adopted by Germany in the mid-1930s that ultimately led to their World Cup victory in 1954. In short, 'each style of play transmits an unshakeable national identity' and, as such, football is an expression of a specific culture albeit in an increasingly global setting. Martialay (2000) believes that the roots of the Spanish national style of play pre-date even the 1930s, though, and explains how Spain's performance in the 1920 Olympic Games in Belgium led to their distinctive national style. Finally, according to *The Times*, in football, the relationship between nationality and style of play is co-dependent: 'National characteristics determine the choice of style' (*The Times*, 13 July 1982). Despite all of these assertions, it is precisely one of the principal tasks of the present study to discover whether these national identities are truly immutable, at least in the sense that they are communicated by football writing, or they evolve over time.

The mediation of different playing styles (perceived as representative of national identities) constitutes a debate, a battle between discourses, a conflict regarding the correct interpretation of the essence of football itself (good, bad, entertaining, boring and so on). Larsen (2001: 59–60) usefully identifies three levels within which the concept of football playing style operates (Table 1). First, there is the strategy or philosophy, the preferred playing style. This is influenced by various socio-cultural factors potentially reflecting *inter alia* class, tradition, history, identity as well as the team's, coach's and players' own aspirations. So, both conscious and subconscious factors determine how any team should play. Second, there are the tactics, the specific principles and team formations chosen for a given match, which involve the conscious selection of players with certain abilities and the delineation of specific rôles. The third level derives from the match itself and represents the realization of the tactics and strategy outlined in potential in the first two levels. At this level, the actions of opponents and, indeed, the match

Table 1 Conceptual model of playing styles

Level 1	Level 2	Level 3
Socio-cultural factors	Consideration for the principles of play	Action/reaction
Subconscious and conscious factors	Formation + players' capacities and skills + rôles of players	Own team + action/reaction opponents + referee
=	=	=
Strategy or philosophy	Chosen team tactics	Configuration of the match/match climate/playing style in situ

Source: Larsen 2001: 59.

officials (not to mention Lady Luck) all influence the way a team performs in the match situation. This actual playing style may or may not be close to the original intention.

Such a conceptual model allows the complex notion of playing style to be studied from a variety of perspectives. The present study will examine the way in which 'quality' daily newspaper press reports of given matches (that is ostensibly focusing on level 3) constantly and consistently link the action they describe with concepts of playing style deriving from level 1 frameworks and, in particular, with those dealing with national identity, history and tradition. Our analysis reveals an overwhelming level of national stereotyping in terms of playing style. However, there were almost as many examples of cases where the reality did not match expectations based on national stereotyping; where level 2 and 3 frameworks are inconsistent with the expected strategy in level 1. In one way or the other, 'quality' daily newspaper reports seem bound always to refer consideration of level 3 events (the match as it unfolds) to the interpretive framework provided by level 2 choices and especially level 1 factors. It is the way in which this is done, most notably via the linguistic techniques deployed by print media discourse reporting on football, typically imaginative metaphors, playful similes and emotive vocabulary, that is the prime object of study in the present volume.

Structure of the book

The book is divided into three sections: Old Europe, Nations within States, and New (Football) Worlds. In Part I (Old Europe), the ways in which the national identities of the principal European football nations of England, France, Italy, Germany and Spain are portrayed in print media discourse on football are analysed from the perspective of both autotypification (or self-image) and heterotypification (imagining the other). Part II examines the extent to which Nations within States – Corsica, Catalonia (hereafter Catalunya) and the Basque Country – are present and depicted as having a distinctive national identity via the football writing that represents the state in which they are located (namely France and Spain). Part III turns the attention to the New (Football) Worlds of Africa, the United States of America and North East Asia, where representations of identity say much about European perceptions and expectations.

At the end of the twentieth century, the media had, indeed, announced that we were seeing the emergence of new football nations, or even continents. Pele's oft-quoted assertion that an African team would win the World Cup might not yet have been translated into reality but the rise of African football in the last quarter of the twentieth century is undeniable. Similarly, the United States participated in the FIFA World Cup for the first time in 40 years in 1990, hosted the tournament in 1994 and then qualified for the next three tournaments, reaching the quarter finals in 2002. In the Far East, the strengthening of Japan, China and South Korea (who reached the semi-final of the World Cup in 2002) following the recent establishment of their professional leagues (in 1983 in South Korea, 1993 in Japan, and 1994 in China) cannot be ignored or omitted from the geographical map of the football world. The 2002 FIFA World Cup, held in Japan and Korea, was declared in the *Guardian* to be 'the momentous one when Europe discovered it could not handle Asia and the Asians' (30 June 2002). The ways in which these football regions are covered in the press in Europe are duly examined.

As linguists with an interest in the cultural, social, historical and political environment in which language is employed, identity formation and cross-cultural comparisons are challenging issues but are highly relevant to us. Without engaging in outdated Whorfian debates over linguistic determinism, in our view language determines, to some degree, our view of reality and we interpret and recreate our world through the way we use language. Language is also a principal determinant of our perceptions of reality. It can both create and reflect reality. For this reason, we would argue that the apparently simple task of football writing is actually much more subtle than might first be supposed. By recycling or modifying existing notions of identity via the football pages in our sample, print media discourse is responsible for the perpetuation, consolidation and evolution of our vision of reality regarding national identities. At the same time, journalists assume a pre-existent shared memory within the readership and expect readers to approach the interpretation of their texts with a common national understanding. Let us explore, then, how, through its ever-expanding coverage of what has become Europe's most popular sport, the discourse of the print media conveys the evolution of national identities during the twentieth century.

Part I

Old Europe

Chapter 2

England

Theirs is not to reason why

There are a number of features and themes which characterize football writing in England throughout the twentieth century and beyond. The importance of the history of football itself is perhaps more significant in English football writing than in the other countries examined in the present study. We are never allowed to forget that Britain is the home of football, the original 'masters of the game' (e.g. *The Times*, 30 November 1955), and, indeed, it is often made explicit that the rest of the world should be grateful to the British for exporting this great tradition to their homelands. Perhaps it is this element of cultural imperialism that permits the English press to deem it appropriate to comment on the football style and development of the game in other countries with a rather patronizing attitude at times. So is England as arrogant about its football and imperial prowess as the rest of Europe might assume? In what ways is a concept of 'Englishness' portrayed in the European print media discourse analysed?

We are fortunate to enjoy the luxury of an abundance of data on these themes, particularly in the later stages of the twentieth century, when political change within the United Kingdom and the European Union contributed to a re-evaluation of English national identity. The key features that recur consistently throughout most of the period studied can be illustrated by exploring the English character as mediated in the football writing: the 'bulldog' or 'lionheart spirit' and the notion of 'fair play', the style of play and the rôle of Wembley in reinforcing a national identity are all significant features here. As the twentieth century drew to a close, the constituents of English identity mediated via the football pages of the English print media, however, became more multifarious and complex. It is, therefore, worth outlining the broader arguments published in *The Times* involving 'post-British' English identity.

The English self-image

There are many ways in which the notion of Englishness (and 'Britishness', since the terms are apparently synonymous for many years in the London-based *Times*) is (re)created in the English press. One of the key elements of this 'Englishness' which was strong in the first three quarters of the twentieth century was the importance attached to the notion of 'fair play' and sporting behaviour. This was seen as a key requisite for playing football the way it should be played but also, as 'foreigners' began to introduce (seemingly) alien concepts such as feigning fouls and injury, it began to be portrayed as a defining feature of the English, one which set them apart from foreigners and, in particular, 'Continentals' and those of a 'Latin' temperament.

The notion of fair play was established in football around the 1850s when the game emerged as a modern mass phenomenon. 'Fair play' included not only avoiding 'dirty' play but also the establishment of the common rules and physical boundaries of the game (Bale 1998). The close association of (amateur) sport with Victorian values and a sporting ethos cannot be overstated. In keeping with the tradition in cricket, footballers were addressed with their title, Mr, and initials as well as their surnames in press reports well into the twentieth century. In this way, sports writers granted them with the respect they earned in their rôle as sportsmen.

This sporting ethos and emphasis on fair play, which it is claimed lay at the heart of the early history of the contemporary game in England (Giulianotti 1999; Mason 1980; Russell 1997; Walvin 1994), are embedded in football culture, and match reports in the press reflect this social value of football during this period. Match reports must be seen as being fair to the opponents and it is usual for them to end on a reference to the sporting nature (or not) of the game: for example, England left the field 'having exchanged shirts with their opponents in a sporting match' (*The Times*, 21 July 1966).

Two apparently contradictory attitudes are, however, often presented as typically English. They are summarized succinctly in *The Times*: 'On the one hand England gave the world the stiff-upper-lip attitude of, "play up, play up, and play the game." On the other hand, England invented the question: "Do we play like English gentlemen (Cheltenham ladies)? Or do we play to win?"' (1 June 2002). So which view prevails in the English print media? Do the English media prefer to depict the English identity as the epitome of sporting behaviour? Or do they prefer more aggressive, ruthless characteristics implicit in the challenge 'do we play to win?'

Both elements of this English image are presented in our data, in England and beyond. However, rather than contrast these two aspects of 'Englishness', we prefer to see them as two sides of the same coin. Holt's seminal history of British sport (1989) suggests that in the Victorian era, while sport clearly helped to build stamina, strength and morale across social divides, it was more than that: 'Sport enshrined the ethic of competition, or more precisely the ethic of *fair* competition' (ibid. 97). Learning to lose graciously as well as win with dignity did not weaken the principle of competitiveness but rather strengthened it. In short, there is no disgrace in defeat, as long as you have done your best and made every possible effort to win, within the limits of fair play. Thus, the ingredient of fair play is crucial to the value of victory.

In actual fact, 'unfair play' was not as alien to the English game as *The Times* might have liked its readers to believe. In 1921, the (English) FA needed to take action to cleanse the game of such behaviour: 'The Football Association have taken very strong action with their fixed determination of putting down foul play' (*The Times*, 21 August 1921). This followed the 'unfair' tactics employed by Huddersfield Town to beat Preston North End in the FA Cup Final at Stamford Bridge in April 1920, which 'degraded the game in the eyes of the public' (ibid.). Since the notion of fair play is presented as such an essential part of the English game, writers are often at pains to emphasize the spirit in which a match is played: 'The Chileans might be vigorous defensively, but it was a sporting game,' the reporter adds hastily (*The Times*, 26 June 1950).

In the run-up to the 1966 World Cup held in England, England (along with Argentina, Portugal and Brazil) participated in a Nations' Tournament in June 1964. At this time England still defined itself, at least in football terms, as a model of fair play. The match against tournament hosts Brazil was described as 'a marriage of poetry and sportsmanship' (*The Times*, 6 June 1964). Ugly crowd scenes pervaded the tournament, though, both on and off the pitch, and the English reporter was at pains to contrast the behaviour of the England team with that of the others: 'England also had a couple of goals disallowed for offside – Hunt at the quarter hour, Byrne five minutes from time. Each decision was taken calmly and sportingly, underlying the difference in attitude and temperament' (ibid.). Even much later, we find examples of English derision of 'unfair' tactics, and a tendency to adopt the moral high ground in such matters. When, for instance, Italy won the 1982 World Cup against Germany in a match 'littered' with fouls, the reporter commented: 'Football's way ahead must not be permitted to follow such a rough path' (*The Times*, 12 July 1982). Again, we see the print media disparage a style of play that is 'unsporting' and the notion of fair play is espoused implicitly.

By extension, then, the way in which football is played is not insignificant. Victory is important but so is the way in which the triumph is achieved. Similarly, defeat, though naturally highly unwelcome, is more acceptable if it is a 'heroic defeat'. Evidence is abundant that 'gallant defeat', battling to the last, allows the print media to turn even losers into heroes: for example, 'valiant near misses seem to command ever greater affection in the hearts of the sentimental British public' (*The Times*, 8 June 1998). Indeed, England's elimination from the 1998 World Cup (by Argentina, following a penalty shoot-out) provides an excellent example of this process within 'a sickeningly familiar tale of heroic failure' (*The Times*, 1 July 1998). Here, patriotic pride is satisfied by the courageous efforts of England's 10 men (Beckham had, famously, been sent off) who, defiantly tenacious, refused to give up. Fighting spirit, courage and determination are prerequisites of English valour. Closely related to these qualities are the symbols of English national heroism.

As we have illustrated in detail elsewhere with reference to a contemporary sample (Crolley and Hand 2002), by far the overwhelming identifying forces within our data invoke the metaphorical 'bulldog spirit' and 'lionheart' attitude of the English. To the sports writers these concepts seem to embody both the identity of the English people and the desired spirit of the England team as mediated by our sample. The loyal and pugnacious bulldog has become an emblem of patriotic, determined Englishness, and appears outside our sample in a variety of milieux such as in advertisements and satirical cartoons. We have detailed elsewhere the ways in which the status of the bulldog was increasingly equated with nationalistic forces while it was controversially adopted as mascot for the England team for the World Cup finals in 1982 (see Crolley and Hand 2002). In a similar fashion, the lion (which came to the fore with the military exploits of Richard I – 'the Lionheart' – in the twelfth century and which was adopted by the FA as part of their 'Three Lions' logo) also represents an overt communication of courage and pride. As well as frequent mention of the qualities associated with the lionheart, England players and teams have often been described unequivocally as 'lions' or even 'lionhearts': for example, 'the lions were rampant' as 'England roar into the quarter-finals' of Euro 96 by beating Holland while players such as Tony Adams, Nat Lofthouse, Alan Shearer, even Steve McManaman have been called 'lions' or 'lionhearts' in the press. The prototype of the courageous English lionheart is an implicit rôle model for journalists.

So when did these symbols become synonymous with English patriotism? Have these qualities always been appreciated by football writers, or are they a more contemporary phenomenon? There is unquestionably a profusion of overt references in our sample to both 'bulldogs' and 'lions'. Quantitatively, we note a rise in the number of cases where references to 'bulldogs' are employed in the 1980s and early 1990s, though it is unreliable to consider quantitative data in a sample such as ours where the coverage towards the end of the period under study is so much greater than that of the early years. However, it seems to be the case that, beyond that period, the use of 'lion' symbolism has become ever more prominent, reaching a peak during Euro 96 when Ian Broudie, Frank Skinner and David Baddiel usurped the term for their chart-topping song 'Three Lions (Football's Coming Home)' which became the supporters' anthem of the tournament. Similarly in 1998, it could still be said that 'a lion-hearted England team plunged out of the World Cup in Saint-Etienne' (*The Times*, 1 July 1998).

Since then, the 'lions' theme has become a (deliberate?) part of the FA branding for the England team. A cursory glance at the news headlines on the England section of the FA website suffices to inform us that the FA now customarily refers to its own England teams as 'lions'. Current England commercial partners Nationwide have also tried to create a synergy between their building society and the England football team by using the slogan 'Pride. Passion. Belief', precisely the lexicon most highly associated with the 'three lions' image.

Searches in the historical archives of *The Times* confirm that the newspaper undoubtedly advocates values that are associated with the bulldog or lionheart images – such as commitment, energy, power and strength – in the football context. Despite occasionally bemoaning the lack of players with individual flair, it generally rates collective effort above individual talent. The respect for football played at a fast pace, for example, is one which dates back many years. There is certainly written evidence in the 1920s which suggests that good football was that which was played at speed: for example, 'The game was keenly contested, and in spite of the heat a fast pace was maintained' (19 May 1924). This overt praise for fast pace continues throughout the twentieth century; Greaves and Charles, for instance, are lauded for their 'dashing penetration' (27 October 1960). In 1960, England's defeat of Spain, 4–1 at Wembley, was attributed to a combination of 'tight, close man-to-man defensive marking' and 'the use of the long through-pass in attack' (1 December 1955). This direct, high-speed football style is valued, sometimes at the expense of more skilful performances: for example, in 1951, Finney was criticized for being 'too often intent on weaving patterns' (4 October). In the early 1950s, the print media seemed to believe that such qualities of speed, dedication and energy met the requirements of a superior football team, and were yet to embrace more 'continental' styles of play. Hard-working journeymen are often good consolation for lack of talent or skill: Armfield and Wilson were praised for being not skilful but 'gallant' in defence (*The Times*, 12 May 1960). Match reports on England are, therefore, peppered with 'fighting', with 'gallantry' and with 'effort' (e.g. *The Times*, 16 May 1960) and continued to be so into the 1980s. After England staggered their way to a 1–0 win against Northern Ireland in 1985, the then manager, Bobby Robson, comforted the country after a poor performance: 'It was a night for hard work and scrapping. They had some big boys, and we all had to fight to succeed. I am pleased that we didn't wilt. . . . From a work point of view we had 11 heroes. . . . We were never outfought and Butcher was outstanding' (*The Times*, 28 February 1985).

However, when a crisis in confidence in England's football supremacy set in (instigated initially, we would argue, by the impact and nature of England's first international defeat on home soil, to Hungary in 1953), pace and effort are not always enough to satisfy the demands of journalists at *The Times* and, while wholehearted commitment is appreciated, occasional frustration creeps in that it is not enough to become a successful team: 'There was plenty of heart but not enough mind' (*The Times*, 6 June 1964, following England's 1–1 draw against Portugal in Brazil). So, just as 'lionheart' or 'bulldog spirit' were referred to within the context of the England players, team or attitude, the qualities enshrined in these concepts continue to be present: tenacity, pride, determination, ferocity and speed were all valued positively.

The link between football abilities and character is incontrovertible. A football match assesses a team's playing skills but its psychological character is also put to the test. There is regular reference in the press, therefore, to a team's psychological strengths or weaknesses. When England won the World Cup, the team is extolled with 'England surmount final test of morale' (*The Times*, 1 August 1966). 'If England, perhaps, did not possess the greatest flair, they were the best prepared in the field, with the best temperament based on a functional plan' (ibid.). Having 'good temperament' and being 'functional' are clearly qualities of which to be proud. The psychological strengths of the English are reinforced throughout the article:

in a 'deep test of morale . . . psychologically Germany should have had the edge in that extra time. But Moore and his men rose magnificently to the challenge. . . . How some of them found the resilience and the stamina finally to outstay a German side equally powerful physically, equally determined, equally battle-hardened, was beyond praise. All were heroes' (ibid.). The fact that England managed to overcome the challenge 'that tested the stamina and will-power of both sides' made victory a worthy one. It was also, hugely ironically given the circumstances surrounding England's third goal (still disputed 40 years on), important to the English press to present the façade that West Germany were 'beaten fair and square' (*The Times*, 1 August 1966). In the main match report, there was no mention at all of the disputed goal, famously awarded by the linesman. Meanwhile, in Germany, the fans were welcoming home their players, equally convinced that they were the heroes.

A characteristic of Englishness perceived from outside England (see below for French and Spanish coverage of English football) is undoubtedly a tone of arrogance. Others clearly believe that the English think they are superior. To what extent is there evidence of this in our sample drawn from *The Times*? Though arrogance can only sporadically be perceived in our later data, an undoubtedly patronizing tone can be detected in *The Times* in the first half of the twentieth century, especially towards other nations who attempted to play football at international level: France, for instance, 'showed a marked improvement' in 1924, and were 'quite up to international standard' (19 May). Less complimentary comments were saved for the visit of the French in 1947:

> France came to Highbury on Saturday in search of the victory on English soil that everyone across the Channel lives for. But they retired a rather sadder and wiser team, for . . . England in the end beat them by three goals to none and the beating was even more emphatic than the score would suggest. France in a word were outclassed. . . . And so, after a ragged start, one more Continental challenge was disposed of summarily.
>
> (*The Times*, 5 May)

First, the general supercilious overtones mask (albeit thinly) something of a superiority complex in football terms. In previews to this match, there was an expectation that England would win (not surprising, perhaps, given the fact that England had never lost at home in an international fixture at this stage) but the tone of the above match report is nevertheless crudely arrogant.

Perhaps the first element to destroy this confidence in football primacy, which bordered on arrogance at times, was, as mentioned earlier, England's first defeat on English soil against a team from outside the British Isles, 3–6, against Hungary in 1953. It shattered English confidence and belief in their (football) supremacy. The ramifications rippled throughout reports for years to come and precipitated a spell of self-inquiry into the antiquated tactical style of play.

In 1955, in a preview to England's match against Spain, we learn that 'Spain will take the field for the first time in history next Wednesday and England will be keen to show that they can still speak with some authority on their own soil' (*The Times*, 26 November 1955). This hints again at a fragile confidence. In 1960, writers were referring to the match as though still in shock when opponents Spain were described as ' the strongest challengers since the Hungarians came to open our eyes to new delights seven years ago' (*The Times*, 27 October 1960). On future encounters we are again reminded of when the Hungarians 'shook the country in 1953' (*The Times*, 19 November 1981).

By 1960, England's football supremacy is no longer assumed. Concern persists apropos the old-fashioned style of English football: 'What has not changed [in the last 30 years] is British football. It remains unaltered, although all other countries have evolved technically and tactically' (*The Times*, 12 May 1960). Although this article mentions 'British' football, it is clear from the context that it is *English* football to which it refers. By this time, the press looked back to an earlier period of global football supremacy. Any attempts to rebuild had been dashed by the Munich air disaster. It is England's 'spirit', 'temperament and fibre' which inspired the team to manage a home draw to Yugoslavia in 1960. However, later that same year, England's 4–2 home victory against Spain led to a sneaking, tentative return of confidence within the match reports: 'at last English football is turning the corner and enjoying a resurgence. . . . England can once again believe in themselves. . . . England, building confidence and dominating a situation which in other days might have been clouded with menace and anxiety' (*The Times*, 27 October 1960). Indeed, it seems to be of utmost importance that England believe in themselves.

By 1966, when the draw is made for the World Cup finals, England are confident enough in their revival to expect to reach the quarter-finals 'but whether Moore and his men can go beyond that and reach the semi-final round for the first time in their history is something that will duly be unfolded' (*The Times*, 7 January 1966). At the time of the World Cup finals in the summer of 1966, England still did not presume overall football supremacy. Perhaps surprisingly, given the home advantage and what we now know about the English press, England were not presented as favourites in *The Times* to win the World Cup. That honour lay with Italy ('Italy to regain World Cup' [11 July 1966]). Though one headline ran 'England's chance never better', the article does not ooze confidence and journalists did not assume, or even anticipate, that England would win the World Cup. Even when the team reached the final, they hoped to win rather than expected it and when belief in victory was asserted, it was rather timid: 'I believe that England . . . will just about win . . . But there could be no more than a goal in it, with perhaps the need of the extra half hour' (*The Times*, 30 July 1966). Even this assertion is couched with uncertainty: 'And even if Moore and his men just fail at this last touch they have done magnificently well even to reach the final in a tough, uncompromising field, a feat many of us thought beyond them' (ibid.). The morning after the victory, *The Times* admitted that England 'are still pinching themselves. So, too, are others of us, the sceptics, who from the start thought the feat beyond our reach' (*The Times*, 1 August 1966). The tone now is far from arrogant.

By the end of the twentieth century, football writing is ambiguous in terms of the levels of confidence or arrogance portrayed on the sports pages. Kelly (1996: 8) testifies to the perpetuation of this great myth of English supremacy when he claims that 'There remains an assumption that Britain – or England – is the best.' However, in football terms, the superiority complex of the 1940s is fading as 'the unfailing optimism of the English football supporter' is more hopeful than realistic and is contrasted by 'those who forecast humiliation in Paris' (*The Times*, 2 September 2000).

There are numerous features of journalistic style and developments in themes within football writing that we have come across during the course of our research, many of which fall beyond the remit of the present study: the presentation of football reports, of names, of scores; the profile and status of the journalists; the depth and length of sport sections in the newspaper. The way in which the rôle of the football manager has been portrayed is one aspect that is, however, worthy of note here and we shall, naturally, focus on the England manager. It is only towards the latter stages of the 1966 World Cup finals that the manager figure begins to gain in importance in football writing. We have seen few references to the manager before this time. Alf Ramsey's predecessor, Walter Winterbottom (1946–62), for instance, enjoyed little limelight. Even in 1966, the rôle of the team captain, Moore, is portrayed as being probably as significant as that of the manager, oft referred to as 'Mr Ramsey' (e.g. *The Times*, 30 July 1966). We frequently read of 'Moore and his men', where the captain is the leader and motivator, whereas references to the manager invariably relate to his rôle as team selector and tactician: 'Mr Ramsey will have in mind . . .' . There are, though, few quotations from players during this period and it is to Ramsey that ultimate success is attributed: 'Ramsey proved right in World Cup' (*The Times*, 1 August 1966).

The impact of the 1966 World Cup win was to resonate throughout English football and become part of the national collective memory in years to come. It also became a national point of reference. Ramsey's winning team was praised for its 'loyalty' and 'effort', if not particularly its skill (*The Times*, 16 June 1982). Retrospectively, the style in which England won the World Cup was blamed for a subsequent generation of unattractive football: 'He achieved it [won the World Cup]. But, like the great war, it wiped out a whole generation of footballers with individualism and flair' (*The Times*, 16 June 1982).

In terms of an English style of play, the English press is not easily pleased and there is some debate regarding individual versus collective effort.

On one hand, a typically English reliance on effort, determination and teamwork are often revered: 'England's stern, stout effort' is praised (*The Times*, 16 May 1960) and 'Every English player certainly fought and bestirred himself to the last breath' (*The Times*, 12 July 1966). The day after England reached the World Cup final by beating Portugal 2–1: 'Here, also, was a triumph for the game of football itself sufficient to silence all the cynics. Instead of a war of destruction here was scientific, flowing football played on the ground, where it is always best. For a change there was no stultifying fear of defeat from either side. Instead, it was the spirit of aggressive adventure, sufficient at last to restore the sparkle of excitement and lift the whole standard of recent times . . . the game itself once more was given a shot in the arm' (*The Times*, 27 July 1966). Notable here is the juxtaposition of the term 'aggressive' alongside 'adventure' to epitomize a desirable style of play. This does not imply a style of play that is necessarily flamboyant in its pursuit of success but one that is destructive and powerful – and this is what the English strive for. Players are even criticized if they demonstrate individualism: Greaves played 'at times too selfishly' (*The Times*, 21 July 1966).

On the other hand, exclusive reliance on collective effort is sometimes acknowledged to be a hindrance. The fact that England were unable to break through a Uruguayan defence led the writer to express a fleeting wish for an individual player, 'a master to galvanize them', with flair and 'an expression of fantasy . . . like Pele' (*The Times*, 12 July 1966). Then later, in the World Cup finals in 1982, following England's 0–0 draw against Spain, 'Their efforts cannot be faulted and nor can their dedication. England's weakness . . . was their lack of one or two outstanding individuals that any side must contain to be confident of conquering the world' (*The Times*, 6 July 1982). After England's subsequent elimination from the tournament, 'The strength of the British champions lay in their teamwork. Their deficiency, as throughout the competition itself, was the lack of outstanding individuals' (*The Times*, 13 July 1982). The ideal for this writer, then, is a combination of collective effort and individualism. The desired balance between these elements is constantly shifting. English football cannot exist without the collectiveness but would like to enjoy the luxury of individualism as well. This balance is picked up in the Spanish coverage of English football discussed below.

Few cases can be as significant to the scholar of English football history as that of Wembley stadium. Wembley emerges from the print media discourse studied as a place of huge significance for the English national identity mediated via the football writing in our sample.

The build-up began even before the stadium had been constructed. As the FA viewed a model, its size (able to accommodate up to 130,000 fans) and comfort (people could shelter from the weather as they do 'at the back of the mound stand at Lord's') were key features, as was the fact that it was accessible from the grounds of the British Empire Exhibition (*The Times*, 18 January 1922). This connection with the British Empire Exhibition, though in early reports linked only via reporting the physical proximity of the stadium to the exhibition area, was later to become strengthened, and before long the Wembley Stadium name was inextricably associated with the British Empire.

There were many articles reporting the progress in the building of the Wembley Stadium (e.g. *The Times*, 14 April 1922; 28 April 1922; 21 August 1922), and this (within the context of the English press in the 1920s) served to sensationalize its construction. Indeed, direct parallels can be drawn between the coverage of the construction of the 'new Wembley' (2004–6) and that of the old. They all reiterate the enormous size of the edifice and emphasize the notions of comfort and luxury in a way that predates the modern experience of football stadia: 'Dining rooms and

tea rooms on a vast scale will provide necessary refreshment for the crowd, in addition, of course, to the restaurants of the exhibition' (*The Times*, 17 August 1922).
Here, it is interesting that there is a perceived necessity to provide refreshments
at all to a football crowd, the emphasis is again on the large scale nature of the
operation and, finally, we note the juxtaposition of the reference to the exhibition
alongside Wembley – once more reinforcing the association in the mind of the
readership. During this period (1922) it became almost common practice to refer
to Wembley as 'the Great Stadium at Wembley'.

Once Wembley begins to be used as a working stadium, there are a number
of features of the football writing that serve to add force to Wembley's status as
a symbol of national identity within the minds of the readership. First, the royal
presence at the opening of the Stadium at the FA Cup final on 28 April 1923
ensured national interest in the project and granted prestige to the occasion in
a way that nothing else could. This royal attendance was commented upon in
all articles in *The Times* during the run-up to the opening and after the event. In
Wembley's early years, it was the norm for royal attendance to lie at the centre
– and usually the start – of coverage of matches held at Wembley, and the royal
connotations remained intrinsically linked to Wembley Stadium, arguably beyond
the years when royalty formed an integral part of the notion of English identity for
many. It was not unusual for this comment on royal presence to be extended to
some discussion of the reception of regal figures by the crowd, as was the case in
1930 when the King appeared unexpectedly following illness: 'The King attended
the FA Cup Final match between The Arsenal and Huddersfield Town at Wembley on Saturday afternoon. . . . His Majesty had a rousing reception from a crowd
of over 92,000' (*The Times*, 28 April 1930). In this particular case two thirds of the
report is devoted to discussion of the King's reception and to the singing of 'God
Save the King'. Second, the participation of a London club (West Ham United) in
the first FA Cup final to take place at the stadium ensured the interest (and hype)
of the London-based media. This was confessed by *The Times* itself on more than
one occasion. Not only did it ensure media interest but it also guaranteed a good
attendance at the match itself. Third, the fact that the Wembley Park Stadium was
the focal location of the British Empire Exhibition contributed enormously to the
construction of a national identity centred around the stadium. The Exhibition
itself was to encourage trade and patriotism among the 58 countries of the British
Empire. At the stadium's inauguration in 1923, it was in fact the first part of the
Exhibition to be opened. Construction had hardly begun on the rest of the site
adjacent. It had been built to schedule and was heralded as a huge success in terms
of engineering and planning. Its luxury and comfort were key features highlighted
in the press before the first match was played there.

The announcement in *The Times* that Wembley would be ready in time to
host the 1923 FA Cup final illustrates several of the points already indicated.
The headline ran: 'Empire Athletic Arena – The Great Stadium at Wembley
– Ready for the Cup Final' and opened with the inscription on the stonework at
the royal entrance to the stadium: 'H.R.M. the Duke of York, K.G. inaugurated

the construction of the Stadium and building of the British Empire Exhibition' (*The Times*, 2 April 1923). Within a few short lines, then, the article again reinforces the connection between Wembley and the British Empire Exhibition, the association with royalty and the 'great'-ness of the project. Its status as a national symbol is unquestionable.

The fourth factor that mythified the status of Wembley involved the sensational events surrounding the first FA Cup final that took place at the venue. This event was at the time, of course, the most prestigious football fixture of the calendar. This match had been glorified in such a way that, in the days when no tickets were issued to attend a football match, with a belief that the 'Great' Wembley stadium would be able to accommodate everyone, and further attracted by the participation of a London club in the final, too many people turned up to watch the match. This resulted in a dangerous level of overcrowding. *The Times* estimated that the stadium was over capacity by some 50,000. Inevitably, severe crushing ensued on the terraces. The photographs that appeared in *The Times* over the following days will have left a strong impression on the readership for many years. Interestingly, the response was not one of panic (since there were no serious injuries) but rather, 'there are still ripples of excitement with regard to the overcrowding of the Stadium of Wembley last Saturday' (*The Times*, 3 May 1923). The reputation of Wembley Stadium remained intact: 'Fortunately, there was no question of any structural defect' (*The Times*, 30 April 1923). The press was quick to reassure the public that 'The Wembley Park Stadium is so well and strongly built that catastrophe of that kind [referring to Ibrox Park, 1902] is quite out of the question' (ibid.). A potential national embarrassment was thus averted.

Also significant to our argument here is that, given the unpleasant conditions within the ground that day: 'There might well have been panic but there was not; and the way in which [the crowd] stood to attention, when the confusion was at its height, to cheer the HEAD of the STATE and sing "God Save the King" was something never to be forgotten' (*The Times*, 30 April 1923). In this way, the print media reported the welcoming reception accorded to royalty while also adding weight to the 'stiff-upper-lip' characterization of English patriotism. These events, which were to be retold and glorified year on year, now form part of the English collective national identity and memory.

Interesting in our data, too, were some of the (many) articles in the aftermath of the 1923 FA Cup final which debated the 'psychological interest' of the 'general question of dealing with crowds in all its aspects', which 'may well be looked upon as a necessity of modern life. For this is the age of crowds and loudspeakers. Every day and in every way they get bigger and bigger . . . huge masses of human beings are being brought together [by sporting events] . . . and call for the most careful organisation' (*The Times*, 3 May 1923). This led to the report of the Departmental Committee on Crowds, which was issued as a White Paper in April 1924.

The next defining point in the history of Wembley Stadium was in 1925 when it hosted the opening ceremony of the British Empire Exhibition. This ceremony, covered extensively in *The Times*, was a 'splendid ceremony of Empire'. Again, the royal presence is important and is established at the outset of all articles in our sample. The scene described in one article serves as a typical example and is worth quoting at length. It could hardly resonate more deeply with royal glamour:

> It is doubtful if the Stadium at Wembley or any other great parade ground has ever seen a finer, more stately ceremony that that of Saturday. It is difficult to say which was the most thrilling moment. When the King, accompanied by the Queen, arrived, heralded by the royal trumpeters in the gorgeousness of their scarlet and gold, and, in the open State coach, swept round the arena amid the clatter of accoutrements, the glitter of steel and the white waving plumes of the Life Guards' escort, while the roar of cheering ran from block to block of the huge enclosure where, banked from ground-level to roof, were massed 100,000 spectators.
>
> (*The Times*, 11 May 1925)

The repetition of vocabulary which evoked the 'splendour' of the 'spectacle' which 'thrilled' the 'great gathering' all contributed to convey the glamour of the occasion but the patriotism associated with it was also evident as the crowd were filled 'by the pride and beauty of the singing of "Land of Hope and Glory" . . . and finally the heartshaking strains of "God Save the King"' (ibid.).

Undeniably the rôle of Wembley Stadium throughout the period of the exhibition was significant in developing the relationship with 'Britishness' within the mind of the readership. Later that year (1925) the Wembley Tattoo, 'a national ritual', took place in the fitting arena, according to one commentator: 'When everything else also belonging to the Empire has found its place at Wembley, why should there not be represented forces of the State, on which in the last resort in time of need the Empire has to rely?' (*The Times*, 7 September 1925). There was created, therefore, a close association between the location of Wembley and the national psyche. The Wembley Tattoo was a very popular event, which appealed to large sectors of the population and was attended by an estimated 1.5 million people in over 50 performances at Wembley (*The Times*, 4 October 1925). During this time, the hymn 'Abide with Me' was sung every night and became part of the Wembley ritual (*The Times*, 12 September 1925). This hymn is still, of course, associated with football and is still played at poignant football moments, as well as at FA Cup finals. The hosting of this huge spectacle ensured that associations of national pride would remain in the national memory for years to come. The 'Wembley equals British' equation was one which endured into the 1990s. Only then did the (English) flags of St George begin to outnumber the (British) Union flags among the crowds, reflecting other changes in the notions of national identities within the United Kingdom and an oft-debated rise in the social acceptability of the manifestation of English identity.

Such is the strong characterization of Wembley that a partial personification process takes place. Wembley assumes traits of a humanized or animated object. For example, when England faced possible defeat for the first time on home soil against Argentina in May 1951, with 10 minutes to go, Wembley internalizes the lionheart spirit: 'A "Wembley roar" kept England pushing forward' (*The Times*, 10 May 1951). England came back to win 2–1. On other occasions, personification is stronger: 'Wembley, indeed, was given back its dignity last night and the game itself once more was given a shot in the arm' (*The Times*, 27 July 1966, the day after England reach the World Cup Final by beating Portugal 2–1).

As early as 1927, it was made explicit that Wembley's atmosphere was so special that it provided an excuse for an Arsenal goalkeeper's error of judgement: 'it is only fair to add that the vastness of Wembley Stadium and its monster crowds always are likely to have a predominating influence upon the mere 22 midgets engaged in winning and losing the greatest football match of the year' (*The Times*, 25 April 1927). It was at this time that the 'most remarkable modern phenomenon of Community Singing' was commented upon (ibid.).

The rôle of Wembley is portrayed as central to the success or failure of the England team and never more so than during the 1966 World Cup. The focus of the preview, and centre of attention, on the morning of the World Cup final was Wembley: 'Wembley Stadium today will stage the eighth World Cup final . . . I believe that England, having played at Wembley all the way, will just about win on their "home" ground . . . on Wembley's flawless turf' (*The Times*, 30 July 1966). Home advantage, and the power of the fans, is recognized as being influential – though the article also mentions the German fans as being a potential determining factor in the support for their team. The atmosphere is almost a participant in the football event: 'nerves crackled in the vibrant atmosphere' (*The Times*, 19 November 1981).

Later, when England beat Hungary 1–0 to qualify for the 1982 World Cup finals in Spain, 'The rafters of the national stadium echoed with the cheers of a full audience and with a patriotic fervour that recalled that sunny afternoon in July 1966 when England lifted the Jules Rimet trophy itself – and never more so than when the two sides walked out of the tunnel to the strains of "Land of Hope and Glory"' (*The Times*, 19 November 1981). In the absence of an *English* national anthem, 'Land of Hope and Glory' assumes a special status. Composed by Edward Elgar (1857–1934), the central theme of the trio section of *Pomp and Circumstance March No. 1 in D* provides the tune to the words written by Arthur Benson (1862–1925). This became incorporated into the *Coronation Ode* in 1902, which was performed at the coronation of King George V in 1911. The song is now known throughout the world as a rousing, flag-waving and patriotic climax to the Last Night of the Proms, the series of concerts held between July and September each year. It now rings out at almost every event celebrating English, as opposed to British, patriotism as an unofficial English anthem.

Reference to all the songs mentioned above ('Land of Hope and Glory', 'Abide with Me', 'God Save the King') are all evocative and constitute part of the shared identity of an English 'imagined community' (Anderson 1983). Wembley Stadium's roots as epitomizing Britishness, then, were eventually nurtured as the ground came to play a central rôle in the creation of an English identity mediated via English print media discourse on football.

Finally, this dissolution of Britishness and development of an English national identity is worthy of attention. The issue of devolution in the late 1990s and consequent assertion of Welsh and Scottish identities during the process of establishing the Welsh National Assembly and the Scottish Parliament led to a certain self-consciousness on the part of the English (*The Times*, 21 February 2001). The strong Welsh and Scottish identities were contrasted sharply by the print media with that of the rather wishy-washy notion of Englishness. This process of political devolution was accompanied by the effects of the expansion of the European Union and a culture of fear of immigrants (again, fuelled by the media). This prompted a renewed fascination with national traditions, characteristics and customs. It also brought much further debate about Englishness. The level of debate over notions of English identity developed significantly during this period. This is reflected in football coverage in *The Times* and is far from confined to its sports pages. Other forms of cultural media were also gripped. Several monographs that pondered the subject of 'Englishness' were published in this period (e.g. Duffy 2001; Langford 2001; Paxman 1998; Scruton 2000; Wood 2000). Debate ranged from identifying a national crisis in a lack of defining characteristics of Englishness, the perceived destruction of all the major symbols of patriotic pride – the church, the monarchy, the parliamentary system, the police force (*The Times*, 17 November 2003) – to the Crick Committee's proposal for the introduction of a citizen's test for immigrants.

Differentiation between British and English national identities and patriotism increased towards the end of the twentieth century. For a large part of the twentieth century, 'English' and 'British' were terms that were employed synonymously in the English media (as, indeed, they continue to be elsewhere – see below for the case of France). It was not unusual for the England team to be referred to as 'Britons' even into the 1980s (e.g. *The Times*, 16 May 1980) and for England to represent Britishness. Wellings (2002: 95) explains this fusion or merging of English and British discourse as the articulation of an 'Anglo-British nationalism', which largely 'hid what one might now understand as "English nationalism" within a "British" discourse of Empire.' This changed in the English press towards the end of the twentieth century, though we see the interchangeabilty of features of English and British discourse remain constant in other European countries. To a large extent this reflected current attitudes of the English football-supporting public. The (stereo)typical England football fan carried Union flags rather than the English flag of St George. Even during the World Cup finals in Spain, 'Union Jacks filled the spaces' (*The Times*, 6 July 1982; 21 June 1982). The Union flags (which until then still held strong right-wing, neo-Nazi connotations for many) were to give way to the flags of St George during the 1990s as an 'English' and 'post-British' consciousness increased.

By 2002, *The Times* reported that an estimated 30 million *England* flags had been sold around the time of the World Cup. It reports, thankfully, that, 'The

English flag has been reclaimed from extremists' (22 June 2002). For some, this popularity of the Cross of St George formed part of 'a softer, more "feminine" national identity, and a new sense of positive pride in our country and our communities' (17 June 2002). The World Cup victory of England's rugby team in November 2003 contributed further to the refinement of the notions of positive aspects of English identity: 'The qualities we now admire in the English are: grit, meticulous preparation and the pursuit of victory' (26 November 2003), though the author confesses that it is unclear in what way these qualities are actually new; 'But when you add modesty, self deprecation and the courteous behaviour of the team in the match's aftermath, then you are in danger of rediscovering a familiar stereotype – the cleancut, stiff-upper-lipped Englishman.' Hence, the 'new' national identity actually resembles very closely the way in which the old was portrayed in the press.

England viewed from France

French press coverage of the English national football team dates back at least as far as the first decade of the twentieth century, given that there was, indeed, coverage in quality dailies of the first ever meeting between England and France, which took place in Paris in 1906 (e.g. Le Matin, 2 November). Throughout the century, England was a frequent opponent of the French on the field of play (34 matches were contested, see Cazal et al. 1998) and, of course, the English were also a major footballing power in international tournaments. There is, then, a quantity of data readily available to the researcher interested in French representations of Englishness in print media discourse on football. On examining the data, a number of interesting themes emerge.

From the outset, England is regarded in France as the model to adopt, the reference to follow with respect to efficiency and effectiveness, given that the English adopted professionalism early and treat football as work. Indeed, it would appear that the English have long been renowned in France for the committed and disciplined way in which they approach the sport of football and the high work rate and great physical effort they put into the game. As early as 1911, for instance, Le Matin noted that the English played a meticulously planned game which took on the status of 'science' when contrasted with the more open, flowing manner in which the French played at the time (24 March) while a later fixture, in 1921, elaborated further on this essential contrast between the English and French styles: 'Two methods came face to face in this memorable encounter [a 2–1 victory for France] . . . the English method . . . orderly, methodical if slow, precise and determined . . . [and] the French method, based on speed, and on diabolic pace' (Le Matin, 6 May). Such is the identification of the English with a mechanistic way of playing that their defeat on this occasion, the first ever to France, is explained via a metaphor of machinery breaking down: 'it would seem that there was a broken spring in the machine' (ibid.). Similarly, reports of matches immediately after the Second World War also refer to the intrinsic qualities of the English in this respect. The mid-1940s match reporters in France were certainly impressed by the English players' physical fitness and strength; these are quite simply real 'athletes' (Le Monde, 29 May 1945; 21 May 1946) whose physical conditioning is to be admired and, indeed, contrasted with that of the French, who are often portrayed as lacking in this regard. In addition to English power and strength, of which the French have traditionally been in awe, the discipline and organizational abilities of successive England teams are also frequently commented upon. In the period under consideration here, it is generally recognized in France that England are the supreme power in world football (paralleling Britain's pre-eminence in the diplomatic, military and, to an extent, economic arenas), which is why it was a 'pleasant surprise' that the French obtained a draw in 1945 (Le Monde, 29 May 1945) and 'to everyone's surprise' that France actually won the 1946 meeting with the acknowledged 'masters' of the game who were as 'mechanical' as ever (Le Monde, 21 May 1946).

By the late 1950s and 1960s, it is expected that England will be a physically strong, tough, disciplined and well organized opponent. 'The England team are *always* a formidable opponent' noted Le Monde in 1957 and 'their *intrinsic qualities* are well known (athletic strength, fearsome striking of the ball, a somewhat me-chanical game played at a steady pace)' (29 November, emphasis added). Again, in the 1966 World Cup meeting between France and England, the French were 'physically inferior' (Le Monde, 22 July) while, throughout the competition, the English provided 'a magnificent example with their courage, ambition, determi-nation and strength' (Le Monde, 3 August 1966). What are perceived to be the typical English qualities of commitment, strength and power are, then, generally admired by French football journalists. One writer notes that 'we really liked the combativeness of this England team' and extrapolated from this starting point to outline the contrasting identities of England and France: 'They showed precisely the qualities that the French lack . . . athleticism, speed of movement, individual technique, all brought to the fore by very good physical conditioning' (Le Monde, 19 July 1966). In short, this 'solid and energetic national team' who demonstrated 'magnificently . . . superb British qualities' were 'worthy winners' of the tourna-ment (Le Monde, 2 August 1966). Similarly, in a 1969 friendly the English were physically superior 'and determinedly committed to playing a direct game, without embellishment displaying the vigour and health of British football' (Le Monde, 14 March 1969 – the use in these two examples of the term 'British' as opposed to 'English' will be discussed below).

Given the nature of the qualities of Englishness foregrounded by the French press and, indeed, given England's position in general as one of the major forces in the game as well as their record against the French (only seven defeats in the 34 encounters of the twentieth century [Cazal *et al.* 1998]), it is not surprising that notions of English superiority feature so frequently in the print media discourse ex-amined. What is, perhaps, more noteworthy is the discursive techniques employed to portray that relative sporting superiority, that is the metaphors and similes used by French journalists when writing about the English playing football.

Primarily, two related images prevail in this respect, first the concept of exhibition or demonstration, the adept and the neophyte, and, second, that of education, the teacher–pupil relationship. After the first ever France–England match, for instance, which resulted in a crushing 15–0 defeat for the French, *Le Matin* reported that 'an exhibition of football' had been witnessed, establishing literally from the outset the notion of the expert English footballers and their aspiring French apprentices (2 November 1906). Reports of the second meeting between the two countries, a 12–0 victory for England this time, contained similar imagery: on this occasion, the French 'were given a masterly lesson' in football (*Le Matin*, 24 March 1908). Again, in 1913, the English were said to have provided 'a very fine exhibition' of football in their 4–1 victory over France at Colombes (*Le Matin*, 28 February 1913).

Comparable images continue to appear in the sports pages of the French press in the 1920s in which England are: 'the formidable Masters of Football' (*Le Matin*, 6 May 1921); 'the teachers who gave a remarkable lesson in football to the pupils, especially with regard to precision and the science of the game' (*Le Matin*, 11 May 1923); 'the English team [that] gave an exhibition of fast, precise, scientific football' (ibid.); the providers of a 'remarkable exhibition of efficiency' (*Le Matin*, 18 May 1928); and 'the Masters of Football, [these] professionals' (*Le Matin*, 10 May 1929).

The now familiar imagery of English superiority over France remains very prevalent in the immediate post-war period as well. Here, the English are still the acknowledged 'masters' of the game (*Le Monde*, 21 May 1946), who play 'a football that is distinctly superior to what is normally seen in France' (*Le Monde*, 6 May 1947), an 'exhibition' style of football provided by players who 'taught the French team a lesson' (*Le Monde*, 21 May 1949). Within this discursive framework, French defeats to England (of which there have been many, 23 in the twentieth century [Cazal *et al.* 1998]) are rarely if ever criticized but are, on the contrary, typically seen as 'honourable', as was the defeat in the finals of the 1966 World Cup (*Le Monde*, 22 July), which, of course, led to the culmination of English football's dominance before the 30-plus years of hurt actually began. Interestingly, even after England's position of pre-eminence in world football had slipped somewhat (but before France came to dominate at the end of the twentieth century), French press reports still display a degree of apprehension with regard to the English. 'Beating England will always represent a great performance' notes *Le Monde* in 1984, 'thanks to the sad track record [against them]' (29 February) and the journalist goes on to use precisely the same image as his predecessors nearly 80 years earlier as a prelude to restating the archetypal English qualities that were also already established in the 1900s: 'the crowd had a right to expect a lesson in British football: classic, rigorous organization, a direct game without embellishment, physical presence, especially in the air' (ibid.).

By the end of the twentieth century, as noted elsewhere (Crolley and Hand 2002), the highly significant Others that are the English in French football culture are at once admired and feared for their reputed qualities of organization, discipline, courage, commitment and fighting spirit. The last attribute, like the others, has a lengthy history in French print media discourse on international football. Images of English fighting spirit that were, for instance, very prevalent in reports of the 1998 World Cup may now be read as mirroring comparable images from the early days of French newspaper coverage of the England team. In 1998, *Le Monde* evokes the 'fighting spirit which inhabits the English . . . with [their] incredible energy, limitless courage and apparently indestructible enthusiasm' (2 July) and proclaims: 'Yes, of course, they were heroic, the English, they always are when they have to fight against adversity and destiny' (7 July). Similarly, as early as 1913, *Le Matin* was noting that one of the defining characteristics of the English team was its 'combative' nature as displayed in a 4–1 defeat of France in Colombes (28 February). The image is reinforced by the same newspaper reporting on a later victory for England: 'the English, operating with that determination *for which they are well known* . . . invaded the French camp' (18 May 1924, emphasis added). Military metaphors such as this, in widespread use across European football writing by the end of the twentieth century (see Boniface 1998; Crolley and Hand 2002; Garland and Rowe 1997; Poulton 1999; Reid 2000) are frequently used in France in the early days of football reporting as well, especially with reference to the English. The English goalkeeper in a 1921 encounter was, for instance, described as 'the last rampart holding back the invasion' (*Le Matin*, 6 May), the 1929 friendly against England was qualified as a 'battle' (*Le Matin*, 10 May) and the English half of the pitch is portrayed in a later game as 'enemy territory' (*Le Matin*, 15 May 1931). The military imagery clustering around the English team and its ready association with explicit references to English determination and courage serve to establish in French football writing a key aspect of the English identity that would survive intact to the end of the twentieth century and beyond.

'English fighting spirit' would seem to be admired in France when applied to a sporting contest but it is also seen as generating a much feared characteristic of many of the England football team's followers in the second half of the twentieth century, hooliganism. Media coverage in the late 1990s of the hooligan element attached to English football abroad is analysed by the present authors elsewhere (Crolley and Hand 2002). Considering the data from earlier periods, it is now evident that the content and the style of that coverage are extensions of the type of discourse that was being used in the early 1980s when, arguably, media attention paid to what was admittedly an escalating problem expanded out of all proportion. An eloquent example of what Armstrong and Harris (1991) term the media amplification of the hooligan issue is provided by *Le Monde*'s preview of the 1982 World Cup match between England and France. The context of the match was certainly noteworthy. The game, the first between the two sides since 1969, was played in Spain immediately after the Falklands/Malvinas conflict and in Bilbao, in the Basque Country, the alleged home base of terrorist activities launched by ETA separatists desiring independence from Spain (see below, Chapter 7). The article succeeded in not once mentioning purely football matters and focused instead, throughout its 10 paragraphs, on security issues and the anticipation of trouble from the English fans. The article's headline is revealing: 'One police officer for every 20 fans' (17 June 1982). With the tone of the piece set, the very first paragraph equates English supporters with terrorists by claiming that the Spanish authorities are just as afraid of the hooligans as they are of ETA and, in particular, of possible confrontations between the English and the large numbers of French supporters in the town. The second paragraph raises the spectre of English fans arriving at the game without tickets while the third notes that there will be 2,500 officers on duty to police 'the thousands of ticketless fans spread all around the ground' (ibid.). Later sections of the article confirm that the match has been labelled as one of the hottest, most at risk in the whole tournament but assert that any trouble is unlikely to come from the Basques, implying that it will come from the English. The whole piece induces fear and apprehension (of the English) in its readers, raises the levels of tension surrounding the game and virtually predicts that violence and disorder will take place.

In the late 1990s, French journalists frequently referred to the British monarchy when writing about the England football team, most notably via playful metaphors describing the English as 'Her Majesty's players' (*Libération*, 10 June 1996). Even English 'hooligans' – who, as we have seen, tend to haunt the French mind – get the royal treatment: at a World Cup game against Argentina, the security forces had to 'eject three rows of Her Majesty's imbeciles' (*Libération*, 1 July 1998). On occasions throughout the twentieth century, the French press also evoke this and other elements of England and Great Britain's political and diplomatic relations, thereby locating sport as an integral part of a wider context of international current affairs. The headline of the match report of the first ever France–England game, for example, was 'The *Entente Cordiale* Match' (*Le Matin*, 2 November 1906), in reference to the diplomatic treaty signed two years earlier linking the two countries in the face of rising economic and military competition from Germany. Around the middle of the twentieth century, references appear to the national flower of England, the rose, which is more specifically a royalist emblem in the form of the Tudor rose, created in 1485 by Henry VII by combining the red and white roses of the houses of Lancaster and York. So, just as the French are often portrayed as 'tricolours' or 'cockerels' (see below, Chapter 3), the English are referred to as 'the Rose 11' (*Le Monde*, 27 November 1957) and 'the team of the Rose' (*Le Monde*, 5 October 1962). Towards the end of the century, military and diplomatic conflicts feature in what are in form, if not entirely in content, supposed to be football match reports. The report in *Le Monde* of the 1982 World Cup match between England and France, for instance, devotes fully the first three of its 10 paragraphs to the politico-diplomatic context in which the 'British' were competing. According to the paper, the Falklands/Malvinas conflict had degraded the climate in which England would play its games in the tournament and was also responsible for 'reviving the dispute with Spain over Gibraltar' (18 June 1982). However, having itself mentioned factors external to football, *Le Monde* seems to use these as a springboard for reasserting elements of the traditional English identity by observing that 'Whereas other footballers would have been distracted by all these external influences, the British made no excuses and showed their usual determination' (ibid.). Having said that, the political overtones of the match report cannot be ignored at any stage within it especially given its headline: 'England 3 France 1 – Rule Britannia!' (ibid.); which connects not only with the lyrics of the patriotic British song of the same name but also with the context of the recent military victory of the latter-day British Empire over Argentina in the south Atlantic.

Finally with regard to French perceptions of England, in earlier surveys (Crolley and Hand 2001, 2002), we noted that French football journalists use the terms 'British' and 'English' as interchangeable synonyms. This can now be confirmed as one of the constants of French football writing throughout the twentieth century as there are many examples of it in match reports of 1909 (*Le Matin*, 23 May), 1927 (*Le Matin*, 27 May), 1933 (*Le Matin*, 7 December), 1946 (*Le Monde*, 2 May), 1947 (*Le Monde*, 6 May), 1949 (*Le Monde*, 24 May), 1951 (*Le Monde*, 3 October), 1955 (*Le Monde*, 15 May), 1962 (*Le Monde*, 5 October), 1963 (*Le Monde*, 1 March), 1966 (*Le Monde*, 22 July), 1969 (*Le Monde*, 14 March), 1982 (*Le Monde*, 18 June) and 1984 (*Le Monde*, 29 February). Technically, of course, it is perfectly correct to refer to English people as being British. In the football context, however, it is wholly inappropriate and demonstrates a lack of appreciation in France of the importance of the distinctions between the four separate football associations in the United Kingdom which themselves play a not insignificant rôle in representing the different national identities within the British state.

England viewed from Spain

A detailed analysis of the Spanish coverage of English football reveals some unsurprising themes but it is nevertheless fascinating to examine the processes that have developed since coverage of international football took root in Spain. Unlike the English and French samples, data for the early years from Spain is scarce. At the start of the twentieth century, there was little coverage of international football at all in the Spanish press. Although football was gaining in popularity at home, Spain's interest in the game on a global level was limited to the intermittent reporting of results of fixtures and rarely extended to sending a special correspondent. This was followed by a period of political and social instability which culminated in the Spanish Civil War (1936–39). For some time after this era, despite claims that football was used as a 'social drug' to distract people from thinking about more serious, political issues (Shaw 1987), domestic matters (including football) took priority over international football, coverage of which within mainstream newspapers would merely have drawn attention to the fact that Spain was ostracized politically and largely from the sporting arena too. So we have relatively little to consider until the 1950s.

Many of the themes and elements of heterotypification of the English mediated via the sports pages of the Spanish press mirror those that appear in the English and French print media, though some subtle differences attract our attention.

As in the English press, an appreciation that England is the home of football is confirmed time and time again: 'English football, home of sport' (*El País*, 8 September 1983); 'The English: founders of football' (*El País*, 8 August 1983); 'The English invented football' (*El País*, 13 June 2004). However, there is a clear view that English football is old-fashioned and that the rest of the world has overtaken England.

It is ironic that the English are criticized heavily in the Spanish press for their anachronistic style of play and for living on past glory, when the press itself is contributing to the perpetuation of the image of the English as legends within football by its persistent allusion to its rôle as the birthplace of football and by referring to England's most glorious moment in football history – that is, its World Cup final victory – with exceptional frequency. Segurola (1999) explains the deep effects that this World Cup win has had on the English: 'The iconography of that final has left a deep imprint on England, who suffer from the nostalgia for this victory' (*El País*, 17 June). What is suggested in this article is that the England team feels pressure to repeat their only significant achievement in world football. The same writer later acknowledges that the media are at least partly to blame for creating a myth around English football: 'There exists a sort of incurable romanticism surrounding England and its national team, perhaps because the world always feels indebted to the country that invented the game of the twentieth century, and probably the twenty-first' (*El País*, 13 June 2004).

An antiquated style of play is exposed as a consistent part of Englishness: 'England is 20 years behind in football' says one (anonymous) Spanish player quoted in *ABC* as early as 1950 (4 July); 'the young players were unable to rejuvenate the British style of play' (*ABC*, 17 May 1955). English football is portrayed as lacking innovation: against France, 'the British team [England] was slow, systematic and lacked original ideas' (ibid.). Similarly, in a preview of a Spain–England match, one journalist writes that for 16 years England has been 'stuck in its classicism' (*ABC*, 8 May 1968).

Spanish press coverage of Spain's 3–0 victory over England in Madrid in 1960 was actually summarized in *The Times*. The article is worth quoting since it covers some important issues that are touched upon elsewhere. The Madrid-based *Hoja del lunes* intones thus:

> British football remains antique . . . there will always be a Britain, nothing ever changes. There will always be a changing of the guard because no one will give a new order. Thus, in a football sense, English football remains the same game as it was almost a century ago. There is no invention. No extemporization, no planning. It is full of heart, but it is monotonous. Yet we offer our condolences for England have sportsmanship which they guard like gold in spite of Spain's *bailando* (dancing, that is) in the last quarter of an hour.
> (quoted in *The Times*, 17 May 1960)

Here, several themes come to the fore. The anachronistic nature of England's football style is bemoaned and this is portrayed as a reflection of British (or rather, English) society in general. Old traditions and ways of life persist because no one takes the responsibility for progress. England is 'full of heart' (the lionheart image is implicit) and clings to a notion of 'sportsmanship' that the Spanish see as retrograde. The pity for the English borders on scorn for their highly prized values.

In terms of the English style of play, there is some development during the period under consideration in the way in which this is presented. For many years (until the early 1990s) a fairly consistent English style of play was depicted in the Spanish print media. For much of this period, a short description of an England performance in 1950 summarizes this style concisely: 'a respectable side, great physical presence, not very imaginative' (ABC, 17 May 1950). This is reinforced in a subsequent match report when, 'England were slower [than Spain], calmer, but more consistent . . . ordered resistance' (ABC, 19 May 1950). This disciplined, organized, unimaginative style typifies how the Spanish described the English for some time.

In some respects, the English style of play shares characteristics with the Spanish style of *furia* (see Chapter 6). Strength, determination and persistence are key features. This is in keeping with what we have seen of English autotypification. The English game is 'combative' and 'physical' (ABC, 31 July 1966). England beat West Germany in the World Cup final because they had 'more enthusiasm, greater desire and fighting spirit' – as well as a 'phantom goal'! (ibid.). There are also abundant references to the lion image which is so predominant in the English coverage: 'the English were like lions . . . they tackled tremendously' (ABC, 9 May 1968). The Spanish appreciate the qualities of good tackling in a way the press from other nations might not because it demonstrates an element of *furia*. The same report went on to acclaim the English style of play: 'They were hard, but played well, together, imaginatively, with speed and movement' (ibid.). This is just what the Spanish admire – the combination of *furia* and skill or imaginative play – 'in a display of physical strength and team spirit' (ibid.).

Though criticizing English football for its anachronistic nature, attempts to modernize the English game are acknowledged in the Spanish press in the 1990s and beyond, even though it suggests that success is only partial: in an article entitled 'Jurassic England', it is purported that 'England wants to modernize but can't' (*El País*, 23 June 1996). England's achievements in modernizing the football industry off the field are lauded (for example, *El País*, 8 September 1983), as is its integration of foreign influences at a domestic level, which is perceived to have had a positive effect on the development of English football: 'foreign blood has been a decisive factor in the reconstruction of British teams' (*El País*, 12 February 1999). The influx of French players into the Premier League is also cited as advancing the English style: 'No country has been more fascinated than England by the success of the French school of football. . . . England has decided to Gallicize in order to shake off the inflexibility that characterized its style of play in the 1970s and 80s' (*El País*, 13 June 2004).

However, England's endeavours to modify its style of play to a winning formula at a national level are classed as flawed: English football cannot be successful if it continues to persist in its obsolete style of play; however, this very style represents the essence of 'Englishness', hence it is a huge challenge to alter it without being unfaithful to the national character. As long as the English highly value players such as Paul Ince, argues one writer sensibly, they will be held back from developing a more sophisticated, modern style of football (*El País*, 23 June 1996). All that has developed, it is argued by the Spanish press, is a style of football that lacks clear definition or identity: 'It is perhaps a lack of definition or sign of identity from which the England team now suffers, led by a Swede (Sven Goran Eriksson), indebted to French influences and represented by players who don't connect well. . . . There is no defined method, influenced by the obsessive diagrams of the manager and the primitive tendencies of some of the defenders who remain anchored to the basic rudiments of English football' (*El País*, 13 June 2004). In other words, 'The English have not done a bad job of updating on a domestic level, better than on the international scene. The influence of continental players has been huge in the Premier League, but the national team has not been able to take that extra step. At best, it is a hybrid between the old roots and a new generation' (*El País*, 17 June 2000).

As we see elsewhere (for example, when the English refute the stereotype of endorsing fair play), even when the English break away from the stereotype, rather than re-evaluate the original premise, the exception to the rule merely seems to reaffirm the original belief: 'England players sometimes stopped the ball dead, as Argentines do, but this does not suit the English' (*ABC*, 31 July 1966). Here, the English played a style that is out of character (and apparently typical of the Argentine style of play) but instead of reporting, in a positive tone, that the English have become more flexible in their approach to football, or have developed a new feature to their game, the Spanish press report it as something improper and inappropriate to their national style.

This discussion regarding a possible evolution in the English style of play raises questions about the possibility that the English identity might also be changing. Is it possible that a changing style of play reflects some deeper social change? Or is this reading too much into what is essentially an exclusively football-related matter? Certainly, a combination of social and football-related change (as a result, for example, of the Bosman ruling in 1995 instituting freedom of movement between European Union member states and leading to a subsequent rise in foreign footballers and managers working in England, along with the rise in the number of international fixtures at club level following the restructuring of the Champions' League) contributes to increased interaction between the English and other nationalities within football. In football terms, it was perhaps inevitable that English football would accommodate some foreign influences. The consequence of this would be the erosion of pre-existent styles and perhaps values too. Social changes might also be pertinent. The stereotypical English style was highly competitive, relied heavily on gritty, rough determination rather than individual talent and flair. English society is arguably becoming less overtly bellicose, violence is less socially acceptable, and some say 'de-masculinized'. This leaves the English style of football wondering where to go in an era in which FIFA have dictated that football involve less physical contact than ever before.

So who are the English, mediated via the Spanish print media? The answer is not simple and credit must be given to Spanish football writers (of the last two decades at least) for their perceptive understanding of the complexities of a nation. However, broadly speaking, there exist two contrasting images of the English, as 'gentlemen' and 'hooligans', both of whom seem to epitomize English-ness for the Spanish press in some way. It is worth developing these two aspects in some detail. Firstly, the English are sometimes 'Gentlemen who watch the match from their bars back home in London' (*ABC*, 27 June 1996). Associated with this gentlemanly image is the notion of 'fair play' and examples proliferate of cognates which emphasize the English sense of and belief in 'fair play'. Second, and in contrast to the upright, chivalrous image of the English, is portrayed the equally hackneyed figure of the beer-swilling, shaven-headed, arrogant hooligan (already noted above as a bogeyman figure in the French press). Let us examine these images in more detail.

The English gentleman is characterized by the strong notion of fair play. This concept is allied to the sense of Englishness throughout the whole period of our sample. Indeed, the notion of fair play is so closely associated with English football that on one occasion it overcame all other national stereotypes: 'Talk of English pride is not appropriate in football, which England began and developed, because England are full of fair play ideals and behave sportingly' (*ABC*, 30 July 1966). Choice of vocabulary illuminates this near-obsession with the English sense of playing the game fairly. When England beat Portugal (2–1) in 'an exemplary match', they 'played in a noble way' (*ABC*, 27 July 1966). It was the combination of 'the English spirit, aroused by good play' which led to England's victory against Portugal (ibid.). It is clear from the text that the 'good play' referred to meant that it was 'a clean game, with few fouls' and 'noble conduct'. The writer, then, attributed England's victory – at least partially – to the fact that they were uplifted by the sporting nature of the game. It is how the English like to play football, ap-parently. When Argentina beat England, 2–0, in 1986, and Maradona scored with the help of the 'Hand of God', *El País* judged that it hurt the English more because one of the goals that beat them was 'illegal' and that this unjust breaking of the rules of fair play rubbed salt into the wounded English pride (7 June 2002). The paper could have a point.

ABC, however, had previously commented on the coverage of the London press following an England defeat by Spain and concludes that the English are 'not as philanthropic or sporting as they were following their defeat against the USA ... they tried to blame poor refereeing' (*ABC*, 4 July 1950). Interestingly, the Spanish match reports did not even mention the controversial penalty deci-sions that it criticizes the English press for covering in such detail. The Spanish press also expressed surprise at the 'incorrect play of the British' (*ABC*, 19 May 1950). Nevertheless, even when the English defy their stereotype (in this case, as proponents of fair play) this merely serves to reinforce the typecast – it was an inappropriate way for the English to behave.

As with the English press coverage examined, adherence to the values of gentlemanly conduct and sporting behaviour does not imply a lack of physical presence in the style of play. As we have seen, qualities such as physical presence, grit and determination are a part of the English identity mediated by the Spanish press, but the Spanish press communicates the notion that these qualities are valued by the English only if they remain within the boundaries set by the regulations of the game. Fair play does not, therefore, equate to any notion of gentility but rather to a strong sense of playing within the rules of the game.

In contrast to the fair-minded, calm and unbiased representation of the English, which has appeared throughout our sample, the hooligan figure is one that does not enter our Spanish football writing until the mid-1980s. By the 1990s, though, the English term, 'hooligan', was frequently used in Spanish football writing to refer to *all* English fans. Although we are told in *El País* that 'hooliganism began [in England] a long time before the Heysel disaster in Brussels' (*El País*, 16 June 1992) we were unable to find specific reference to English hooligans prior to 1985, and the term '*gamberros*' (the Spanish word for 'hooligan') was still used to describe violent England fans. In the early 1980s, English trouble-makers were described simply as 'fans': '45 English fans were arrested in Denmark' (*El País*, 24 September 1982); 'Three British fans were injured after the Spain–England match' (*El País*, 28 March 1980). In 1986, one article in *El País* which mentions 'hooligans' still provides a rough translation ('*gamberros*') for those readers who were not familiar with the term as it emerged into use (*El País*, 22 June 1986). In the late 1980s, the English term 'hooligan' became increasingly common. Since then, a semantic drift has taken place in Spanish as the original meaning of the term 'hooligan' shifted to refer to any particularly passionate fan and sometimes to mean any (English) football fan at all, and many writers use the terms 'hooligan' and 'English fan' interchangeably. It is interesting to note, however, that not all journalists share this habit of referring to all English fans as 'hooligans' and some maintain a semantic distinction between 'fan' and 'hooligan'.

Regardless of the terminology employed, it seems that *El País* is reluctant to update its perception of English hooligans. Two decades of associating English fandom and violence takes a long time to fade. Although the Spanish press lacks the sensationalism of many aspects of its English counterpart and sometimes acknowledges a decline in violence, in many ways it perpetuates the belief in the continued violent nature of English football fans. 'Violent scenes that were so common a decade ago are disappearing from English football, but there are still problems when English fans travel abroad' (14 October 1997); 'Hooliganism has become more sophisticated. The Beast has not died. Far from it: it returns with a difference' (4 August 1993). It is only very recently that the Spanish print media have begun to change the style of their discourse. Coverage of England fans in Japan, for example, presented an image which approximated that of the sporting gentleman more than that of the hooligan: 'English fans behaved well . . . They approached Argentine fans to have their photographs taken with them . . . they picked up cans and litter' (24 June 2002). This behaviour was contrasted with the hooligan image of English fans. In fact, for almost a decade, evidence of changing English fandom has appeared to surprise some writers in the Spanish press.

This hooligan element of English fans is one small part of a larger picture depicted in the Spanish press regarding the English character. On a positive note, in recent years the Spanish have been looking to the English as a rôle model of social integration and this seeps through the sports pages of the newspapers. Spain has only recently begun the quest to eradicate racism from football (and this forms part of a broader anti-racism social policy) and recognizes that England has already made enormous headway in turning this social aspiration into reality. Racism is, indeed, a serious issue in Spanish football and the prevailing attitudes in England and Spain are contrasted: following the Spain–England match in 2004 when the English media lambasted the Spanish fans for booing black players, *El País* explained a cultural difference 'the rival [England] is used to zero tolerance of racism in their country' and suggested that Spain should try to 'go down the path taken in British football grounds' (20 February 2005).

English pride, even arrogance, old-fashioned nature, strong sense of tradition and notions of fair play are all characteristics of the English identity that feature strongly in our Spanish sample. To a large extent, too, overlap exists with the heterotypification of the English and the portrayal of their style of play. It is assumed that because England is the home of football ('the inventors of football', *ABC*, 4 July 1950), the English think they are the best and assumed English arrogance is often close to the surface in Spanish football writing: 'The English have a great opinion of themselves in all aspects of life and football is no exception' (*El País*, 9 June 1996). In our early data, this assumed pride and arrogance spills over into the assertion that the English *are* the best: 'the British masters of intelligent football' (*ABC*, 4 July 1950). Though in later years this myth erodes, the notion that other countries use the English as a yardstick of their own success is present, as others 'measure themselves against the English and their legends' (*El País*, 13 June 2004). This begins to connect with the Spanish portrayal of the English national character. Indeed, the realization that England might not reign supreme globally in football appears to dawn on the Spanish print media at a similar time to when the English suffer their own crisis in confidence following their devastating home defeat against Hungary in 1953. Interestingly, however, the Spanish sense England's vulnerability before the English believe it: 'England are no longer unbeatable' (*ABC*, 19 May 1950). When Spain beat England 1–0 in the World Cup finals in July 1950, 'the lesson, so hard for the old tradition and legitimate pride of football in England, defied all predictions' (*ABC*, 1 July 1950). The decline in football supremacy led to 'the broken pride of the former British maestros' (*ABC*, 17 May 1955). Much later, however, that pride stubbornly remains: 'England has suffered the German hatchet too often, but they refuse to accept the rôle of underdog. Pride does not allow it' (*El País*, 17 June 2000).

The English might not be the most endearing nation, as portrayed in the Spanish sample, but the Spanish press conveys the sense of a population passionate about football for whom football grounds have special status. Atmosphere is seen as an important part of English football and is portrayed with a combination of awe, fear and curiosity – and never more so than at Wembley, 'the boiling pot of football' (*ABC*, 26 July 1966). As in the English print media discourse, Wembley assumes an important status and prestige in the Spanish press (e.g. *ABC*, 30 November 1955). When England hosted the 1966 World Cup, the atmosphere of the historically loaded venue of Wembley was credited with the team's success; whether it be the flags, chants, songs, clapping, constantly mentioned as part of England's achievements, or the belief that 'England are practically unbeatable in the well-built fortress of Wembley' (*ABC*, 26 July 1966). The aura of Wembley makes *others* believe in England's invincibility. Furthermore, it was the fact that FIFA allowed England to play all their matches at Wembley that led to the first murmurs of discontent regarding the organization of the tournament and suspicions that FIFA had manipulated the competition to let England win (ibid.). In more recent times, Wembley has assumed the status of a 'mythological setting' in the words of *El País* (16 June 1996). However, England's lack-lustre performances at Wembley in Euro 96 led one reporter to decry: 'You could make out a few thankless players roaming around Wembley with a lack of respect for its history . . . a holy sanctuary . . . . The Wembley pitch was unjustly treated' (ibid.). Thus, Wembley's iconic status is far greater, and more consistent, than that of the England team, who are not seen as worthy to play there in this case.

Finally, England's perceived status within the British Isles and Europe as a whole is worthy of some discussion. As in French print media discourse, the label 'England' is interchangeable with 'Britain' throughout our sample to the present day. For example, England are often named 'the British *selección*'; 'Castilla will play the winner of the British Cup' trumpets *El País*, referring to the *English* FA Cup (10 July 1980); 'British football lost its position in European football following the 1985 European Cup final' (6 May 1996), clearly should read English football to be accurate, since only English clubs were excluded from playing in Europe following the Heysel disaster. Hence, on occasions, it is difficult to discern whether the Spanish press is making comment about British or English identity. Very few writers are careful enough to distinguish between Englishness and Britishness.

In terms of England's position within Europe, surprisingly little emerged from the sample. There is a perception that England is politically and psychologically isolated from the rest of Europe and that it does not want to be part of Europe. In terms of English identity, while the Spanish press fails to define satisfactorily a European identity or even style of play, English identity and style of play are frequently juxtaposed to the 'European'. We can also detect a level of frustration with the perceived English anti-European stance: *ABC* comment on a friendly played in 1968: '"England v. the Rest of the World" seemed too arrogant. It would be better if it admitted that England is part of Europe' (*ABC*, 5 May 1968). Not only does this allude overtly to English arrogance but it also refers to the way in which Spain perceives England as setting itself apart from the rest of Europe.

So, the Spanish print media coverage of football offers some consistent images of English football and contributes to the creation of national stereotypes. The English have an important place in the history of the global game but their style, heavily reliant on determination, speed and fighting spirit, has been portrayed as antiquated for the last half-century. However, the picture of Englishness is not static. The English gentlemen coexisted with hooligans in the late 1980s and the 1990s but recently there are signs that the image of the thug is in decline. Though there are constants within the way the English style of play is portrayed, evolution is observed too as English football integrates foreign influences and seeks a new identity, one appropriate to the twenty-first century.

Chapter 3

France

The style counsel

Football was played in France in the late nineteenth century but it was not until 1904 that the first official international match was played by a French national team (a 3–3 draw in Belgium). The governing body, the amateur, multi-sport US-FSA (Union des sociétés françaises de sports athlétiques), favoured athletics and rugby over football and failed to take any initiative in establishing a national team. It was content to send a club side, Le Club français, for instance, to participate in the 1900 Olympic Games and it was primarily thanks to the Belgians that a French national team was finally sent into action to play in what was originally designed as an annual trophy between the neighbouring countries, the Evance Coppée Cup (Cazal *et al.* 1998: 15). The creation of FIFA later in the same year (inspired by the Frenchman Robert Guérin, a journalist at *Le Matin*) gave further impetus to the notion of international competition and France was a founder member of the new governing body of world football. The establishment of the French FA (Fédération française de football) in 1919, under the leadership of Jules Rimet, who would go on two years later to preside over FIFA itself, gave further impetus to the development of the sport in France both internationally as well as domestically and France became one of only four European countries to participate in the first ever World Cup finals, held in Uruguay in 1930.

It was, however, some time before France could lay claim to being a power in the football world. The World Cup itself was hosted by France in 1938 as were the first ever European Championships (established by another Frenchman, Henri Delaunay) in 1960. France was, though, eliminated at the quarter final stage of the former and, even more disappointingly, at the semi-final of the latter. The third place obtained at the 1958 World Cup was, therefore, regarded as the high point of French football until the first trophy was won in the 1984 European Championships, held on home soil. By the end of the twentieth century, France had, of course, finally established itself as a formidable force on the world stage by winning both the World Cup (in 1998, again at home) and the European Championships (in 2000) in quick succession.

Of particular pertinence to the present study is the identity of France as a footballing country, the image of Frenchness that is portrayed in sports media texts, notably the quality daily press, both inside and outside France itself. At the end of the twentieth century, that image was unequivocal. Football writing in France's daily press in the last five years or so of the century serves to feed the patriotism of the national imagined community primarily by recycling myths from French military history and, thereby, reinforces an ideological consensus around the concept of the nation defined by Renan as the memories of the (supposedly) great things we have done together (Renan 1882). Next, in its exuberant coverage of the issue of ethnicity, the French press also presents football as an idealized metaphor for late twentieth-century society. France's trophy winning football team is represented as a way for people of diverse origins to live and work harmoniously together in pursuit of a common aim. Finally, style, flair, creativity and quality are felt to be vital and non-negotiable elements of the essentialist French identity although this is accompanied by a realization that creativity is not incompatible with the discipline and hard work necessary for success at the highest level (Crolley and Hand 2002: 63–74). In the light of the above, it will be interesting to consider a representative sample of football writing in the French press from the 1900s to the late 1980s to discover whether or not these features of French autotypification are constants. Additionally, given that the principal attributes of Frenchness outlined above are shared by other countries, it will also be instructive to examine the extent to which English and Spanish perceptions of French national identity have evolved over the same period.

The French self-image

Wahl (1989: 159–60) points out that it was in the early days of international football, which coincided with the rise of chauvinism in Europe prior to the Great War, that the national team's performances started to be identified with the fortunes of the French people and it is interesting to note in this respect the use of what might be termed an inclusive discourse in the match reports and previews of the 1900s and 1910s. Reporters speak of 'our opponents', 'our players', 'our forwards', 'our compatriots' (Le Matin, 24 March 1908) and 'our representatives' (Le Matin, 16 May 1910), for instance, linking the newly formed national team, the print media and the supporters in a common bond by the simple use of the first person plural possessive pronoun 'our'. Such usage is not confined to the early days of football match reporting, though, as it continues into the 1920s and appears consistently in the French press right up to the mid-1960s. It will suffice to provide one or two examples from each decade to substantiate the point. The term 'our players' is noted in one match report (Le Matin, 16 May 1921) and 'our representatives' is used to describe the French team playing Spain in 1923 (Le Matin, 29 January). Similarly, France is 'our team' in the Germany match of 1933 (Le Matin, 20 March) and 'our boys' against Italy in 1938 (Le Matin, 5 December). Reporting in the post-war period continues in the same vein – 'our goalkeeper' (Le Monde, 21 May 1945), 'our forwards' (Le Monde, 24 May 1949) – while the 1950s see no decline in the usage: 'our centre forward' (Le Monde, 5 October 1951), 'our footballers' (Le Monde, 13 April 1954). A particularly striking example of the usage dates from 1961 and a report of a match against Spain in which no fewer than 10 instances are noted in the one article: 'our team', 'our men', 'our 11', 'our football', 'our defence', 'our attack', 'in our favour', 'our forward line', 'our boys' and 'our nets' (*Le Monde*, 2 April). It would seem that this type of writing style disappears somewhat by the 1970s, though, and therefore belongs to a particular era. However, it is also true that, although inclusive discourse is no longer the norm in football reporting by the late twentieth century (as it demonstrably was in the first half of the century), it is still used at times of heightened national awareness and pride such as the aftermath of the 1998 World Cup and the 2000 European Championship victories, for instance (see Crolley and Hand 2002: 63–74), and has, therefore, not fallen completely into disuse.

The 'our boys' discourse of football writing so prevalent in the first 60 years of the twentieth century might well have virtually disappeared by the 1970s but a historical constant in portrayals of the French team throughout the century is to emphasize notions of national community and collective identity through the simple technique of referring to French players in terms of the national flag. They are often, then, 'the tricolours' (*Le Matin*, 22 March 1937; *Le Monde*, 21 May 1946; 6 May 1947; 3 April 1948; 24 May 1949; 19 March 1955; 17 May 1955; 17 February 1956; 20 April 1984; 25 March 1988), 'the tricolour team' (*Le Matin*, 6 May 1921; *Le Monde*, 30 April 1947; 21 May 1949; 21 June 1949; 1 July 1958; 5 May 1962), 'the tricolour 11' (*Le Monde*, 7 October 1952), 'the tricolour attack' (*Le Temps*, 17 March 1931). This is a standard and customary usage which is also noted in the late 1990s (Crolley and Hand 2002: 63–74) and right into a friendly against England in 2000 which duly speaks of 'the tricolour attacks' (*Le Monde*, 5 September 2000). Admittedly, it is often the house style of French newspapers to employ stylistic variation, here the adjective 'tricolour' being used in place of 'French', but nonetheless the cultural connotations of French national identity, unity and, indeed, history represented by the famous blue, white and red flag cannot be divorced from this usage.

Next, the military metaphors that are used so widely in the European media to describe action on the football pitch at the end of the twentieth century (see Boniface 1998; Crolley and Hand 2002; Garland and Rowe 1997; Poulton 1999; Reid 2000) are also in evidence in the earlier periods under consideration in the present study, demonstrating sports journalists' predilection for war imagery. The report of a 1921 encounter with England, for example, refers to the goalkeeper as 'the last rampart' and 'the English territory [being] invaded' (*Le Matin*, 6 May) and that of the 1925 meeting with the same opponents refers to 'well-matched forces' and 'invaded territory' (*Le Matin*, 22 May). A 1937 game against Germany is likewise qualified as 'combat' (*Le Matin*, 22 March) and in a 1947 match the English forwards were said to have displayed 'their skill in finding the breach' in the French defences (*Le Monde*, 6 May 1947). Similarly, in the 1949 meeting with the same opponents, the French 'invaded the British camp' (*Le Monde*, 24 May 1949) whereas their Spanish opponents later in the same year 'flew like arrows opening up deep wounds' (*Le Monde*, 21 June). Again, in a 1954 match against

Germany, 'Our players fought and, faced with the massive and repeated assaults of the enemy, they held their ground', 'regrouped their forces' then 'brought out their trumpets to sound the charge' and themselves 'occupied enemy territory' (*Le Monde*, 19 October). In a 1955 game, the French players were said to be unaffected by conceding a goal and 'returned to the fight to make incursions into Spanish territory' (*Le Monde*, 19 March). Match reports of France's games in the 1966 World Cup, too, are replete with references to the French fighting bravely and courageously (e.g. *Le Monde*, 17/18 July 1966; 22 July 1966).

As well as this general military terminology, the use of which must have become a cliché by the end of the century, there is also evidence of more specifically French socio-cultural references being deployed in print media discourse on football. Wahl (1989: 155–61) notes that, around the time of the Great War, the press establish a parallel between the preferred style of play of the national team and certain French characteristics derived from military history. In both, apparently, the French typically engage in heroic, fervent and courageous attacks against opponents – usually German or English – who are generally better organized and more powerful. Images of French courage in the face of adversity in conflict are, therefore, very prevalent in football writing from the 1910s up to the 1960s. Around the Great War, French players, 'like soldiers charged with the mission of defending the interests and reputation of the homeland . . . appear eminently endowed with the qualities representing the nation' (ibid.: 159). What are these qualities? According to *La Vie au grand air*, 'notably the desire to win, which reflects that of our victorious army, as well as an enthusiasm that often disorientates opponents. The English, Czechs and Belgians were superior man for man in terms of skill on the ball, understanding and executing play but we upset them by the way in which we play football' (20 November 1919, cited by Wahl 1989: 155). The 1921 home match against England is duly reported in the national daily press as a clash of two styles, the English one of 'method and order' contrasting with the French way which is 'based on swiftness, excess speed and furious pace' (*Le Matin*, 6 May). Ultimately, 'French ardour' and 'the fury of our players' overcame the English as France obtained its first ever victory over England (ibid.). A report of a subsequent game against the same opponents four years later employed similar terms and also couched much of its content in an extended metaphor referencing the Napoleonic wars: 'The Old Guard, to whom we have finally appealed, are not quite old enough for the pensioners' home [and] deserve a citation in sporting dispatches' (*Le Matin*, 22 May 1925). (The Old Guard were Napoleon's favourite and most experienced troops who almost saved the day at the battle of Waterloo in 1815; the pensioners' home mentioned in the original French is the Invalides, also a military museum and the final resting place of Napoleon himself.) Two further defeats at the hands of the English towards the end of the decade allow journalists to foreground the qualities of courage and bravery in battle that appear to be important elements of French autotypification at the time: 'energy, courage and heart' were displayed in the 5–1 defeat in 1928 (*Le Matin*, 18 May) and 'the

French team defended courageously' in losing 4–1 in 1929 and 'were in no way diminished by the battle' (*Le Matin*, 10 May).

Reports throughout the 1930s and 1940s continue to expound the same theme. A 1–0 home victory over Germany in 1931 in the first ever meeting between the two countries, for instance, was acclaimed as 'the fine order of the German team was annihilated by the energy and courage of the French' (*Le Temps*, 17 March) while the draw obtained against England in 1945 was apparently achieved because the French can do anything when they are 'moved by zeal and enthusiasm' (*Le Monde*, 29 May 1945). Similarly, the victory over the same opponents a year later was readily attributed to 'the fury and inspiration of the "tricolours"' (*Le Monde*, 21 May 1946). Even (or especially?) in games in which performances are poorer, the French quality of courage is still highlighted throughout by *Le Monde*. In the 1947 defeat by England, 'we defended courageously' (6 May) and, losing to the Spanish in 1949, the French nonetheless 'counter-attacked with a certain courage' (21 June).

Finally, the French print media discourse of the 1950s and 1960s provides further examples of patriotic pride being taken in courageous, although sometimes futile, endeavour. A victory over Germany in 1954 is seen 'primarily as a victory of heart . . . the players fought with ardour against the world champions' (*Le Monde*, 19 October) whereas in 1966 the players were 'courageous' in defeat against Uruguay (*Le Monde*, 17/18 July 1966) and 'valiant' losing to England as the French team 'fought courageously throughout the match' (*Le Monde*, 22 July 1966). Again, in a 1969 friendly against the English, the French were engaged in a contest that was simply 'above their capabilities' but '[these] boys . . . nevertheless fought with courage against rivals superior in every domain' (*Le Monde*, 14 March 1969).

Courage, valour, enthusiasm, ardour, fury, energy and zeal, especially when displayed in adversity, are clearly leitmotifs in French football writing (at least until the 1970s) and constitute a veritable semantic field operating within print media portrayals of Frenchness even though individual examples might well appear in different locations (different organs of the press) as well as at different times (from the 1920s to the end of the 1960s). There is, however, another typical element that characterizes Frenchness, especially in the sporting context, which it is important to examine forthwith.

Style is a typical French trademark at the end of the twentieth century. French footballers are expected to demonstrate on the pitch the qualities associated with style, creativity and flair and are roundly castigated should they fall short in this respect (for discussion of examples relating to the last three major tournaments of the twentieth century, the European Championships of 1996 and 2000 and the 1998 World Cup, see Crolley and Hand 2002: 63–74). One of the important questions to be posed in the present study is whether these concepts are historical constants or relatively recent constructs. It has to be noted that overt references to French style and flair are few and far between in the early days of international football (from the 1900s to the 1920s) and that, even then, references in the data up to the mid-1950s are still less frequent (and less exuberant) than those from the late 1950s onwards and particularly from the 1980s. However, the notions are still present in significant ways and are worthy of examination.

We have already acknowledged the importance of courage in adversity as a defining feature of Frenchness in the football context. French players are, though, praised further by the daily press when they add to this quality the concept of putting on a good show, a vibrant display or an entertaining spectacle. The team that lost away to Spain in a 1923 friendly, for instance, was lauded in this way: 'they made a good impression and deserve congratulations for their admirable courage' (Le Matin, 29 January). The idea that a French team is praiseworthy even in defeat so long as it has provided a good spectacle is further reinforced by a report of a match against Italy in 1932: 'The crowd were not too disappointed. It mattered little to them that the French team were beaten so long as the match was splendid' (Le Matin, 11 April). Indeed, by the late 1940s, the link between French football and creativity and flair seems well established given that it is a source of disappointment to journalists to witness a French team that fails to display these attributes. The lack of imagination shown by the team that crashed to a 5–1 home defeat against Spain in 1949, for example, was qualified as simply 'inconceivable' by the reporter in Le Monde (21 June).

It would seem that it is the 1950s that see the real flourishing of the discourse of style and flair in the football match reports and related articles of the French daily press and yet, in the early part of the decade, although these characteristics are now recognized as typically French, there is still some ambivalence over what is the primary attribute defining Frenchness, style or courage. A report of the 1952 victory over Germany illustrates the point. 'Everything that gives French football its character was on view yesterday: ball control, clever passing, body swerves, dribbles, switching the play into open spaces . . . but the greatest merit was perhaps to have maintained courage throughout' (Le Monde, 7 October). The turning point in this issue almost certainly came with France's unexpectedly good performances in the 1958 World Cup finals in Sweden. Led by the highly respected duo of Albert Batteux and Paul Nicolas off the pitch and by the brilliant playmaker Raymond Kopa and record-breaking goal scorer Just Fontaine on it, France reached the semi-finals, to be eliminated by Brazil, and demolished West Germany 6–3 in the playoff to take third place, which would remain the best ever performance by a French team in international competition until the European Championship was won in 1984. Le Monde's report of the Germany match (1 July 1958) might be read as setting the standard for French national teams of the future in that it closely identifies a particular type of football with Frenchness itself, defining the French self-image in the now familiar terms of creativity and flair bringing (relative) success which, although present in earlier periods as we have seen, had previously to vie with the notion of courage in adversity (and frequent defeat) as the principal defining feature of French national identity in print media discourse on football. 'In Sweden, France found her style' trumpets the headline of the report in question. This 'splendid performance' is lauded as 'the finest in the history of our football' and the article continues with the somewhat prophetic statement that 'our national team has found its own style, its personality, which has charmed the world and which from now on should be its trademark'. What constitutes this style? First, the importance of the 'marvellous playmaker', Kopa, is stressed. Kopa, 'one of the most remarkable footballers in the world', who 'shines like a thousand torches', is 'the man around whom the French team is based'. Notwithstanding his own merits, Kopa, 'the Napoleon of French football' according to Lanfranchi (2002: 19), also prefigures future French playmakers who, in their turn, would be portrayed as living embodiments of Frenchness by sports media discourse, such as Michel Platini (see below) and Zinedine Zidane (see Crolley and Hand 2002: 65, 72–4). Next, the open, flowing, attacking style of play, 'always looking to score' is duly cited by the newspaper as the second defining feature: 'Above all, it's a simple, direct, incisive attacking style made up of short, neat passes, executed on the move with clever and quick movement of players.' In short, 'French football has [now] staked its claim to fame' with the result that, after 1958, the expectations of French national teams in respect of style, creativity and flair are high, much higher than they ever were before. Indeed, the importance of the 1958 World Cup cannot be overestimated in this respect: as Hare notes (2003: 122), the interest generated in France by the relative success of the national team did much to raise the status of football to that of 'a vector of national values'.

When the expectations of national values being upheld are met, praise will flow in the French press in extravagant abundance; when they are not, castigation and even denigration will be just as swift to follow. Following France's elimination from the 1966 World Cup, for example, Le Monde rounded (ever so politely) on the manager, Henri Guérin, criticizing him for his lack of creativity and his attempts to impose too rigid a defensive system on his players. He did not have the 'radiant personality' of his predecessors such as Paul Nicolas. Style in French football writing is often conveyed using images of radiance, brilliance and shining lights (see Crolley and Hand 2002: 63–74); Guérin did not display the required brilliance and Le Monde, along incidentally with the specialist magazine France Football (Cazal et al. 1998: 201), called for his immediate resignation: 'Mr Henri Guérin should have the wisdom to resign' (3 August 1966). He would not be the last French manager to be on the receiving end of a press campaign directed against him for not sufficiently accentuating the now widely expected qualities of style and creativity (for an overview and discussion of the mid-1990s print media criticisms of Aimé Jacquet see for instance Crolley and Hand 2002: 11, 66–71; McKeever 1999: 161–83; Tournon 2000: 211–15).

Le Monde goes further in its reflections on the 1966 World Cup to extrapolate from the early French and Italian eliminations and the English victory what it calls 'The failure of Latin football'. 1966 represents the 'decline' of the Latin game, incapable of competing with 'the rigour of the meticulously organized defensive systems' of the top northern European teams, England and West Germany. Then, in a highly revealing sequence, the newspaper asks the rhetorical question 'Should we really rejoice in this?' before providing its own answer in the negative: 'This game should above all be rich in attacking movements, open, ambitious, alert, imaginative with the heady taste of trying to win rather than only seeking to avoid being beaten' (3 August). Clearly expectations in the French sports media are that football should be an arena in which the spectacle of creativity, style and flair is displayed and it is a source of some consternation that what *Le Monde* later calls 'the liveliness, the inspiration, the gift of improvisation, typical French qualities as we all know' (14 March 1969) are often not enough on their own to overcome the power, strength and organization displayed by teams such as England.

If the 1966 World Cup marked the eclipse of Latin football, at least in its French guise, then the mid-1980s saw its triumphant return to prominence as France reached two World Cup semi-finals (in 1982 and 1986) and won the European Championships (in 1984). The French team was led by its captain and playmaker and, therefore, heir to Kopa, Michel Platini, whose rôle was constantly acclaimed by the press, often via metaphors of light and illumination that typically embellish the narratives of successful heroes inside and outside the sporting context in France: 'The French captain is unequalled in raising the temperature on the pitch and in the stands. . . . Never has he shone with as much impact as in the national team'; 'Platini lights up the play in a flash' (*Le Monde*, 23 February 1982); 'Platini's passing is luminous' (*Le Monde*, 10 July 1982).

The 1982 World Cup semi-final encounter with West Germany, watched on television, according to Wahl (1989: 322), by 30 million people in France, marks the high point of press reporting on the association of style and flair with essential Frenchness (until the apotheosis that is the 1998 World Cup triumph, which is the subject of another study; see Crolley and Hand 2002). The three articles covering the match appearing in *Le Monde* communicate as much information about French perceptions of the Germans as they do about French identity itself and these will be explored later (see below, Chapter 4). Focusing on France, the front page headline after the match simply read 'Bravo!' 'French romanticism' had triumphed in defeat, apparently, as 'the French team joined Brazil in the land of legendary fabulous losers beaten as much by their own passion for the game as by their opponents'. The newspaper compliments the Germans on their victory but not without considerable irony: 'you won because we were better' (10 July 1982), the implication being that the French played the game in the correct open and attacking way whereas the Germans' approach was negative, over-physical and mean-spirited. The match report on the inside pages picks up the principal theme with its first sentence reading, 'What a team, but what a team!' 'It's only football but, for once, we can play the patriotic card', the report continues, France 'were exemplary and magnificent, they were superb on Thursday night, this team . . . the stylish French team of whom magical things are expected. . . . It could not be clearer. From the French we expect a spectacle.' Once Platini had equalized the early German goal, the expected spectacle unfurled: this was 'a superb and lengthy exhibition' of football, humiliating the supposedly best team in Europe; this was 'the start of an extraordinary French fantasia typified by the sparkling Tigana, an attacking whirlwind, a delight and a masterful show of attacking football'. France even went 3–1 up in extra time only to be pegged back to 3–3. *Le Monde*'s explanation for the failure to win the game in extra time revolves around the very nature of what it is to be French: 'a team has to be able to hold on to a lead but, when it's a French team, it will have faults deriving from its own qualities, an inability to close the door, to shut up shop, an inability in short to keep a calm head. . . . France had got to the final and then lost out by their own hand. . . . [T]he sublime spectacle was [then] brought to a brutal end' by defeat in the World Cup's first ever penalty shoot-out (ibid.). However, in the final analysis, because France had gone down with style, because the team had been defeated playing open, spectacular football, they can be only praiseworthy in the eyes of the print media (especially when contrasted with their somewhat cynical German opponents): 'All in all, between the permanently arrogant, contemptuous and scandalous behaviour of the German team and the desire to play well, the attacking spirit and the sense of spectacle of the French team, the choice is easily made' (13 July 1982). Demonstrating great intelligence and creativity in a battle against overwhelming odds that may well still lead to ultimate defeat is a source of heroism in French eyes, a marker of the 'Asterix complex' (Hare 2003: 124) with which many in France readily identify.

Reports of the successful 1984 European Championship campaign continue to accentuate the notions of style and creativity although the performance in the final of the tournament is portrayed as something of a disappointment in this respect. Reviewing the tournament up to the final, *Le Monde* indicates that, after 80 years of expectations, the national team is finally consistently delivering performances worthy of a French side: 'Never since the first match in 1904 has the French team been as celebrated as it is now for its performances in major competitions and its string of good results. [The manager] Michel Hidalgo has provided a style and a personality that are *universally appreciated*' (28 June, emphasis added). It is as if France's footballers have finally caught up with the expectations placed upon them by the media and the supporters. There is a template of French identity that the national team has to slot into. When it does, all is well and print media discourse overflows with praise for what is perceived as the full realization on the football field of the most praiseworthy aspects of French national identity. *Le Monde* explains the characteristics that find such favour in French eyes: 'this is football where pleasure in playing the game remains the priority . . . where the players aren't prisoners of tactical straitjackets but can take their own initiatives . . . and truly flourish' (ibid.).

Within this context, the manner of the victory achieved over Spain in the final of the tournament was not particularly appreciated by *Le Monde* as it did not live up to the demanding expectations placed on French footballers. That France and Spain should be contesting a major final is seen as a source of pride in a particular type of football, confirming 'the return to prominence of the football of the Latin countries' (29 June), but the match itself was portrayed as failing to provide the desired exhibition of French flair comparable with that displayed in the earlier rounds (notably against Belgium) or, indeed, in the 1982 World Cup. The match was won 'commando fashion' rather than by creativity and inspiration and was marred by niggling personal battles and duels. Worse, leading 1–0, the French began to play 'in the Italian way', the 'anti-football' way and closed the game down rather than continuing to attack. Ironically, it had been noted, of course, that the absence of such a tactic had led to ultimate defeat in 1982 against West Germany whereas here it guaranteed victory and France's first major trophy. Even so, in French print media discourse on football by the late twentieth century, winning is neither sufficient nor satisfying if it is achieved without flair and creativity; conversely, as in 1982, losing can be glorious and fulfilling if the French go down in style. The consolation gained by becoming European champions merely tempers rather than eradicates the disappointment felt on witnessing a French team, *the* quintessential French team of the mid-1980s no less, betraying its inheritance. The disappointment is voiced by the telling rhetorical question posed in the very last sentence of the match report in *Le Monde*, which says so much about French expectations of their sporting heroes: 'Is this really the final [Hidalgo] dreamed about for French football, for the crowd and for the millions of kids who are behind us?' (ibid.).

It is interesting to note that, taken as a whole, the samples of the print media discourse on football in the twentieth century support the interpretation of French national identity offered by Pierre Daninos (1954), who claims two dominant aspects of Frenchness, *le relèvement*, that is France fighting courageously in adversity particularly against superior opponents, and *le rayonnement*, which is France shining like a beacon providing a glorious example for the world. Both of these aspects of essentialist identity are heroic. The former is symbolized by Joan of Arc, the prototype resistance leader and national heroine who fought to rid France of the English invader in the Hundred Years War and the latter by Napoleon Bonaparte, the great military and political leader who, initially at least, spread French glory and influence around much of Europe in the early nineteenth century. In terms of the press coverage of French football, we see both aspects of character highlighted. In the earlier periods, in which France found it difficult to make its mark on international football, the accent is on courage, fervour, zeal and enthusiasm in battle, whereas from the late 1950s onwards, when performances improved and France finally became a major player on the world stage, the focus is more on the exemplary qualities of flair and style and taking pride in French greatness in these respects. It is too facile to state that one aspect gave way completely to the other at any particular point in the twentieth century (even though the 1958 World Cup is a good candidate) as clearly there is considerable overlap between the two. What it is fair to say, though, is that the imagined identity of France seen in auto-typification through football writing has to be based on one of these two aspects of character. If neither characteristic is present, then the French press is merciless in its condemnation and this is as true in 1984 (see above) and in the mid-1990s (see Crolley and Hand 2002: 65–7) as it was in the early days of international football: 'The French played their part badly. Their game was jerky, imprecise . . . pitiful . . .

and their clumsiness was not compensated by any courage or ardour' (*Le Matin*, 10 April 1911).

A final theme to consider is that of ethnicity. By the end of the twentieth century, the majority of commentators (inside and outside the media) view the inclusion of ethnic minority players in the French national team as a positive development. Indeed, the success of the ethnically diverse squad in international competition seemed to focus attention on the relationship between ethnicity, citizenship and inclusion and demonstrated the power of what Gastaut (2005) calls 'the symbolic charge' invested in footballers from the ethnic minorities in France. For instance, immediately after France won the 1998 World Cup with its team of *blacks, blancs, beurs* (blacks, whites and second generation North Africans; the alliteration and word play on the colours of the national flag, *bleu, blanc, rouge* – blue, white, red – are woefully lost in translation), *Le Monde* and *Libération*, among many others, treated their readers to a flood of utopian moralizing on the subject of immigration. The mediation of the football team's success elevated it to the status of exemplum, a symbol dispensing invaluable instruction in the lessons to be learnt from French history and politics. France's footballers, therefore, incarnate 'the French concept of a nation: a country built on immigration' (*Libération*, 10 June 1998); 'the French people are discovering, in the faces of their team, that they have become a mixed race Republic, that this works, that we can all love one another, and that we can win' (*Libération*, 10 July 1998). Morally, this French model is seen as superior to others because this 'multicolour team [is] a mirror of the mosaic that is France' (ibid.), a personification of 'the ideal of the French melting pot' (ibid.) which, by virtue of its having 'virtually no equal anywhere in Europe' (*Libération*, 10 June 1998), is viewed as a singularly positive defining feature of French identity (for further discussion, see Crolley and Hand 2002: 72–4).

The presence in the national team of naturalized immigrants and players from France's ethnic minorities is by no means a new phenomenon, though. The much acclaimed team of the late 1970s and early 1980s included Marius Trésor (from Guadeloupe), Manuel Amoros (of Spanish descent), Jean Tigana (Mali), Michel Platini (of Italian descent) and Luis Fernandez (Spain); the 1960s saw Nestor Combin (Argentina), Jean Djorkaeff (of Russian descent); the 1950s Raymond Kopa (of Polish descent), Just Fontaine (born in Morocco of a Spanish mother), Rachid Mekloufi (Algeria), Roger Piantoni (of Italian descent), Abdelaziz Ben Tifour (Algeria), Mustapha Zitouni (Algeria); the 1940s Rudi Hiden (Austria), Larbi Ben Barek (Morocco), Julien Darui (born in Luxembourg of Italian and Portuguese descent); the 1930s Alfred Aston (of English descent), Gusti Jordan (Austria), Hector Cazenave (Uruguay); and the 1920s Henri Bard (Switzerland) (Cazal *et al.* 1998; Saccomano 1998; see also Marks 1999). Indeed, in 1986, the daily sports paper *L'Equipe* published a survey demonstrating that a third of the players who had represented France up to that point were of foreign or immigrant origins (cited by Mourlane 2003 and by Hare 2003: 133). Even so, prior to the 1990s, at least on the basis of the data examined for the present study, the issue of ethnicity hardly features at all in the football writing of the general French national daily press (although there are, as Marks [1999] observes, noteworthy articles devoted to the issue in the specialist press). Indeed, it is only rarely that the ethnic origins of players representing France are even mentioned and when they are, no further comment is deemed necessary. For instance, Michel Platini is often referred to as 'France's Italian' (e.g. *Le* Monde, 17 June 1986) while the unfortunate scorer of an own goal against England in 1951 is 'the Algerian Firoud' (*Le Monde*, 3 October). Again, De Bourgoing, playing against Italy in 1962, is qualified simply as 'the Franco-Argentine' (*Le Monde*, 5 May). Reporting on a victory over Germany in 1952, *Le Monde* even accompanies its article with a box indicating the ethnic make-up of the side (five players from the Nord, two Parisians, one from the Ardennes, one from the Morbihan and two naturalized immigrants, the Pole Cisowski and the Hungarian Ujlaki) but no interpretation whatsoever is given of the significance, if any, of these facts (7 October).

In seeking to understand why the issue of ethnicity becomes such an important one for the general daily press only from the 1990s onwards, it could be argued that it is only then that the topic is at centre stage politically, placed there by the emergence of a strong presence on the far right of French politics in the shape of the Front national. Although it was founded in 1972, the Front national did not break through electorally until 1986 when its near 10 per cent of the vote at the general elections saw it receive 35 MPs in the French National Assembly. From that point onwards, the party scored between 10 and 15 per cent of the vote at general and presidential elections, making it one of the top four parties in French politics and providing a platform for its charismatic leader, Jean-Marie Le Pen, to preach a form of nationalist discourse that excluded immigrants and many ethnic minorities from participation in the national family. Indeed, Le Pen even turned his sights on the French football team during the European Championships of 1996 declaring that many of its 'foreign' members did not want, or even know how, to sing the national anthem (*Le Monde*, 25 June). It seems feasible, therefore, to state that print media discourse on football in France appears, in this respect, to operate with an ideological function: to promote a consensus around a shared image of the nation based on the traditional French concept of creating unity from diversity, a concept which is felt to be under threat in the 1990s from an increasingly powerful force in politics that would seek to undermine just such a consensus. In a way, the euphoric utopianism of the late 1990s discourse on France's 'Blues of all colours' (*Libération*, 10 June 1998) may be read as a liberal (over)reaction against the depressive dystopian discourse of the Front national on the perils of multiculturalism. In much the same way as the print media are all too ready to castigate French footballers who do not live up to the expectations of them to personify the ideal of Frenchness based on courage in adversity, style and flair, so, too, are the press only too ready to manipulate football and present it as the vehicle for communicating a sentimental vision of national harmony within ethnic diversity – but only when that vision is seriously called into question by a threatening force outside the mainstream of French society.

France viewed from England

Our analysis of the way in which France and the French are represented in the English press may be divided into four periods: pre-war (1920–38), post-war (1945–55), the emergence and pinnacle of French-style football (1968–84) and the contemporary period (1996 to the present day). These categories by no means correspond to clear delineations in the way the English press deals with 'Frenchness' but they coincide with certain patterns which emerge in our data.

In the early, pre-war period, though the press articles examined are relatively short and lack detail, we have enough material in fixtures between England and France to be able to propose some tentative suggestions regarding the way the English print media portrayed the French. Coverage of France's fixtures against other teams reveals little as it is limited largely to reporting of results and/or a team sheet at best. We must rely heavily, then, on the coverage of fixtures between England and France (although matches against Scotland also provide a small amount of data in the early years).

In early football coverage of international fixtures, a clearly patronizing tone could be detected towards French football. Following an England victory over France in Paris, for instance: 'The French showed a marked improvement [from the previous year], their team work being quite up to international standard' (*The Times*, 19 May 1924). However, as long as the French imitated the English style of football, within the text, we note the subliminal respect for their style of play – generally long balls, strength and speed: the English hailed the French for their 'fine clearances' and 'vigorous' play and were particularly respectful of Diagne, who was a 'tower of strength' (*The Times*, 27 May 1938). At this time too, the French appeared to share the English sporting ethos within football. As usual during the pre-war period, the 'sporting spirit' (by both teams, in this case) was commented upon and *The Times* similarly praised the French for their hospitality: 'The visitors received a warm welcome, and were applauded heartily when the game was over' (27 May 1938). In terms of Anglo-French relations, there was no hint of animosity towards the French in this period, which was still marked diplomatically by the *entente cordiale* first signed in 1904.

Interestingly, a report on England versus France 'Ladies' in 1920 largely mirrors the values depicted in the men's game ('There was charging too – charging of a Corinthian kind – fair but vigorous . . . . It was a hard, sporting game') and the playing styles of the English and French are contrasted: apparently, the crowd was 'delighted with this French civilisation of our rough and tumble sport' (*The Times*, 7 May 1920). The qualities of English ladies' football are reported as having something in common with the men's – it is a 'rough and tumble sport' – but the characteristics of the French are evidently more stylish than those of the English. Whether the French have a civilizing effect because they are French or because they are French *women* we can only conjecture. What is clear is the perception in 1920 that French women were more sophisticated than their English counterparts.

By 1938, football was considered important enough for *The Times* to send its own correspondent to Paris to report on England's 5–1 victory over France (*The Times*, 27 May 1938).

In many of these pre-war articles, while the match reports offered little material on the development of French characteristics in the print media, they nevertheless offer snippets of socio-historical value. It is usual for the reporters to comment on what we might today consider peripheral issues, such as who wins the toss and the wind direction. In the days when the 'field' or 'turf' was offered little protection from large stands and roofing and the long-ball style of play was the rage, who had to 'face the wind' first assumed great importance.

In the immediate post-war period, it is clear from the coverage of the England versus France match that took place on 27 May 1945 that the war itself was understandably uppermost in the minds of the reporter. Indeed, the proceeds of this 'friendly' match were to go to British and French war charities, we are informed (*The Times*, 28 May 1945). *The Times* mentioned the fact that a French band from the 156th Infantry Regiment of the French First Army was to play at Wembley before the match and that they were travelling straight from Germany where they had been 'fighting until the surrender' (*The Times*, 25 May 1945). The Allied Football Associations who were in the United Kingdom during the war were to present a flag to the (English) FA prior to the game. The French were portrayed as close friends and allies of the English. The fact that 'friendly' matches were played in the immediate post-war period with such frequency also suggests familiarity and a good working Anglo-French relationship in football terms at least.

On a football-related note, though, it is clear that England still assumed football supremacy over their neighbours across the English Channel in this period: 'It will be something of a surprise if England do not win with something to spare this afternoon' (*The Times*, 26 May 1945). Perhaps predictably, given hindsight of several decades of 'over-hyping' journalism, England underestimated their opposition and did not win. The outcome was a draw, and, typically, the French were given due credit for their performance.

In 1946 another 'friendly' match took place between England and France. At a time when cricket dominated the sports page of *The Times*, with rugby, 'Association' football, golf and greyhound racing enjoying a short paragraph each, the match report consisted of one paragraph (plus a team sheet which included players' names and the domestic club they played for; names only in the case of French players) supplied by Reuters; *The Times* itself did not send a correspondent. France won the match 2–1 and *The Times* again sportingly admitted that 'France won a well-deserved victory' (20 May 1946).

The following year, the two sides met again, on 3 May 1947, on the same day as domestic league fixtures took place. This time the match – significant as being 'the first international match in which substitute goalkeepers will be allowed in the event of injury' – seemed to attract more attention than previous encounters: a column of some 300 words, plus the team sheet. Throughout, the French are referred to as a 'Continental' side, and apparently they displayed appropriately

'Continental' characteristics. England were advised to release the ball reasonably quickly to their forwards, 'for Continental sides recover quickly to form a barrier inside the penalty area which is often hard to penetrate' (*The Times*, 3 May 1947). The tone of the preview is cautionary, warning England not to underestimate their cross-Channel neighbours. Aware that they were unbeaten 'by a Continental side' in England, and reminding readers of the aforementioned draw, *The Times* insisted that England were keen not to have their 'colours lowered on English soil, but two years ago the flag was at half-mast, for the French held us to a draw at Wembley Stadium.' At this time, then, there appears to be awareness that the French are un-English and that they pose more of a threat in football terms than ever before but there is still little evidence of a specifically French identity. The French are part of the 'Continent'. For a long time, and bridging the pre-war and post-war periods in our data, the French were categorized as 'Continental' by the English print media rather than more narrowly defined as French.

There was a marked change of attitude in the match report in 1947. Victory inspired more than a touch of arrogance in the tone: 'France came to Highbury on Saturday in search of the victory on English soil that everyone across the channel lives for. But they retired a sadder and wiser team, for though they defended successfully – if somewhat unethically – until just after half time, when at last their goal fell, England in the end beat them by three goals to none and the beating was even more emphatic than the score would suggest. . . . France in a word were outclassed' (*The Times*, 5 May 1947). Even with such smugness – and scorn at the unsporting style of play – the reporting style has room for magnanimity – 'Conceded their centre-half, Gregoire, was injured' – but there was thinly veiled criticism of the short-passing style of the French: 'in the first half they mounted an attack in which we saw the side string together a series of short passes. But in truth this short-passing of theirs merely took them round the England defence, never through it at speed' (ibid.). While this hints at what later becomes a recognizably intricate French style of play, it is implicit that the effective way would have been to go straight through the English defence, at pace – that is, the English way! Indeed, in contrast, 'Swift [Manchester City's goalkeeper] busied himself occasionally by gathering loose balls and – much to the crowd's enjoyment – kicking them downwind very nearly into the French penalty area' (ibid.). Later on, England's 'beautiful passing *at speed*' (our emphasis) is lauded. This says a lot about the style of football appreciated and valued by the English at that time and, more appropriately to our discussion here, it informs us of how the French style of football was portrayed, contrasted to the English style and viewed as plainly inferior.

For the first time, we perceive a hint of an imagined French national identity seeping into the football writing: 'Why were the French able to go in at half-time on level terms, with their hearts still high and their many tricolours waving defiantly in the breeze?' (*The Times*, 5 May 1947). This alludes to a specifically conferred French, rather than 'Continental' identity, with French identity now closely associated with the national flag.

Much less informative is the coverage of the corresponding fixture in 1949 in

France. Unlike the match just three years earlier, a correspondent from *The Times* was actually present at this game and the report again holds some interesting features. Indeed, the account is significantly longer than in previous years, occupying a whole column of *The Times* for the first time in this series of 'friendlies' against France. Though 'the French fought hard' and the 'thrust and counter-thrust' at speed of their attacks was appreciated (*The Times*, 23 May 1949), the match reporter does not pass by the opportunity to comment on the 'Continental' style of playing, increasingly becoming a euphemism for cheating: 'It was not a great match – there was too much obstruction and unethical continental tackling for that' (ibid.). One of the rare comments that emerges from the scant coverage in *The Times* of the Scotland–France fixtures of this period alerts the reader to the fact that 'France made quick progress along the ground' (28 April 1949). The French style of play is becoming evident.

By 1951, English supremacy on the football field is no longer assumed with quite the assurance of the pre- and immediate post-war period: 'On the face of it, France would not appear seriously to threaten England's unbeaten record against foreign challenge on these shores' (*The Times*, 3 October 1951). However, football writing now refers to an 'overseas threat that has grown apace in the last 20 years.' Sure enough, the French were no pushovers and the match was drawn.

By now, the 'Continental style' is 'traditional' and of the French *The Times* predicted: 'Doubtless they will show all the traditional cleverness of the continental footballer, but it remains to be seen whether they will be able to finish their attacks strongly against a well-organised English defence' (*The Times*, 3 October 1951). This questions the extent to which the (rather ambiguous) 'cleverness' can overcome a traditionally English defence. A strong element of what Perryman (1999: 24) describes as a 'problem with things foreign' permeates the English print media when it comes to describing the style and quality of football of other nations. Hence the French short passing is disdainfully looked upon as ineffective. There is a denigration of the Other that escalates throughout the second half of the twentieth century (for further discussion, see Crolley and Hand 2002).

The shame of only drawing the 1951 match to the French is almost tangible. On one hand, the report indicates how 'France played valiantly' but, on the other, for the England players, 'It was a match they will wish to forget as quickly as possible' (*The Times*, 4 October 1951). The reporter admitted that there were 'many lessons to be learnt' – not least of all 'the England defenders have not yet learnt how to penetrate Continental defenders who trade space for time.' It reminds the reader that England's 'unbeaten record against the overseas challenge still stands intact within these shores. In fact, the apple at the top of the tree still remains out of reach to the invader' (ibid.). The undefeated home record, portrayed typically via metaphors of military impregnability, is almost becoming a burden as the 'Continental' opposition strengthens visibly.

In 1955, a 'British Correspondent Resident in Paris' wrote a fascinating article on the 'Evolution of Football in France: Effect of British Influence' (*The Times*, 11 May 1955). Within this article, the English were no longer viewed as unbeatable by the French. The gap between 'the pupils and their masters' in football terms had narrowed. There was also an acknowledgement that the French style of play differed from the British and that it included features of the game so far unappreciated in the UK: 'French national teams unusually play what critics have called the Latin game – colourful, varied, and very fast. The French still admire the ball control of our players, their giving and receiving of hard passes, the heading and loyal virility. They believe, however, that the Latin style, well exploited, beats the cold efficiency even of Britain's best players' (ibid.). Although the characteristics which define France according to our sample are by now obvious (for example, 'a quick-moving and skilled attack' [*The Times*, 16 June 1958]), Frenchness is yet to become nation-specific. It is still part of a broader 'Continental' definition or, in this case, it is 'Latin'.

This all changes by the time we enter the third phase of our data on France in England. Towards the end of the 1960s, the Continental nature of French football is secondary to its Frenchness. The football team and the nation they represent are by now closely identified. Anglo-French relations also seem to have deteriorated. Perhaps reflecting the frosty diplomatic relationships between Britain and France during the de Gaulle presidency (1959–1969), there seems to be a particular delight conveyed in beating the French: 'The 85,000 crowd were in full throat, fixed it would seem by a special desire to teach the French a lesson. And certainly by the end Gaul had been carved up into many pieces' (13 March 1969).

During this period, French football rises from mediocrity (at best) in the 1960s to supremacy in the 1980s. *The Times* initially laments how football in France seems to be in a moribund state: 'Lacking success at various levels – international or even Continental, in the various European competitions – public support and interest in the game are peeling away, like an onion by layer . . . and football is virtually in its coffin' (1 January 1969). However, there is already some appreciation of French artistry – 'they caressed the ball around smoothly' (21 July 1966) – and this is a salient characteristic which will dominate writing on French football for the next two decades and beyond.

In the mid-1970s, for instance, *The Times* claimed that for a generation, since Stade de Reims reached the European Cup final in the 1958–59 season, 'French football has lain silent and becalmed in a trough. Now it is alive again' (12 May 1976). Similarly, when Saint-Etienne were beaten by Liverpool in the European Cup quarter final, in a match famous for its atmosphere at Anfield, French football had become 'tactically engrossing' and 'attractive to the eye' (*The Times*, 3 March 1977). However, it was in the 1980s when French football really reinforced its typecast and the flamboyance of French football shone through with one headline in particular catching the eye: 'France, flying the tricolour of flamboyance' (*The Times*, 13 July 1982).

Commentary on French football in the 1980s is, indeed, peppered with lexical items that conjure images of extravagance and beauty. Giresse 'teases' us with his dribbling abilities (*The Times*, 9 July 1982), for example. Then, in a 'mesmeric evening' when the French beat Yugoslavia 3–2 in the World Cup finals, 'France strolled through the first half looking pretty' and at the start their 'performance bordering on arrogance had alienated their adoring supporters' but 'once roused, the sleeping beauty of French football reawakened' (*The Times*, 20 June 1984).

This is the period when *The Times* can trumpet: 'France's attacking spirit brightens up the game' with their 'blatant over-confidence' (25 June 1984). By now the French are all about confident, attacking splendour: 'the French are committed . . . they do not know how to be negative . . . will always attack . . . with an irrepressible spirit.' Their 'exhilarating destruction' of Belgium 5–0 at the European Championships was heralded as a 'triumph of technique over tactics' (*The Times*, 18 June 1984) as France apparently proved that 'there is no tactical answer to individual ability.' While the likes of Platini, Giresse and Tigana typified 'a short passing game of supreme accuracy', France 'strolled' to victory. Not only was the smooth ease of the victory the trademark of French football but the 'spontaneous', 'artistic', 'creative' style in which it was accomplished is a leitmotif in our data (e.g. *The Times*, 13 June; 16 June; 28 June 1984). The press presents a French team which combines successfully individual flair and team effort in a way that the English find so difficult to accomplish. The 'spontaneity' and 'improvisation' of the 'artists' are uplifting for journalists of *The Times*, who 'yearn to see technical extravagance and grace with the ball' (16 June 1984). The English print media, then, present French football in a dreamy light: 'football, which, as France has so beautifully proved in the past fortnight, can still achieve romantic and dramatic proportions' (26 June 1984). One of the most persistent myths reiterated by the English press is that of the French national team's flair and style: 'It is the generic obsession with style which gives them such international appeal' (*The Times*, 12 June 1984). Undeniably linked here to representations of the French nation, whom the English tend to envy for their higher standard of living and better quality of life (Gallie 1997), football writing identifies French football as superior in quality, with their 'elegant and eloquent' performances (*The Times*, 28 June 1984), the vocabulary chosen to describe football here echoing other general descriptions of the French. In a similar fashion, we note repeated synonyms relating to the 'romance' and 'artistry' of French football. Question marks, however, take the form of a tendency among the English football writing to query France's stamina and morale when things do not go smoothly. Despite their positive qualities, the French are at times 'tentative' or 'emotional'. The English press thus extends prevailing attitudes towards the French (that they are emotional and somehow fragile in character) to their style of football.

France 98 (when France, of course, emerged as winners of the World Cup) provided further opportunities to make the connection between the French nation and the concept of style. *The Times* assumes that the French expect their football to be representative of their nation: 'The French nation may be looking for style as well as victory from the host team' (13 June 1998). In many ways, the coverage of France 98 repeats and consolidates the leitmotifs that have been accumulating throughout most of the century within football writing. The coverage is saturated with references to the 'style', 'extravagance', 'elegance' and 'vivacity' of France. France's football is 'packed with French flair and the romantic notion that winning actually mattered' (25 June); France's 'advances were sweeping and vivacious, but naturally they were profligate in front of goal' (13 June).

France 98 also saw a (temporary?) end to the reasserted belief in France's lack of self-confidence. We have detailed elsewhere (Crolley and Hand 2002: 56–7) the ways in which the English print media tried to explain France's ultimate victory after building up decades of reporting the fragile nature of France's self-belief and distrusting their ability to overcome the final challenge of winning the World Cup final. As France won the World Cup, the media had to try to justify this apparent anomaly, so inconsistent with their portrayal of French identity hitherto. The disturbing explanation posited was that it was France's black players who provided the mental strength that France had lacked for so long.

France's performance in the 2002 World Cup, however, appeared to offend deeply the English print media. France's elimination from the World Cup after the group stages, without managing to score a goal, led to harsh criticism in the English press, who personalized the issue enough to question the attitude of individual French players as much as their standard and style of play: 'The truth is that France only have themselves to blame for the most pathetic defence of the crown in World Cup history' (*The Times*, 12 June 2002). The 'complacency', 'malaise' and 'lack of hunger' have done 'seismic damage to the reputation of French football and footballers. Could anyone trust the appetite of a French World Cup winner after this? . . . They have surrendered reputations it took a decade to build' (ibid.). The writer then adds, cuttingly, that 'French players insulted us all and devalued their own currency in the process.' It is alleged, then, that in under-performing so drastically, with 'casual incompetence', the France squad humiliated their whole nation. The author of this particular article suggests that France could have done much better 'had their Gallic shrug not been so evident' (ibid.). We have returned to the clichéd reporting which attributes poor performances to the supposedly weak French mentality. Their ultimate defeat is, therefore, portrayed as something of a natural consequence deriving from their national character.

Our sample overall provides evidence of some shift in the way in which English attitudes towards the French might have changed. The notion of amicable neighbours who share the sporting ethos during the pre-war period deteriorates in the post-war period and beyond. The pre-war and immediate post-war eras are characterized by the 'Continental' label attached to French football. In these periods, little French identity is recognized, though there is evidence of what later emerges as a constant: French style, flair, individualism, sophistication and vulnerability. We are yet to see whether 2002 was a 'blip' in French football or a significant step in the evolution of French identity portrayed by the print media. The constancy of portrayal suggests that English writers will not be tempted away from the stereotypes easily: images of French elegance, artistry and fragility cannot be shrugged off lightly.

France viewed from Spain

Given the fact that Spain played several 'friendly' matches against France in their formative years on the international football scene, the amount of coverage in our sample is quite disappointing. 'Reports' on the six matches which took place prior to the Spanish Civil War in 1936 are limited to basic team sheets and results. Moreover, in a preview to a 1942 match played in Seville (one of the first 'friendlies' contested in Spain after the end of the Civil War), the newspapers went to considerable lengths to describe the fact that the team and its entourage visited monuments built to commemorate the Spanish Civil War (*ABC*, 13 March 1942). This is the only hint at the politicization of this fixture at this time and there is little indication as to the broader relationships between France and Spain, except, perhaps, the fact that the friendlies took place at all.

It is not until the 1940s that we are offered any trace of a French identity mediated via the Spanish press. We are going to explore the extent to which these early reports contributed to the establishment of a French identity in football literature and the degree to which notions of 'Frenchness' might have evolved over the period. Initial evidence of a French style of play emerges in the Spanish print media discourse in our data in the early 1940s. By this time, French football had become 'one of the most respected on the Continent . . . the French work hard, cover a lot of ground but without the effort or enthusiasm that is so important to our style of play' (*ABC*, 17 March 1942). Here, the Spanish press acknowledges similarities in the style of play between themselves and their Latin neighbours but draws a line; the French 'lack the enthusiasm, effort . . . vibrancy . . . vigour . . . spirit and impetuousness' of the Spanish (ibid.). The French are Latin without the *furia* typically demonstrated by the Spanish (see below, Chapter 6). Already, however, there is evidence of the creative streak that comes to typify French football and is associated with a more general view of artistry among the French. The notion that the seeds of a French identity are germinating in Spain at this time is strengthened by the allusion to the French laid-back attitude that is apparently inherent in their style of play. Again, this concept is one which will burgeon over the next 65 years.

Following a French victory over England (1–0) in 1955, one article in *ABC* alludes to the 'play, tone and spirit of the French' as though these features are by now recognizable and the readership would share the understanding of what this means (17 May 1955). More specifically, it was 'the speed', 'the initiative' and 'the inventive' French style of play that contributed to their victory in this match (ibid.). Again, and typical of reporting in Spain of domestic football, the notions of 'the French initiative' and 'creative capacity' are reinforced in a report following a Reims–AC Milan fixture in the Copa Latina in Paris (*ABC*, 24 July 1955). In this sense, coverage of the French domestic teams replicates the characteristics of the national side: Saint-Etienne is 'a quick team, who play lively football with a good sporting spirit' (*ABC*, 25 June 1957).

The Spanish press seems to have an affinity with the Latin nature of the

French. Ignoring the true complexity of France's ethnic composition, the reader is frequently reminded that the French are Latin, whether in national heritage or style of play (for example, 'the English . . . were surprised by the Latin improvisation' [*ABC*, 17 May 1955]).

The 1960s was an unsuccessful period for French football and is portrayed as such in Spain – exemplified in an article entitled 'French football is in decline' (*ABC*, 22 July 1966) – but from this low position France rose to become a beacon of European football, representing a new era in terms of creativity and innovation. By the early 1980s, Spain's coverage of French football had shifted to consider the team as one that might play well but is not always effective in getting results: on occasions, they have 'played good football, but without a result' (*El País*, 16 January 1982). As French football reaches its peak, however, the eulogies increase, as does the identification of apparently typical French characteristics in their style of play. The French are 'brilliant', 'creative' or 'imaginative' though even at their most revered they are far from perfect. Their inconsistency is a source of comment for the Spanish press: too many players 'can either play brilliantly or pass by unnoticed' (*El País*, 16 January 1982) and even the great midfielder Alain Giresse is 'too fragile and can't handle being marked'. Again, as we saw in the early 1940s, there are suggestions that the French do not take their football seriously and their lackadaisical attitude is interpreted as half-hearted by the Spanish print media, features that seem to have become established in reporting on French football.

When French footballers demonstrate characteristics that do not square with their stereotype, then the Spanish reporter displays a tendency to rationalize by positing alternative explanations for the atypical traits. Michel Platini, for example, was in many ways the personification of French football, 'with exceptional vision, an outstanding team player, and precision touch on the ball and when shooting at goal' (*El País*, 20 June 1984). However, *El País* claims that it was in Italy, where Platini spent the latter part of his playing career, that he learnt the 'less French' attributes of 'patience, keeping possession and economizing effort' (ibid.). Interestingly, of Zinedine Zidane *El País* also claimed that his 'time in Italy strengthened him', particularly mentally (18 June 1998). Mental strength is not an attribute typically associated with the French, therefore *El País* seeks to justify its presence in a player seen as typically French in so many other ways.

In this period of 'magnificent' French football, *El País* is replete with vocabulary that invokes the 'inspirational' style of football. While it is 'wonderful' or 'splendid' football, it is always marked as French: 'They will keep creating and inventing until they score' (27 June 1984). On more than one occasion, the French style is likened to that of Brazil ('France move the ball about like Brazil' [13 June 1984]). It is only when the Spanish team are beaten by France in the European Championship final that the Spanish press accuse them of dirty tactics: 'France, like any other ordinary team, resorted to time-wasting, cheating and arguing with the referee' (13 June 1984). Yet this sort of representation of France is the exception rather than the rule – and probably helped the Spanish come to terms with losing the match. The norm in this period is for France to be extolled highly for their method of play: 'The French manager has inculcated his team with a love of spectacle' (17 June 1984); and for this reason, even when they were winning, they continued to attack 'as though they were playing against the clock', and against Belgium 'they scored goals almost at will.' For the image of the French, in contrast to that of the Germans, for instance, is that they do not play just to win games. They play to delight and enthral; if they win, so much the better. This impression of French football has endured to the present day, when expectations in Spain are that the French should, first and foremost, entertain. French football is measured by the standards set by the now legendary performances of Tigana, Platini and Giresse (El País, 8 July 1998).

When France do not perform in the way that is expected of them, as we have seen in other cases, Spanish journalists do not review the stereotype or attempt to modify it. Instead an explanation is proposed. For example, France's poor performance against Croatia in the 1998 World Cup finals was blamed on the French suffering because 'the system was stifling the team' and 'the team was prisoner to the system' (El País, 9 July 1998). No one doubts the (natural) ability of the French footballers, just their ability to perform on cue. In Spain, as in France itself (see above), the manager, Aimé Jacquet, shouldered most of the responsibility for submitting France to a system that did not allow them to be France. The Spanish press reflected the French view that Jacquet was not French enough for the French. 'The professor' was portrayed by El País as being 'too conservative and cautious', thus offending the sense of how football should be played by France's national team (18 June 1998). His desire to 'thwart the opposition' lacks the creativity necessary to be respected by the French (27 June 1998). Indeed, it lost respect from the Spanish press, too, where France was chided for being 'a team who betrayed its traditions for a handful of results' (ibid.). These 'traditions' had also been betrayed earlier, apparently, when the 'fabulously skilful' footballer, Michel Platini, turned manager and 'substituted skill for an obstructive mentality' (El País, 20 February 1991). The whole of Spain was 'shocked' by the transformation of France between 1984 and 1991.

The Spanish print media acknowledge that the French are different, and that they must try to convey an impression of 'the French mentality' (El País, 19 June 1984). Importantly, the French have a different relationship with football from the Spanish – and in both 1984 and 1998, when France enjoyed their first two major international triumphs, this aspect of 'Frenchness' is discussed in detail, as is the 'Frenchness' of celebrating national victory.

Several reports draw on the symbol of French football, the cockerel, to illustrate this point (see Hand 1998 for a detailed historical and cultural analysis of the importance of this image in France). On occasions, this image is developed astutely: 'the French cock-a-doodle-do broke out last night in the Parc des Princes following the victory of the national football team' (El País, 28 June 1984). This article goes on to explain how 'the French cock-a-doodle-do is something akin to Spanish passion for the same sport, but passed through the sieve of rationalism'. The image of the French cockerel crowing – above and below – is an attempt to Gallicize the occasion. It is not the French way to celebrate by going onto the streets: 'Because the French are rational and Cartesian, they did not take to the streets last night to celebrate the "historic day" in French football, when, for the first time, they won this international trophy. Here, what works is the crowing, which is not as exhibitionist as Hispanic passion, but is inexorable.' This article compares the French and Hispanic passions for football and asserts that 'that French respond to Hispanic football-passion with a nation-passion.' The point is made that French pride in football is reflected in national public life via a public 'crowing' – whether that be on the front page of the newspapers or via politicians. In 1998, the Spanish press had to modify this presentation of France's relationship with football: 'So distant towards football traditionally, so cold, so indifferent, so paternalistic, even, in its observation of the passions that this game incites in others, France has taken the lid off its emotions with the excitement of the successful run of its national team' and there was an 'enthusiastic fervour that football has never been responsible for before in this country' (*El País*, 10 July). The French were said to have discovered an 'unexpected passion' for football (*El País*, 14 July).

The French are different from the Spanish in other ways, and via our analysis of football writing we have been able to identify several of these features. The Spanish press portrays the French as more 'civilized', 'educated' and 'philosophical', 'entertaining' journalists as they like to partake in 'fluent discourse'. Those (men) involved in football are also portrayed as being more in touch with their feminine side: Aimé Jacquet apparently crossed his legs in a shockingly 'unmacho' way, 'a position in which [Spain's then manager] Javier Clemente would never have been seen' (*El País*, 6 July 1998).

A final theme that arises towards the end of the twentieth century and is, as in the French sample, particularly salient during the 1998 World Cup, is that of ethnicity. In 1998, the French national football team is portrayed as representative of French society in a broader sense. The fact that French football fever affected the whole of the country, uniting all sectors and ethnic groups within society, is seen to be a reflection of the constitution of the multi-ethnic French national team: the crowd that took to the streets and met in the focal places in each town consisted of 'young people from as many backgrounds as the national team itself. For one night the *beurs* (second generation Maghrebians), black Africans or Antilleans felt the same emotions, and even the same fraternal emotions, that the players shared on the pitch with all their effusive huddles and embraces' (*El País*, 10 June 1998). Not only does the Spanish press present the national team as a microcosm of the diversity within French society, it goes further and suggests that football is fulfilling a function of social cohesion: 'Although it is difficult to measure the effects of this collective catharsis, surely the sum of identifications with the likes of Zidane, Desailly, Blanc, Djorkaeff and Barthez, the convergence in a shared objective, contributes to the integration and social cohesion which this society needs so badly' (ibid.). A few days later, this sentiment is repeated: 'The victorious combination of the three skin colours in the [French] national team: white European, black African or Antillean, and dark Maghrebian, seem to have provided an antidote to rampant racism and xenophobia' (*El País*, 14 July 1998). According to the Spanish print media, football has helped France by providing a new framework in which national identity can be reinterpreted in a broader, more modern social context and include French people of all races: 'The newspapers talk of a "lesson in unity" given by the Algerian Zidane, the Breton Guivarch, the Basque Lizarazu, the African Desailly, the Armenian Djorkaeff . . . France is multiracial and will remain that way' (ibid.).

'Triumph unites France' trumpets the headline of *El País* (14 July 1998), which goes on to add that 'Never since the Second World War have millions of French of all races shared the same dream.' In a society that the writer describes as 'socially dismembered', football has provided the catalyst for a collective outpouring of shared emotion. He sagely wonders how long this cohesion will remain intact and how the French might be able to capitalize on the football event in order to reaffirm France's national identity. As we later realized when images of rioting youths from suburbs around France were beamed across the world in 2005, it would take more than football success in France to ensure social integration and encourage the harmonious co-existence of different races. The Spanish print media identified in 1998 that the French have underlying social problems and suffer from a lack of consensus around national identity in a modern, inclusive sense: 'What is evident is that French society needed to identify with a common cause, to share in an achievement which would return its self-confidence as a nation.' The degree to which football success might transcend the sporting context in France is questioned. After all, in France, we are led to believe by the Spanish print media, football is not an all-consuming passion for the population: 'The great fiesta, the immense solidarity that has united all sectors of the population over the last week must not be allowed to evaporate with the coming of summer' (*El País*, 14 July). The 'colouristic' national team irritates the extreme right National Front party to such an extent that its leader, Jean-Marie Le Pen, 'never tired of pointing out that most of the players could not sing the words to the Marseillaise'. This perspective also received considerable attention in *El País*, who conveyed the 'chauvinism which flourishes in all corners of this country [France]' (ibid.). *El País* calls on French politicians, media, businesses, artists and intellectuals to take the initiative and ensure that the effects of the World Cup are prolonged.

Spanish coverage of French football, therefore, shares features in common with English coverage. Both countries ooze references to French characteristics of style and artistry and identify psychological fragility as vulnerability.

Chapter 4

Germany

Past performance equals future value

Germany is Europe's most successful football nation. Playing as Germany from their affiliation to FIFA in 1904 up to 1914 and again from 1920 to 1942, as West Germany in the post-war period (from 1950) and, once again, as Germany from 1990 following reunification of the country's East and West, the Germans have participated in seven World Cup finals since 1954, winning three of them, as well as in five European Championship finals since 1972, again winning three. As the German FA itself notes, this success on the international stage 'is an important basis for the international reputation that German soccer has gained worldwide' (Deutscher Fußball-Bund 2005). However, is the Germans' reputation to be ascribed solely to their enviable record of success or are there other features of note in the imagined identity of Germany? When European football writers report on the Germans playing football throughout the twentieth century, what are the key features of the portrayal and how have they evolved? Initially, this chapter will present an indication of how the Germans view themselves through the fortunes of their own football team before moving on to consider representations of Germany in the quality daily presses of England, France and Spain.

The German self-image

In terms of German autotypification, Gebauer (1999) identifies three stages in the development of the relationship between the German national team and German society as a whole. It is important to note in the context of the present volume that the close connection between German football and wider German society as a whole is a relatively recent one that did not exist 50 years ago according to Gebauer (1999) and Eisenberg (1990, 1999), who state that football in the immediate pre-war era was a sport appealing to a limited section of society only, the 'working class', and therefore not representative of the entire nation. Additionally, in the 1920s, the Weimar Republic's perception that sport's principal value lay in its contribution to the physical training of the populace as a sign of Germany's rebirth after the Treaty of Versailles, followed in the 1930s by the Nazi regime's privileging of the cult of the body, physicality and hard labour as well as its overt politicization of sport in general, also contributed to the lack of esteem in which football was held by intellectuals and journalists up to and into the 1950s (Eisenberg 1999).

For Gebauer, things started to change at a very precise moment: the World Cup final of 1954. From this point onwards, the national football team was adopted by and recognized as the representative of the German nation both in defining itself and in presenting an image of itself to the world at large. More specifically, henceforth the élites of German society began to accord football a value and a prestige that it had hitherto lacked and which permitted it to take on the rôle of national representative. In Berne in 1954, of course, the Germans won their first World Cup by defeating the hot favourites Hungary, unbeaten in over four years and widely regarded as technically far superior to them. So surprising was the result (especially to the Germans themselves) that the victory was dubbed the *Wunder von Bern* (the Miracle of Berne) and, according to Merkel (1994), this footballing miracle was quickly read as part of the wider socio-economic miracle (the *Wirtschaftswunder*) that was unfolding as Germany rapidly reconstructed after the Second World War. The World Cup victory, of course, did not contribute materially to the physical rebuilding of the country but it did provide a new model of Germany to display to the world and, indeed, a new way for Germans to think of themselves. Interestingly, though, as Gebauer indicates, the elements of this German self-image were historically long-standing and well established. It is the use to which they were put and the context in which they operated that were novel and allowed Germans to take pride in and see themselves in their footballers. The German footballers, notably Walter, the captain, became heroes during the tournament and were subsequently worshipped as such when they overcame the disastrous start of losing their first game 8–3 (to the Hungarians, in fact) and went on to win the final against the odds having been 2–0 down. The ghosts of the hero worship of the 1930s and 1940s were laid to rest not by abandoning the concept altogether but by applying it to a sporting context in a relatively acceptable manner (although both the decidedly politically incorrect chanting by German fans of 'Deutschland, Deutschland über alles' and the tabloid headline in *Bild* of 'We Are Great Again' might be felt to have crossed the line [cited by Eisenberg 1999 and Winkler 2005 respectively]). Even so, from 1954 onwards, Germans *are* allowed to celebrate their heroes once more (and, by the 1970s, have no compunction, for instance, in nicknaming one of them, Franz Beckenbauer, *der Kaiser* or, indeed, in the 1990s, in referring to another, Matthäus, as 'the new messiah . . . redeemer and saviour' [*Süddeustche Zeitung*, 20 November 1995]). Similarly, the style of play of the victorious German team is resonant with images that previously had found expression only in military affairs but were now becoming the hallmark of German activities in the respectable areas of sport and economics. The German team had its leader, the legendary Sepp Herberger, coach from 1938 to 1964, whose word was never doubted and the players themselves were ordinary 'working-class' men, semi-professionals from the provinces, whose industry, discipline and team spirit combined with a speedy, mobile game to overcome the flashy wizardry of the Hungarians. The typical German qualities were now being employed in the acceptable sporting context (rather than the unacceptable way in which the same qualities had been employed by the Nazis in the political, diplomatic and military arenas) and thereby facilitated Germany's rehabilitation into the national community. From 1954 onwards, Germans can once again be proud of their reputation for discipline, collective effort, industriousness and speedy, ruthless efficiency. The values that had been corrupted by Nazi rule were now finding a new home in the football world (see Crolley et al. 1998: 179). Moreover, with the former leaders, the Führers of all kinds, political and military, gone and discredited, the typical, historic German values were now being upheld and demonstrated by the workforce, ordinary people, simple citizens, working tirelessly and unassumingly together for the benefit of the nation as a whole. Such were the values on which the German élite of the new Federal Republic under Chancellor Adenauer (voted the greatest ever German in a 2003 ZDF television poll) placed great stock. These values were now represented by the successful (West) German football team. It was the Miracle of Berne, not the Nuremberg Trials or the establishment of the Federal Republic in 1949, that represented emotionally and psychologically the end of the Second World War as 'Through its victory, this little football team had symbolically healed the wounds inflicted [on Germany] during and after the war' (Gebauer 1999: 107). Indeed, the notion of healing is very much the theme of Wortmann's film version of the Miracle of Berne (Wortmann 2003). With its publicity straplines of 'Every child needs a father, Every people needs a dream, Every nation needs a legend', the film weaves the story of a family reconciliation after the return home of the PoW father with that of the World Cup victory and demonstrates, according to Winkler (2005), the important psychological rôle played by the German football team, whose success was both a symbol and a validation of the reconstruction of West Germany after the war.

The second stage in the identification of the German football team with the nation dates to the early 1970s, culminating in the second World Cup triumph of 1974. Politically, the period was marked by the policies of Chancellor Brandt (1969–74) aimed at creating a more open and inclusive German society and, of course, by the diplomatic rapprochement with Eastern Europe (the Ostpolitik). Socially and culturally, German youths and intellectuals discovered the values of the protest movements of the United States of America and immersed themselves in popular culture, pop art and music. The hippy generation had been born. The German football team seemed to reflect the new artistic and intellectual context of German society in that, without ever sacrificing the traditional values of discipline and hard work, players such as Franz Beckenbauer and Gunter Netzer added individual flair to a team that was encouraged by its coach, Helmut Schön, to be more open and less defensive than its predecessors. According to Gebauer (1999: 107–8), this new mixture of intelligence, artistry and industry directly appealed to the new Germans who, in turn, saw themselves reflected in the qualities of what was clearly now *their* football team. The Italy–Germany meeting in the World Cup semi-final in Mexico in 1970, widely acknowledged as the match of the century (Saccomano 1998: 120), saw the start of the most elegant, stylish and adventurous football Germany had ever played and precisely at the time of a period full of optimism, promises and willingness to reform on many social and political fronts. Germany's image abroad was also improving considerably, simultaneously on the football pitch and in the political/diplomatic arena, and the country could now be seen finally to have liberated itself from its history, from the Nazi mentality and from previous administrations rooted in the past.

Finally, the third stage in the evolution of the image of German football and its relationship with national identity unfolds in the last 15 years or so of the twentieth century. Under the direction of Chancellor Kohl (1982–98), German society was dominated by the notion of continued success. 'Continue as before, Germany' was one of his successful electoral slogans. His other forte was to sit out any crisis he encountered (and there were many). Whatever negative thing might have been said about Kohl (mainly lack of vision), there was always one thing which justified everything he did: success. Being successful, being the best and winning mattered more than anything else. It was, therefore, highly appropriate that Kohl congratulated the German football team's coach, Bertie Vogts, after a dull, defensive performance against Italy at Euro 96 by speaking of the national team's 'super performance' and adding: 'It's not important how one wins but that one wins', thereby justifying his own policy with the help of the people's game and revitalizing one of football's most contentious formulæ (*Süddeutsche Zeitung*, 21 June 1996). The *Süddeutsche Zeitung* in this instance views politics and football together. The strategy in both appears the same: win at all costs. Interestingly, Kohl, on subsequently seeing Germany win Euro 96, went on to use the national team's footballing success as a metaphor for the future direction of the country's politics by calling on his government to match and therefore be worthy of Germany's footballers (Gebauer 1999: 101).

In German sport by the 1990s, the focus had clearly moved away from the ordinary workers of the 1950s and the popular cultural creatives of the 1970s towards a greater concern with personal success, wealth and glamour obtained by sporting celebrities cultivating their image or, indeed, their brand, and demanding a high price for their services. The German football team, with its heavily commercially sponsored, super rich star players became simply another high-profile example of the transformation of sport into a business. In a sense, the values and characteristics of the German team (and, by extension, of German society more widely), for all their longevity, became so many elements of the brand, of the commercial image, a process that operates in the interests of commercial sponsors such as Mercedes, of course, given that the qualities upon which it has built its own image (technical efficiency and reliability) are precisely those communicated by the typical German footballer. The popular and intellectual reaction to this process – reflected by journalists – has been one of cynicism. There is disappointment that traditional German virtues have been hijacked into the service of commercial aims and, indeed, that sport itself has succumbed to the imperatives of the marketplace. Indeed, full professionalism in the game was officially permitted in Germany only from 1972 (Eisenberg 1999) and, therefore, still seems somewhat alien to many German commentators' eyes. When the German press of the late twentieth century reports on football, then, it does so with a certain irony, with a certain awareness that the long-standing German attributes of discipline, efficiency and industry are now virtually caricatural traits cultivated by very highly paid professional footballers primarily interested in furthering their own celebrity status. One of the most frequent topics of debate in the mid-1990s in the *Süddeutsche Zeitung*, for instance, is the way footballers use their skills for self-marketing purposes. It is, therefore, no surprise that so many metaphors and similes relating to the world of business may be found in German match reports and related articles: a football club is a 'firm', footballers are 'employees' or 'salaried employees' and the manager is the 'head of department' or a 'leading employee'. A lost away game is a 'sad company outing'; a footballer can be described as a 'kicking entrepreneur'; 'damages' are part of 'the salary'; a manager can suffer from *'Betriebsblindheit'* (being blind to the shortcomings of one's own company). A football match is a 'Saturday shift' which takes place on a 'working day' and an injured player has to hand in what the Germans so beautifully call an *Arbeitsunfähigkeitsbescheinigung* (a sick-note) like any other employee in the world of business. Success in sport is a 'lubricant for successful business transactions'. The fan is the 'customer', either angry or happy, depending on the quality of the product. The whole of the football experience is quite simply summed up in the words 'football theme park' (*Süddeutsche Zeitung*, 25 September 1995; 6 November 1995; 13 November 1995; see also Crolley *et al.* 1998: 177–9).

By the end of the twentieth century, there would appear to be little doubt that the German national team represents German society especially in terms of the image Germans have of themselves (autotypification) and of the dominant values of their nation but perhaps in ways that are rather more complex than might first be imagined. It will be interesting to discover whether other European countries' views of the Germans are equally complex or, on the contrary, based upon a relatively limited set of characteristics.

Germany viewed from England

In terms of Germany's heterotypification, the case of coverage in England is enlightening. Our sample, which excludes tabloid sensationalist press, of course, covers the period from the first time England showed any real interest in German football (that is, when England played Germany for the first time in an official match in 1930) to the present day. As noted earlier, between 1950 and 1990 Germany was divided into the Federal Republic of Germany and the German Democratic Republic (represented in football by West Germany and East Germany respectively). Although we sought data relating to both East and West Germany in our sample, the evidence presented is drawn almost exclusively from coverage of West Germany since in football terms it provided the stronger teams, participated in more official competitions and enjoyed greater, more in-depth media coverage. Following the reunification of Germany in 1990, the German football team was recreated. Early coverage of German football in England informs us in two ways. First, it indicates political relationships involving Germany and, second, it depicts a German style of play, one that is not static but evolves significantly during the period. Both of these elements combine to create a recognizable German identity mediated by the English print media.

England first played Germany in an official competition in 1930 but, probably because the tie was played in Berlin, the fixture warranted no more coverage in *The Times* than a dry notation of the result, a 3–3 draw (12 May 1930). A search through the archives to uncover coverage of the first match on English soil, however, was more fruitful. This match took place in 1935, a period of political turmoil throughout Europe and a controversial time for England to host Germany given its transition into a Nazi regime. The potential political ramifications of this fixture clearly preoccupied the sports pages of *The Times*. Protests against the fixture were organized by the Trades Union Congress (TUC), who planned anti-Nazi demonstrations outside Tottenham Hotspur's ground where the match was to take place (*The Times*, 2 December 1935). The TUC were in turn criticized by the Counties Association of Football Clubs for their interference in football and for not understanding 'the psychology of the British people'. It suggested that the TUC should not 'besmirch the honour and degrade the tradition of British sportsmanship by attempting to affront our German guests' (ibid.). *The Times*, however, does attempt to focus on the sporting event and to distance the sporting from the political by adopting a tone of disdain towards the Germans for not applying the same principle of disassociation between sport and politics: 'In view of the political character of sport in Germany, it was clear that the fixture was being made use of by the German Government for political purposes' (3 December 1935). After the event, during which both England and Germany (teams, fans and officials) behaved impeccably, according to *The Times*, it was commented that attempts by trade unionists to politicize the match had failed miserably and, indeed, had backfired since, at a time of German desires for a political rapprochement with Britain, 'for Germany, it was an unrestricted political, psychological and also sporting success' (6 December 1935).

The political connotations of the next fixture between the two sides, three years later in 1938, are underplayed by *The Times*, which once more attempts to portray the match as disconnected from the political scene. Again it admits that 'The international football match between England and Germany [has] for the German public thrust politics into the background' though the England team 'immediately made a good impression by raising their arms in the German salute while the band, after playing "God Save the King", played the German National Anthem' (14 May 1938). *The Times* is at pains to emphasize the 'friendly' nature of the fixture, which was played within the 'traditional sporting ethos' of the sport of football.

The political ramifications of sport are more commonly discussed around England–Germany fixtures than any other in the English data examined in the present study. This political comment surrounding the pre-war fixture continued in the post-war period. For example, 'The appearance of Germany's international football side at Wembley Stadium this afternoon adds its bit to Anglo-German relations' (*The Times*, 1 December 1954). Although *The Times* goes to some length to reassure the readership that sport is not politicized in Britain, commenting on the matter at all clearly increases the political nuances of the fixture.

As far as the football itself is concerned, the German stereotype, with which most general readers of football writing will be familiar, has not yet emerged in the 1930s. Germany had not yet developed the confidence, even arrogance, of later years, it would seem. Though England only drew in Berlin five years previously, Germany was still portrayed in 1935 as a nation learning the game of football and we are reminded that the British are still the masters of the game: 'The players had come to England to try to show that they could play football. Germans learned to play football from the English . . . and England should win with a little in hand' (*The Times*, 3 December 1935). Contrary to the tone of later coverage in our sample, German football in the 1930s is not renowned for its strength in defence: 'Defence is where Germany is at her weakest' (*The Times*, 4 December 1935). An 'attractive game' was expected, again in stark contrast to later depictions of Germany. Unlike our sample of French print media discourse (see below), where characteristics associated with Germany date as far back as the earliest football reporting, at this stage in our English data, not only is there little evidence of the German stereotypes which emerge later, but a specific German identity is yet to develop. Like the portrayal of France in the pre-war period, the Germans are simply 'Continental' in the 1930s and 'What Continental sides still seem to lack is that all-important thrust near goal and a co-ordinated system of defence' (ibid.). Again, the disparity between this portrayal of Germany and that which developed in the post-war period is quite dramatic.

Fortunately, the report of the above match was unexpectedly detailed for this period in terms of its analysis of football. The anonymous correspondent from *The Times* enlightens the reader with an in-depth insight into the strengths and weaknesses of both the English and German teams. The expectations outlined above were only partially fulfilled. The match was not so 'attractive'. The German defence was unpredictably effective – though this was 'due not so much for strate-gic brilliance as to the physical fact that the body of a footballer, however good or bad, has substance, and that a number of them manoeuvring in the small space are bound to make it difficult for a shot to get through' (5 December 1935). The Ger-mans tried to pack their defence with players and stifled England's attacking play, though the Germans did concede three goals on this occasion. Perhaps the reality of the German performance, that is, their physical strength in defence, provides the tiny embryo which is nurtured in the 1950s to become a more recognizable stereotype of German football and identity later. Equally contradicting later im-ages, however, the Germans 'started shakily' and lacked confidence.

There is little detailed coverage of Germany's football in our data until the 1950s. To a large extent, Germany's winning of the World Cup in 1954 was a piv-otal moment in the reporting of German matches in England as it was in Germany.

Here some of the characteristics which were to become clichés of German football were embedded in English football writing. Perhaps the most pervasive trait is that of German power – both physical and mental. This is reflected in the use of lexical items which convey the image of physical strength, speed, control, determination and endurance. A few examples from *The Times* suffice to give a flavour of reporting during this 1954 World Cup: German football is 'fast, enthusiastic and direct in attack . . . and lacks subtle refinements' (23 June); 'Germany were hard tackling and direct in purpose' (1 July); 'Germany took complete command' (ibid.); Germany 'played fast, intelligent football when they attacked . . . with unflagging energy' (4 July).

Surely the nature of Germany's World Cup victory – to come back dramatically from 2–0 down after eight minutes against a technically superior team in Hungary – contributed to the creation of the myth of German invincibility. The Germans proved that their self-belief and their willpower could lead them to victory against any opposition: 'They refused to be mesmerised by the Hungarian passing . . . the Germans fought back to fame by their tremendous enthusiasm, drive, stamina, strength, and their willpower' (ibid.). Over the space of several days, this image of German power football was reinforced over and over again (for example, Germany's triumph was accountable to the 'fast direct and intelligent game of the Germans, backed by stamina and will-power' [6 July]). Hence, the myth was born. Over the next half-century, Germany would go on to build on the confidence this victory gave them, in much the same way as England's humiliating defeat the previous year against Hungary left them to dwell on their former glories for the rest of the century. Indeed, the legacy of this victory on other nations is explicitly and prophetically expressed by one journalist who warns, 'remembering the way [Germany] arose against all the odds to become World Champions in Switzerland last June, one will be prepared for anything' (23 March 1955). The rest of the world seems to have played Germany ever since with this warning in mind.

Germany played England at Wembley the December after the World Cup victory in 1954. By now, clues to what later becomes a German stereotype are surfacing: 'The Germans are defensively strong'; 'the German defensive covering near goal – a veritable Siegfried Line at times – was gallant in the extreme' (2 December 1954 – note this early reference to military history, which will never be far from the preoccupations of English journalists writing on German football in the next 50 years). They also have grit, 'determination', 'resolve' and 'spirit' (e.g. 1 December 1954). At this stage, an element of perceived 'luck', or 'fortune', is introduced for the first time into the commentary on German football. By this time, then, a German identity is beginning to trickle into the writing, containing elements which combine physical and psychological strength, though it is not yet identified as specifically German, nor portrayed as a stereotype. Indeed, correspondents from *The Times* still refer to Germans as 'Continental' deep into the 1950s.

It is clearly, then, during the post-war period that the German style of play becomes established. Over the next couple of decades, we are able to choose from an overwhelming number of examples in which the stereotypical German style of play and character are reinforced via football writing. The portrayal of Germany clearly connects with views held about German identity outside the football context. Most of the characteristics that are repeated with such frequency to create a mythic version of reality can be summarized rather crudely as power-related. These might include aspects of both physical and psychological power and descriptions of Germany often combine both of these elements. Some examples will illustrate this point: 'The Germans, *as ever*, boast high fitness, rigid discipline, and forthright play' (*The Times*, 30 May 1962, emphasis added); They are 'dedicated, physically powerful, and trait to an inch' (*The Times*, 25 July 1966). This 'iron will' becomes 'an institution in terms of psychology' (19 June 1970); 'West German spirit lifts the cup' (*The Times*, 8 July 1974); the 'iron will of the Germans' apparently enabled them to beat France in the 1982 World Cup semi-final (*The Times*, 13 July 1982); 'Aggression is West Germany's natural game' (*The Guardian*, 14 July 1966); 'The powers of endurance exhausted the patience of the onlookers' (*The Times*, 22 June 2002). Germany's extreme mental strength manifests itself in terms of its self-belief: 'The Germans are hungrily confident' (*The Times*, 30 May 1970); Germany's 'defence is too strong and confident to be ruffled or pierced' (*The Guardian*, 14 July 1966). Their 'confidence', however, soon becomes 'over-confidence' and then arrogance: 'Germany . . . fell into the trap of overestimating even their own phenomenal powers of endurance' (*The Times*, 19 June 1970). They have a 'belief, bordering on arrogant self-assertion that binds [them] again and again' (*The Times*, 2 July 1996). The opposition often fears defeat by Germany not necessarily because of their superiority on the pitch but because Germans think they are superior and are confident that they will win (*The Times*, 6 July 1996).

The Germans' machine-like efficiency is an image which is relatively late in emerging in our sample of English press discourse. Though one early reference acknowledged the Germans as efficient ('knowing the efficiency of the Germans' [*The Times*, 23 March 1955]), this aspect of German characterization does not appear regularly in English football writing in our sample until the late 1960s and 1970s when, for example, 'The efficiency of the East German victory in Wales' is noted (*The Times*, 24 November 1969). By the 1980s and 1990s, however, the image becomes a cliché upon which most commentary on German football draws in some form: 'Traditional efficiency should win them the [European Championship] title' (*The Times*, 27 June 1996) as they are a 'tournament machine' (*The Times*, 2 July). When the Germans defy their stereotypes and do not demonstrate their usual 'efficiency', they are accused of 'betraying their history' (*The Times*, 22 June 1996) or it is said that 'there was an obvious need to revive old traditional values and these, it seems, include the habit of winning grimly' (ibid.). In any case, stereotypes that have built up and been maintained over such a long period take a long time before they even begin to decay.

We have discussed elsewhere the prominence of military metaphor in football writing and in particular in matches between England and Germany (see

Crolley and Hand 2002) and, indeed, wondered if this had become exaggerated following the Second World War when images of Germany and warfare become inextricably linked in press discourse. However, even though match reports in the 1930s were relatively short and limited in content, there is clear evidence in our data that, in fact, military metaphor pre-dates the Second World War: for example, 'The Germans bombarded the English goal' and 'Germany took the offensive' (*The Times*, 16 May 1938). These military references become the norm, though, following the Second World War, when explicit references become much more frequent. As football writing expands in volume and the quality and scope of sports pages improve drastically, some writers, conversely, resort to lazy journalism as a short-cut to create a familiar image in the mind of the readership. Thus, we see a significant rise in the use of military images and metaphors in our data: 'The German defence, as solid as a tank' (*The Times*, 8 July 1982); 'The German guns may be pointing in the wrong direction but they have a habit of finding their target' (ibid.); 'Stielike was on permanent watch as usual throughout the night. Kaltz and Briegel, released from full back duty, formed part of the reconnaissance group' (*The Times*, 9 July 1982); 'Germany emerge bloodied but unbowed to fight another day' (*The Times*, 12 June 2002); 'In a misty, humid atmosphere, laden with tension, Germany battled through to the second round of the competition . . . wounds included a bloody nose and a cut head and there was a stand-off between Christian Zeige and Lauren' (*The Times*, 12 June 2002). The myth of German power (and near invincibility) is frequently communicated via the use of politico-military terminology. Germany's rôle in the two world wars is evoked unashamedly – such as the reference to the Siegfried Line mentioned earlier – or, latterly, in a more understated manner. We suggest a quantitative difference in the frequency of military lexical items employed in reports on German football compared to other national teams (for instance, vocabulary such as 'sorties', 'forays', 'ambushing', 'a battle on two fronts', 'marching on . . . in the hope to conquer Europe' [*The Times*, June 1996] appears to cluster more around Germany than any other nation).

The close association with Germany's military history is illustrated not only in the proliferation of metaphorical military terminology but also in more subtle ways, referring, for example, to the Germans' 'strategic planning' ('the German strategy was as obvious as it was rigid' and they had 'inflexible plans' [*The Times*, 9 July 1982]). Depiction of the Germans as bullies probably also has its roots in military campaigns – as the tactics employed in the 1982 World Cup finals were slammed as 'German intimidation [and] fearful tackles' (*The Times*, 10 July 1982) and at a later tournament they 'moved relentlessly on, spoiling innocent hopes and dreams such as those of the gallant Mexico' (*The Times*, 30 June 1998). It was similarly an 'aggressive' Germany that 'overpowered' Iran in 1998 (*The Times*, 29 June).

So, much has been said about the German style of play and little of it is complimentary. The Germans are criticized for their reliance on strength and for stifling creativity in their opposition. Even the praise is usually back-handed. Despite Germany's 2002 World Cup record of scoring 13 goals in five matches while only conceding in one of those games, their style of play is not admired in the English press: 'Germany's record is easier on the eye than their performances. . . . Statistics are supposed to bring clarity but, in this case, they are the thickest of smokescreens . . . and Germany have a shortage of skill' (*The Times*, 22 June 2002). Equally unflattering is the description of the German team that reached the World Cup final: 'Germany are dull, dull, dull and desperately hard to watch. . . . They are the antithesis of Brazil – mentally tough, organised and thoroughly unpopular with it' (*The Times*, 30 June 2002), though the writer reluctantly concedes that 'one has to admit to a sneaking regard for their stickability and professionalism . . . and only a fool would deny they can play the game' (ibid.).

Many of the characteristics that now constitute a German identity in the English print media discourse date back to the 1930s, though it was not until the late 1950s and beyond that the print media conveyed these images (relating to power, teamwork, efficiency, spirit, determination and boring football) as being specifically German.

Germany viewed from France

The history of France–Germany fixtures dates from the early 1930s. On either side of the Second World War, and in contrast to the English case, important elements in the construction of a recognizable German identity already feature in French press accounts of these early matches. The first ever meeting in 1931, which resulted in a 1–0 home victory for the French, was covered by *Le Temps*, for instance, and already, from the very outset, the essential but contrasting characteristics of the two nations may be seen in the match report: 'Against the very sure technique of the German players, the French countered with their "guts" and their furious speed . . . the fine discipline of the German team was destroyed by the liveliness and courage of the French' (17 March 1931). A basic opposition is established between two contrasting styles of play, which themselves might be felt to represent two contrasting sets of national characteristics, and this opposition would be played out on numerous occasions in the subsequent 60 years, culminating, as we shall see, in the apotheosis of the match reports and articles on the two World Cup semi-finals between France and Germany in the 1980s. The three other France–Germany games of the 1930s provide additional information contributing to the elaboration in the sports pages of a certain German identity. First, the typically German concern for etiquette and protocol is noted. A journalist reporting on the 1933 match in Berlin was struck by 'the manners of the crowd [which] were exemplary throughout [with] the French team being applauded and thousands of voices shouting the word Frankreich, meaning France' (*Le Matin*, 20 March 1933). Similarly, the fans at the 1937 encounter in Stuttgart were described as 'enthusiastic' and offering 'a charming welcome' to their French guests (*Le Matin*, 22 March). Interestingly, it would appear that no hint of the wider politico-diplomatic tensions existing between the two nations in the 1930s is to be found in the football writing of the period studied. What the discourse of this time does do, though, is firmly establish some of the traits that the French will continue to associate with the German football team up to and beyond the end of the twentieth century. In defeating the French in 1935, for example, the Germans apparently demonstrated that they are somewhat ponderous, 'slow into action' (*Le Matin*, 18 March) but nonetheless determined and resourceful: 'they knew what they had to do' (ibid.). Two years later it was apparently not surprising that the Germans won because of their 'physical domination' of the game in question, a match 'played in a good spirit but in which the Germans were the more virile' (*Le Matin*, 22 March 1937).

Discipline, determination and reliance on physical attributes, familiar traits from the 1990s (see Crolley and Hand 2002: 93–9) are, then, already apparent in the German identity inhabiting the football writing of the French press in the 1930s. The first two France–Germany matches of the immediate post-war period will amplify these traits and add to them, this time, in contrast to the 1930s, by employing overt references to wider political issues operating within the Franco-German relations of the time.

The first post-war meeting between France and (West) Germany on the football field, in 1952, was treated by *Le Monde* at least as a very special event in that not only was a half-page preview of the game provided but also two match reports occupying almost a full page of sports coverage. The preview is unequivocal about the match's wider significance as it 'marks the official resumption of sporting relations between the two former enemies' (5/6 October) and the first match report notes the 'intense curiosity' generated by the game, within which 'there are complex feelings mingling with the fanaticism of football' (7 October). The primary projects of post-war West Germany were economic reconstruction on the one hand and rehabilitation into the international community on the other and these are commented upon in this football match report. Germany is 'anxious to recover the sympathies it lost and to have its sportsmen please the world' and this football match can play a part in 'chasing away the bad memories' of the recent past (ibid.). It is significant that against the economic and political background of France and West Germany joining forces in setting up the European Coal and Steel Community, the forerunner of the EEC, *Le Monde* uses the following image to set the scene for its match report: 'The tender, misty, shiny autumn light played around the chimneys of the Sartrouville factory, planted there as a backdrop to ensure that the lads from Dortmund or Wuppertal and our boys from the mines of the Nord would feel at home' (ibid.). The report highlights the common experience of French and German workers down the mine or in the factory and, in so doing, focuses on the areas of economic activity in which the French and Germans at large were starting to cooperate internationally. As such, the report places the accent on a somewhat poeticized vision of reconciliation between the two countries and, therefore, clearly allows its coverage of the football match to be informed by politico-diplomatic developments outside the sporting arena. In terms of reconciliation, it is interesting to note that, according to the journalist, the game was initially played in a distinctly cool ambience but that the atmosphere warmed up when the German captain, Walter, offered to shake hands after committing a foul on a French player: 'the atmosphere become noticeably more sporting and cordial when Walter was seen to help up and comfort one of our wingers he'd clattered with a heavy tackle' (ibid.). It is almost as if the German has to make the first move, to acknowledge his guilt for previous aggression before relations can be normalized. In other words, once again, the events on the football pitch in this important match are seen to reflect wider developments in the new and rapidly evolving post-war relationship between France and Germany as nations and international partners.

Having said this, the second match report of the 1952 encounter uses far less conciliatory vocabulary and imagery when describing the German team and its activities notably by using a sub-headline that screams 'The Siegfried Line cracks at last!' and continuing with a reminder that 'History has already taught us all about the failure of fortified defensive lines' (ibid.). The latter is a reference to the failure of the Maginot Line to prevent the German army from invading and overrunning France in 1940 while the former refers to the German defences of the Great War which were also used in the Second World War. In other words, from the outset, a football match involving France and Germany is reported in terms of the major military conflicts between them of the first half of the twentieth century. Once established in this way, the military imagery of the report flows freely throughout. By employing a sweeper, the Germans laid 'an ambush' for the French. The sweeper himself is 'a sniper' playing 'behind the main combat zone' who intervenes in the 'battles' fought by his defenders (ibid.). For all of the focus on common ground and reconciliation displayed by the first match report, there is still, in the second, an accent on Franco-German conflict and division that is conveyed largely by military metaphors relating to the two world wars, a feature of French print media discourse that remains prevalent in subsequent reports.

In previewing the next meeting between the two teams, in 1954, Le Monde, for instance, unashamedly employs the vocabulary of the Second World War in its descriptions: with the Germans playing at home 'in the Vaterland . . . one can easily imagine the atmosphere of 80,000 spectators saluting their footballers as "Ubermensch" and hailing their Triumph' in the recent World Cup (14 October). The report of the match itself, a 3–1 victory for the French, is replete with military metaphors and images of German power and strength: 'Our players fought and, in the face of the massive, repeated assaults of the enemy, they held their ground . . . the bugles were produced to sound the charge [towards] Turek, the giant German keeper . . . our troops regrouped [and] occupied enemy territory . . . noting the Germans' power and their irresistible momentum' (ibid.). Events on the football field are, therefore, clearly still portrayed in terms of the recent military conflict between the countries involved.

The physical strength, imposing efficiency and determination bordering on arrogance of the Germans continue to feature in the 1960s and 1970s. The German team of 1967, for example, which recorded Germany's first victory over France for 30 years, was described as 'alert, athletic, resolute . . . efficient', one that caused apprehension amongst the French players who 'arrived at the Berlin stadium worried, in awe of their opponents and the surroundings' and who were ultimately 'dominated physically by Germany . . . the challenge provided by this sturdy German team being just too great' (*Le Monde*, 29 September 1967). Once more, opportunities to make reference to the Second World War are not allowed to slip by as the superiority of the Germans left the result in no doubt 'in this immense stadium built to honour the Third Reich' (ibid.). Again, in a 1970 preview of the German team competing in the Mexico World Cup, a familiar picture is painted: 'As for the Germans, we know all about them. It's not that they lack creativity but, with them, muscle is always more important . . . their winning temperament predisposes them to great victories as they have always insolently demonstrated' (*Le Monde*, 17 June 1970). Similarly, in a 1977 encounter with France, the accent is placed upon 'the power and precision of the Germans', 'their athletic players' and the attitude that 'the Germans would never have considered they might lose the game' (*Le Monde*, 25 February). In short, the Germans are now acknowledged as 'the best in the world', 'the gold standard' and 'worthy of their reputation' (ibid.).

By the 1980s, the discursive stage, therefore, had clearly been set for the two epic World Cup semi-final matches between France and Germany in 1982 and 1986 which, as has already been noted elsewhere (Crolley and Hand 2002: 95–6), are widely regarded in France as directly experienced proof of the hypothesis, well established by then, that German football teams will always be physical, intimidating and aggressive; they will inspire fear and will be almost impossible to beat.

In the 1982 match, France led 3–1 late in extra time only to end the game locked at 3–3 with Germany eventually winning the tie in the World Cup's first ever penalty shoot-out. The style of play of the Germans, itself seen as an extension of German identity, was denigrated by the French press, most notably by *Le Monde*, which consistently employs a series of binary oppositions in the text of its match reports and related articles, thereby foregrounding the essential contrasts in the imagined identities of France and Germany and, to an extent, displaying what Hare refers to as the 'atavistic bitterness' of some in France towards their German neighbours (2003: 124). A front page taster of the match report found on the inside pages uses literary references contrasting 'French romanticism and German realism', for instance, while under the heading 'Force and fantasy' the match report itself notes that 'Germany deserves the respect one would grant a huge army on the march while the smart French team inspires fantasy. . . . It could not be clearer. From the French we expect spectacle, from the Germans we expect success' (10 July 1982). The fact that this attitude was shared by the German side, though, was not appreciated by the French journalist: 'their absolute confidence and serenity come close to arrogance. . . . German football, by all appearances, knows nothing about modesty and draws its power from a rather exasperating belief that it is the best' (ibid.). This self-belief then translates into a style of play that is portrayed by *Le Monde* as mechanical and aggressive: 'the piston, Briegel, makes the whole machine work in the [German] way, sure of themselves and imposing. They are formidable, this phalanx of muscle and iron' (ibid.). German muscle found its personification in the shape of the goalkeeper Harald Schumacher, at least according to *Le Monde* which regarded his literally bone-crunching challenge to prevent the French player Patrick Battiston from scoring not as an isolated aberration but as a metaphor for Germany's aggressive and bullying approach to its more refined, sophisticated French neighbour. Just as Schumacher had earlier 'struck' Didier Six and 'downed' Dominique Rocheteau, this tackle on Battiston was 'deliberate', 'scandalous', 'indecent' (ibid.) and revealed much about perceptions of the different national identities on display in this football match. The 'exemplary, magnificent [and] superb' football of the French, therefore, 'contrasted sharply with the hatred in the heart of Harald Schumacher. . . . There was injustice here and perhaps more than that, a certain vileness displayed by one man, the German Schumacher, an excellent keeper but all things considered a sad gentleman. This big, strapping lad saved his team but at what price?' (10 July 1982). In a later summary of the tournament as a whole, *Le Monde* fires a telling final parting shot in the battle for hearts and minds opposing France and Germany: 'between the permanently arrogant, contemptuous and scandalous behaviour of the German team and the desire to play well, the attacking spirit and the sense of spectacle of the French team, the choice is easily made' (13 July 1982; see also Saccomano 1998: 52–3, which contrasts the 'magical', 'joyful', 'brilliant' French 'geniuses' with the 'mechanical', 'imposing', 'violent' and 'aggressive' Germans).

The 1986 World Cup semi-final between France and Germany, while not so memorable for the quality of its football – a rather stale match won 2–0 by the Germans – is still significant from the perspective of the present volume for the way in which it was portrayed in the print media in France, essentially as the latest in a long line of Franco-German conflicts both on and off the pitch. *Le Monde*'s preview, for example, notes that 'the whole of France is waiting for the hostilities to resume' against 'Kaiser Beckenbauer's troops' and twice uses the key term of 'revenge' (24 June 1986), ostensibly in the context of the semi-final defeat at the hands of the Germans four years earlier but also implicitly in reference to the ideological discourses of politics and militarism of the turn of the century which were replete with the concept of gaining revenge over Germany for the Franco-Prussian War following which Alsace and Lorraine were annexed by the German Empire. Subsequently, the Great War of 1914–18 was portrayed in France as a mission to retrieve the lost provinces. This implicit subtext of Franco-German military hostility is then made quite explicit by the article in question noting that a 'ready made slogan exists' for this game: 'Germany will pay' (ibid.). 'Germany will pay' was the much-used phrase in the post-Great War period referring to the terms of the Treaty of Versailles whereby parts of Germany were occupied by the allies and extensive financial reparations became payable by the Germans themselves. So, the latest football match between France and Germany is clearly portrayed by *Le Monde* as being an extension of the troubled history of the political and diplomatic relations between the two countries.

In terms of reporting the match itself, both the expectations of the German opponents with regard to their perceived qualities and the wider rôle played by

Germany in French history are realized in the unflattering discourse employed by *Le Monde*: 'These German players, with no creativity and no weaknesses . . . at least have a perennial quality, their physical strength. As a wine has body, Germans have strong legs and lungs full of air.' The French simply underestimated 'the square heads opposite' and were defeated by 'the best known of our denigrators, the most common of our persecutors' (ibid.). As Dauncey and Hare note (1999: 6), the comprehensive defeat of 1986 serves in this way to strengthen 'the French psychological block over their inability to beat their neighbours and old enemies across the Rhine'.

Germany viewed from Spain

The relationships between Spain and Germany in the twentieth century have differed radically from those between Germany and England or France. Hispano-German relations were generally well-disposed throughout the twentieth century. While the two countries cannot be said to be close culturally, they enjoy cordial relations. On the political scene, for a period in the 1930s, Spain had something of a special relationship with Germany, though there was never any great alliance between the two countries. Germany's Nazi regime assisted General Franco in his attempt to take control in Spain (1930s) but at the same time Spain was wary of Germany's plans to turn Spain into an economic colony as it controlled trade between the two countries and interfered in Spain's mining industry (Leitz 1996). According to Bowen (2000), it was only Franco's indecisiveness that prevented Spain from entering into more formal alliance with Germany and becoming part of the Axis during the Second World War. Certainly, the Falange arm within Franco's regime was supportive of such a coalition and Spain signed the Anti-Comintern Pact in 1939. However, Franco resisted Germany's advances, avoided close involvement in the Second World War and retained strong control of Spain. Though Spain became 'neutral' in the war by around 1941, and entered into a period of benevolent neutrality towards the Allies, Spain was banned from the United Nations and excluded from the Marshall Plan in 1947. This ostracism from the political arena meant that sport assumed a symbolic significance in Spain. When Spain played international 'friendly' matches, they meant much more than that to many Spaniards. It is surprising, then, that we do not have a greater bank of data with which to work during this period. Disappointingly, there is relatively little material in our sample that can enlighten us regarding the way German identity was portrayed in Spain for many years. Spain did not play Germany in a competitive fixture until 1966 when they met in the World Cup finals in England. Prior to then, the four 'friendly' meetings between the countries in the 1930s and 1940s received scant attention from the press in our sample.

Unlike English and French football writing, which focuses tightly on military metaphor and imagery when reporting German football, Spanish coverage is not particularly belligerent. The fact that Hispano-German bilateral relations are not clouded by historical resentment, a superiority complex or guilt means that the reports focus more intently on the dry accounts of the style of play. Indeed, Spain judges the English and German press rather scornfully for their obsession with past history and comments on their poor taste in making constant references to the war in the build-up to the World Cup final in 1966 (ABC, 29 July). We do, however, see elements of German identity being portrayed in the few data at our disposal. This early evidence provides useful indications as to how football writing would depict Germany for several decades and beyond.

First, Germany's reputation for playing effective but uninspiring football was established in the 1950s. When West Germany won the World Cup in 1954, it was 'a dull team' who relied on 'solidarity in numbers'. At this time, ABC made the connection between the national football team and the German nation at large. It reported that Germany's World Cup triumph had helped the Germans rediscover a sense of pride in their nation and the seeds of a new German identity were sown. Still in the 1950s, Germans were noted as playing with, 'skill, tactical ability, aggression' (ABC, 3 June 1957). The tactical awareness and aggressive nature of German football are to become a leitmotif in Spanish coverage. By 1966, German football is still aggressive but 'slow, with low levels of skill' (ABC, 26 July 1966). Germany's enigmatic winning strategy of playing poor quality football contributes to the aura of invincibility that surrounds the German team for most of the second half of the twentieth century.

Though the Spanish press acknowledges the myth of the 'invincible' Germans, there is little hard evidence to reinforce that image, apart from constant regular references to the cliché. In 1998, for example, El País refers back to the myth of invincibility in the World Cup finals of 1982 when 'the myth of the Germans was well and truly alive' (El País, 9 July 1998). Similarly, in 2002, El País claimed that it was the World Cup performances of 1982 that had created this myth of an indestructible Germany (El País, 28 June 2002). However, our evidence clearly demonstrates, not surprisingly given previous German football performances, that the stereotype pre-dates this by some two decades at least. In 1966, one reporter for El País concluded that Germany reached the World Cup final because it 'possessed the indomitable strength which has characterized all German teams' (ABC, 2 August 1966). The energy, pace (though admittedly limited to Franz Beckenbauer) and determination of this 1966 team differed from the apparently 'predictable' style which typified German football prior to that date. Indeed, El País also makes claims in 1970 and 1974 that these German teams had 'created a dynasty' or 'a standard by which to be measured' and, retrospectively, in 2002 it was argued that 1986 provided the German team which would 'establish definitively the genetic map for future German teams' (El País, 28 June 2002). Though the Spanish print media appear somewhat confused as to when the German image was created, we find evidence dating to the 1950s and 1960s.

Other aspects of German mythification appear as true in Spain as in France and England. In particular, we are reminded that Germans are physically 'strong' and 'powerful' (e.g. El País, 19 June 1984). This physical strength is attributed, in a sinister way, to Nazi Germany's policy of cleansing the nation of 'racial impurities'.

Overt allusion to this is made in one case when a report refers to 'the physical superiority of the Germans . . . because they have racial concerns that we have never had in Spain' (*ABC*, 23 July 1966). Germany's victory over Spain is thus attributed to a history of racist politics. Germans' physical power and size were constant features of Spanish coverage in the 1980s in particular, when references abound to Germany's 'overwhelming physical presence', 'physical capabilities', 'gigantic' or 'Herculean' presence, for example. The Germans' defensive qualities are emphasized and they are reprimanded for stifling creativity and 'lacking individualism'. They are, instead, 'indefatigable', 'determined fighters' but 'well organized' and 'not lacking in skill'. When Germany won the World Cup in 1974, the Spanish print media argued that this was 'not the best team in Germany's history', that they won despite their poor performances and that managing to overcome the impressive Holland must count for something. Again in 1982, when Germany reached the World Cup final, Spanish writers accused them of doing so 'without playing football'. Though lacking the overt, politically enhanced rivalry inherent in the English and French press, the Spanish print media manage to convey an unambiguous disdain for Germany's style of football: 'Again, the same old story: without an ounce of football, Germany is knocking on the door of the final. The tale of German football, as rudimentary as it is successful. In one of its usual tedious, miserly performances Germany knocked Croatia out of the tournament' (*El País*, 24 June 1996). German football gives as much pleasure as having your teeth pulled out at the dentist, according to *El País*, which is notably scathing about German efforts to play football: 'Nothing they do on the pitch gives pleasure. Everything is rough and crude' (ibid.). The reporter also, rather amusingly, draws on another image of the Germans, one which we see figuring in the data in France and England, to illustrate his point: 'Watching [Germany] play we are not allowed to forget that they are really Mercedes manufacturers dressed up as footballers' (ibid.). German football is, therefore, mechanical and reliable but predictable.

So, we see reporting of German football develop relatively little over the decades. It is portrayed as being effective but mechanical, predictable, oppressive and lacking in individualism or creativity. These are qualities and standards by which German football is now measured. When Germany does not conform to its clichéd form – usually because its style is 'not effective as is the norm' – the Spanish press maintains the stereotype nonetheless rather than accept a changing style and weakening of the traditional image of German football.

Chapter 5

Italy

High drama, fine art, classic design

The history of football in Italy covers the entire twentieth century. The Italian FA (*Federazione Italiana Giuoco Calcio*) was founded in 1898 and the country affiliated to FIFA on the governing body's inception in 1905. The inter-war years saw the first successes of the national team on the global stage with consecutive World Cup titles won on home soil in 1934 and in France in 1938. After a period of relative decline in the immediate post-war era, Italy saw its status as one of the top powers in the game sealed, first by the growing strength of its domestic league and the successes recorded from the 1960s by its club sides in European competitions (notably Juventus, AC Milan and Inter Milan) and second by further international titles being won by the national team (the 1968 European Championships and the 1982 World Cup).

By the end of the twentieth century, with regard to portrayals of Italy's identity in the press, Italians are frequently depicted by football writing in Europe as gifted and potentially highly artistic characters. They are, though, also expected to be theatrical, volcanic of temperament and suspect in terms of morale, favouring a cautious, cagey or overtly negative approach to their football (see Crolley and Hand 2002: 46–8). It will be interesting in the present chapter to discover whether or not these are long-standing traits attributed to Italians throughout the twentieth century by considering English, French and Spanish sports media discourse in the quality press.

Italy viewed from England

Italy have played England 22 times in international football and their rivalry over the last century was tempered with mutual respect for contrasting styles of football. So let us examine the ways in which Italy's image has been established in English print media discourse on football.

Evidence of Italian typecasting is unveiled from the outset. Prior to the first ever game between England and Italy in 1933, England still believed they were the superior side: 'Naturally, I expect England to win' reports *The Times* (10 May 1933), though this was quickly amended afterwards, when the same newspaper admitted that 'the Italians were distinctly superior' on the day itself (15 May

1933). However, it was the nature of this quality that was to provide the basis for coverage of Italian football for much of the rest of the twentieth century. Coverage of that very first match between England and Italy in 1933 already provides a skeleton of an Italian image in terms of its 'dash and confidence' as well as the strong defensive work: 'They stuck very closely to our men throughout' (ibid.). For the only time in our sample, England 'possess a superior technique. In their dribbling and especially in their headwork the English side were distinctly better than the Italians' (ibid.).

After this, the Italians overtake England in terms of technical ability. Their 'passing was much more precise' and they 'combined cleverly' with 'great assurance' (*The Times*, 15 May 1939). Again, the Italians were praised for their 'great defensive work' as they 'centred their efforts on stopping the English attack' (ibid.). There is even a hint of criticism, which again we are to see repeatedly in subsequent years, that the Italians were too defensive: 'they made the mistake of dropping back entirely on the defensive after they had taken the lead' (ibid.). This Italian style is refined further in 1948 and 1949 with their 'quick passes' and when their 'approach play began to click smoothly and to worry the England defenders' (*The Times*, 17 May 1948); England are taken aback by the 'speed and clever inter-passing of Lorenzi . . . and [Italy's] quick control and smoothly rolled passes' (*The Times*, 1 December 1949). It is at this point that we also find the first references to the stereotypical Italian volatility, reflected this time in their 'hurried *temperamental* finishing' (*The Times*, 17 May 1948, emphasis added). Though in 1933, 1934, 1939 and 1949 the Italians were still labelled as 'Continental' in *The Times*, there has nonetheless emerged a style of play that is distinctly marked as Italian. Each report elaborates on and strengthens the build-up of images. By 1949, *The Times* acknowledges the 'superior technical skill and speed' of Italian football (1 December).

By the 1960s, images are becoming stereotypes, clichés even, and range from Italian obsession with pasta to their demonstrative gestures, penchant for style and the hint of a fickle nature. In 1961, for example, 'Arms wave, shoulders shrug, fingers are pointed as tactics and the possible outcome are argued' (*The Times*, 23 May) – and that is during just the preview to the match! Again, at the 1962 World Cup finals in Mexico, we see 'The Italians, installed in the Air Academy here with ample supplies of pasta, oil, meat, wine, and mineral water brought with them' (*The Times*, 30 May 1962). The Italians are by now 'remarkable artists' who 'stroked their passes from every angle' and 'with an attacking pedigree' (*The Times*, 25 May 1961). The game was 'more predictable' and 'played largely at one pace' (ibid.). Italy's apparent reliance on defensive tactics is bemoaned in *The Times*, for example, following Italy's defeat against 'unfancied' North Korea: 'Fear of defeat has turned giants into pygmies. Concentration on defence has stifled the flair of their game' (*The Times*, 20 July 1966). By the 1970s, the archetypal Italian performance has been truly established: 'It was a *typical* Italian chessboard performance – subtle, defensive interlocking at the back, which *as usual* contained the frustrating and often blatant body check. . . . But once they were ahead the Italian tails went up with a click' (*The Times*, 14 June 1973, our italics).

By the 1980s, English print media discourse on football has accepted Italy's football superiority as the norm: 'Victory over the Italians [is] never more than a distant hope' (*The Times*, 17 June 1980). England manager Bobby Robson's prediction prior to an England–Italy match in 1985 summarizes the (by now traditional) Italian style of play: 'Italy will be as defensively strong as usual and they will rely on breaks. That is their classic style. They will give us nothing' (*The Times*, 4 June 1985). It is also in the 1980s that frustration creeps into the English football writing: 'The Italian mentality is based on the belief that the opposition will not score. Therefore they cannot lose. A glance at their domestic results tells us the negative tale' (*The Times*, 13 July 1982). Respect remains, though, as the physical side of Italy's play strengthens: 'The unyielding shield of the Italians' beat Brazil in the 1982 World Cup semi-final (*The Times*, 13 July 1982) and *The Times* acknowledges Italy's 'begrudging power that hovers on the edge of outright violence' and 'vigorous tackling' (17 June 1980). Even then, though, Italy benefit from their 'touch of imagination' that the English envy (ibid.).

In addition to coverage of the Italian national team, the numerous Italian footballers who have played in England in more recent times (in particular in the 1990s and beyond) have also contributed to reinforcing a stereotype. On an individual level, the portrait depicted is rather complex since the individuals tend not to display all the characteristics of the Italian national team. They are not defined as being defensive or as hard tacklers, for example. On the contrary, the qualities of style and flair are foremost, in keeping with a more general view of Italians' approach to fashion and design: for example, 'Chelsea's gifted Italians' are 'elegant' and have 'flair' (*The Times*, 10 November 1997). While Italian footballers are typically extolled for their high levels of skill, they are also portrayed as temperamental, unreliable, extravagant, rather superficial and with a penchant for the theatrical (when not portrayed as plain cheating). Benito Carbone and Paolo Di Canio, for example, were described by one reporter as 'highly paid, highly strung performers', 'often walking an emotional tightrope', who produced 'theatrical gestures and grimaces' (*The Times*, 29 September 1997).

The final Italian stereotype, which is worthy of brief mention since it appears sporadically in our data, involves references to the mafia and conspiracy theories, generally instigated when Italians challenge authority or try to dupe officialdom, particularly when they complain about refereeing decisions: 'Italy practically invented the conspiracy theory, and there were Machiavellian mutterings about big guys pulling invisible strings from the moment the Croatian comeback in the second group match made the Azzurri's progress look uncertain. That is normal, it goes with the territory' (*The Guardian*, 30 June 2002). This mentality is clearly presented as being part of the Italian character. Both at team level and on an individual level, Italian footballers are never far from accusations of stretching the rules of the game beyond the limits within which the English print media feel comfortable. There is evidently something of a culture clash when it comes to the English print media commenting on Italian football and footballers: Italy 'leads the way in the manipulation of the rules' (*The Guardian*, 30 June 2002).

The depiction of Italian fans is also fairly consistent throughout our data. They are portrayed as fanatical, flamboyant, but sometimes inconsistent. One reporter's comment that Italian fans sang only when their team was winning insinuated a passionate but fickle support (*The Times*, 25 May 1961). The depiction of Italy as a football-mad country actually pre-dates coverage of football. An article in *The Times* (18 April 1925) entitled 'The Spread of Football: Keenness on the Continent' explained how football was becoming popular among the indigenous Italian population. The flamboyance of the Italian support is reinforced in the 1970s in particular: 'The Italians take their football passionately: they will be screeching their heads off, loosing off rockets, firecrackers and the rest' (*The Times*, 13 June 1973); 'The noise rippled and quivered as rockets sped to the sky and the green, red and white banners waved' (*The Times*, 14 June 1973).

English coverage of Italian football and footballers, therefore, clearly identifies supposedly typical national characteristics. The talented, skilful and technically superior Italians are over-defensive, theatrical and temperamentally volatile. This characterization was built up and strengthened during the twentieth century, though it will be interesting to study developments beyond our sample in a period when greater integration of a European labour force might eventually lead to an erosion of national stereotyping at an individual level at least. Early signs suggest that national stereotypes at international level will take much longer to fade.

Italy viewed from France

The geographical proximity of Italy to France and the cultural similarities between the two predominantly Latin nations make Italy an important opponent in the French football psyche and provide France–Italy matches with a unique dimension, a dimension that, in keeping with football's wider capacity to communicate information about national identities, says much about French perceptions of their neighbours on the other side of the Alps. But what do the French think of as typically Italian? The links with ancient Rome (doubtless fuelled by the comic book adventures of Asterix the Gaul)? Temperaments that are as volcanic as the southern Italian landscape? A cautious, defensive mentality that is transposed into a style of play in football terms? Certainly all of these may be found in the football writing of the quality daily press in France in the twentieth century but with varying degrees of coverage and of complexity.

Ludic metaphors likening Italians to their ancient Roman ancestors are not uncommon in European football writing. In the report in *Le Monde* of one World Cup match, for example, the metaphor was extended across the whole article resulting in the playful portrayal of a football match involving Italy as a gladiatorial combat in a stadium taking on the qualities of the Colosseum itself: the match, opposing Italy and the United States of America, was said to have been played in a 'Roman arena' where the Americans constituted 'the sacrifice' that the crowd, 'thumbs to the ground, demanded be finished off'; 'the little Sicilian gladiator', that is the forward Schillaci, duly obliged by scoring the winning goal (16 June 1990).

Similarly, the stereotypically volcanic characteristics of Italians also feature in the French press, especially when the venue of the match under consideration is Naples, with its geographical proximity to Mount Vesuvius. A reporter for *Le Matin* in 1938 could not resist commenting upon the setting, for example: 'Evening fell on the last ten minutes of the game [that Italy won] and the red glints from Vesuvius lit up the plume of white smoke emanating from the volcano' offering the backdrop to the temperamental crowd which 'whistled madly at the end for no obvious reason' (5 December 1938); while a homologue from *Le Monde*, separated by 40 years of time, employed similar tactics to transpose the physical features of the volcano into the psychological characteristics of the Italian fans: 'In this Bay of Naples groaning with life and bathed in sun, the sight of Vesuvius is ever imposing. With its 70,000 fans, the San Paolo stadium is also transformed into a volcano . . . and the Italians' excessive passion for football remains undiminished' (10 February 1978).

Having said this, perhaps the single theme that most exercises the minds of French football journalists from the early twentieth century onwards (with regard to Italy) is that of the true nature of the Italian temperament and, slowly but progressively, a debate is engaged about the extent to which the defensive style of play commonly adopted by the Italians betrays their Latin heritage, as will be demonstrated by the following chronological survey.

The first football match between France and Italy was played in 1910 in Milan and resulted in a 6–2 victory for the home side. However, little attention appears to have been paid to the encounter by the French press; the major daily *Le Matin*, for instance, devoted no more than seven lines to the occasion (16 May 1910). Subsequent matches also failed to attract much interest despite their being an annual event up to the eve of the Great War in 1914 and there is, therefore, little of note in this section of the European press with regard to the portrayal of Italian national identity. Even in the early 1920s, match reports remained short, curt and descriptive and refrained from commenting on the attributes or characteristics of the Italian players (see, for instance, *Le Temps*, 20 January 1920 and *Le Matin*, 21 February 1921).

It is really only from the mid-1920s that anything resembling an Italian identity in the making is depicted in French press reports of matches involving Italy and France. For instance, one report in *Le Matin* spoke of 'the impetuous Italians' (23 March 1925) while another in the same newspaper remarked upon their 'nonchalance' and 'lack of conviction' (25 April 1927).

By the end of the 1930s, of course, Italy had become a global power in football with two World Cup triumphs to its name. However, one of the means by which that success must have been achieved, selecting professional footballers for the national team, was not at all appreciated by the press in France where the game, at international level at least, remained resolutely amateur. A crushing 5–0 defeat at the hands of the Italians in 1931, for example, was said to have been achieved by Italy 'playing their own game' based upon 'their physical and technical superiority' (*Le Temps*, 27 January 1931). A year later, *Le Matin* was scathing about the consequences of introducing professionals into the international arena. The Italians who beat France 2–1 on this occasion were qualified as 'less ardent, less nippy' than their amateur predecessors and the game as a whole disappointed the French crowd who had turned up to witness a fine display. The newspaper suggested that the change in the Italians' style of play was attributable to professionalization, which encouraged a more disciplined approach, a more mechanical technique and a more cynical outlook than that exhibited by Italian sides in the past: 'One would have thought we were watching a good, professional, third division English team' was the less than complimentary summary (11 April 1932). Clearly, by the end of the twentieth century, Italian defensive discipline and caginess were givens (see Crolley and Hand 2002). It is interesting to note that, in France at least, the origins of this typically Italian way of playing football were not appreciated but were rather seen as a negative consequence of the switch to professionalism at international level.

Match reports covering Italy–France games after the Second World War continue to engage with the question of Italian identity and, in particular, of whether or not the style of play deriving from it is laudable or even authentically Italian. In the first match opposing the two teams in the post-war period, a 1948 encounter in Colombes watched by over 60,000 spectators which Italy won 3–1, the Italians were said to have demonstrated 'remarkable liveliness, acrobatic skill and moves conducted in a flash' which made the present 'Azzurri worthy of their predecessors' (*Le Monde*, 6 April 1948). When Italians fail to demonstrate the qualities expected of them, though, French journalists are swift to condemn them: 'generally lively and quick . . . today, they were slow and fearful' (*Le Monde*, 8 May 1962). Indeed, throughout the 1960s, French journalists were concerned that Italy (and, on occasion, France also) were almost betraying their Latin heritage by not playing in a quick, fancy, open way, favouring instead the more cautious, economical and disciplined approach to the game introduced by the development of professionalism in the 1930s. The friendly played in Paris in 1966, which ended scoreless, provides a notable example. Previewed by *Le Monde* as 'a serious head to head of two neighbours . . . of two Latin teams separated by bitter rivalry . . . a clash that always stirs the passions' (19 March 1966), the match was clearly expected to be open, lively and spectacular. The festival of Latin flair did not materialize, however, and *Le Monde*'s match reporter was clearly disappointed. 'Maybe the strong personalities in the Italian team would set off the fireworks we so expected to see', notes the report (22 March 1966) but it was not to be: 'fitter and individually technically superior . . . [the Italians] remained faithful to their tactics of strong defence and determined counter-attack . . . [the match] was honest but not showy and this was not generally what had been hoped for from a spectacle in which the Latin temperament should have been expressed to the full' (ibid.).

The expectations placed by French media discourse on Latin teams to play in a certain way continued into the 1970s and 1980s. After a 2–2 draw in Naples between France and Italy, for instance, the Italian team was castigated for 'not shining like their forebears' (*Le Monde*, 10 February 1978), demonstrating once again the importance of the precedent set by past teams which current ones have to live up to in order to be true to their essential identity (see Archetti 1996). Similarly, the same newspaper in 1982 identified the common traits shared by France and Italy and attributed these to their comparable ethnic backgrounds: 'these two teams play the same Latin football based on technical skill allied with a liveliness of spirit and action' (25 February). However, it was also noted that the Italians differ from their opponents by being 'more attentive to the need for organization, especially defensively', which itself might well lie behind the match reporter's qualification of Italy as 'a disappointment' in footballing terms (ibid.). Further condemnation of the overly defensive Italians came during the 1986 World Cup in Mexico, during which France recorded only their fifth victory against their neighbours in 75 years of competition. 'Troppo, too much!' screamed *Le Monde* before going on to denigrate the style of play labelled *catennacio*, which involves locking up play with 'huge padlocks' that serve only to narrow ambition and for which the Italians must be made 'to pay dearly' (17 June 1986). Finally in this respect, by the end of the twentieth century, whether or not the excessively defensive traits in question were originally Italian, and irrespective of the extent to which they counter expectations of Latin football, they are undeniably and inextricably associated with Italy: the team competing at France 98, for instance, was simply summed up as 'typically Italian, aggressive, often cynical' (*Le Monde*, 19 June 1998).

Italy viewed from Spain

Italy are one of Spain's most frequent international opponents. The two sides have met 26 times since their first encounter in the 1920 Olympic Games in Antwerp, Belgium. By then, Italy had the advantage over Spain of a decade's international experience. The seeds of Italian football identity were sown here in Antwerp in terms of Spanish print media discourse: 'The Italians, frustrated at not being able to break through our defence, resorted to dirty play' (*ABC*, quoted in Martialay 2000: 275). Though there were encounters between Spain and Italy during the 1930s and 1940s, we have few data to work with in this period. There is, however, a wealth of material available from the 1950s and beyond.

Even by the 1950s, Italy's status in Spain as a strong footballing nation was becoming established – 'the Italian aces' (*ABC*, 24 July 1955) – as was their name for playing a distinctive style of football with defensive prowess, a reputation which persists throughout the twentieth century: 'the excellent Italian defence' (*ABC*, 4 July 1950); 'The Italians focused on man-to-man marking' (*ABC*, 27 January 1955). The Italians' defensive capabilities date from a long time ago. It has been difficult to situate the origins of this precisely, given the lack of material available on Italian match reports in the first half of the twentieth century in our data. However, by the 1950s, examples abound as we hear of the 'the purple Italian wall', when Real Madrid play Fiorentina, whose defence was 'compact, firm, capable of closing gaps with absolute precision' (*ABC*, 31 May 1957). Already the Italians are famed for their counter-attacking danger and 'their incredibly quick attack from defence' (ibid.). This reliance on defensive tactics, accompanied by a tougher side to their game, punctuates many reports in Spain: 'the man-to-man marking was ruthless' (*El País*, 26 January 1978); Italy were 'defensive . . . relying on the counterattack . . . . Then the game got tougher, and even dirty' (*El País*, 22 December 1978); Italy's defence was 'practically impenetrable' (*El País*, 9 July 1994).

Nevertheless, there is more to Italian football than defensive tactics. Italians are portrayed as being skilful and talented footballers, particularly when plying their trade at club level. When reporting on Fiorentina's performance in the European Cup final of 1957, for instance, the Italians were said to 'pass the ball with the huge skill that doesn't need a first touch' (*ABC*, 31 May 1957). Italians 'pay attention to detail in their football . . . have the ability to benefit from a sudden touch of genius . . . because of the subtle spectacular nature of their football' (*El País*, 11 October 1997). Italians are also depicted as having a good understanding of the game: they are the 'Italian tacticians' (*El País*, 11 October 1997); Italy 'played a very tactical game, paying great attention to detail' (*El País*, 10 July 1994); and in the same World Cup finals in 1994 it was commented that they 'performed with tactical efficiency, paying special attention to saving their efforts for tricky situations' (*El País*, 9 July 1994). Just as in France, it is the potential spark of individuality and flair that makes Italian football so attractive to Spanish journalists despite its defensive tactics and predictability. *El País* summarizes the principal ingredients of what it calls the 'transcendental' Italian character thus: 'firmness, discipline, good defensive tactics and character' (9 July 1994). It is the last of these traits that provides the unpredictability, the individuality or the flair that inspires admiration from the Spanish reporters. Without this flair, Italy are denigrated as risk-averse as they disappoint the Spanish print media who are perplexed as to why they do not play with the style that they have 'naturally' been given as Italians (e.g. *El País*, 18 June 1998; 19 June 1998).

Another aspect of the Spanish portrayal of Italy considers Italians to exhibit a stylish confidence, bordering on arrogance: 'Italy thought they were superior and began playing with too much confidence' (*El País*, 13 June 1980). However, when Italians act contrary to this image, this, too, is the subject of comment: for example, *El País* remarked on their 'unusual lack of confidence' and when they were 'afraid of attacking and leaving themselves vulnerable' (11 October 1997). Unlike in our English sample, where Italians are notable for their fashionable style and elegance, this features relatively little in the Spanish data (for example, via a reference to their Armani suits [*El País*, 9 July 1994], or to the flamboyance of the 'Italian divas' [*El País*, 22 December 1978]).

When Italians do not conform to the expected traditional style of play, they are inevitably portrayed as letting someone down – either the fans or the players themselves. In 1994, for instance, Spain criticized Italy's predictable style of play and *El País* in particular claimed that 'this reduces the opportunity for the spontaneity that the talented [Italian] players need' (9 July 1990). In this article, there is an assumption that Italian players are naturally gifted and that playing a predictable, 'boring' style did not play to their natural, national strengths as a Latin country. It was for this reason that the former Italy manager, Arrigo Sacchi, was 'hated' in Italy – he did not allow the players to play the football that Italy wanted and the fans yearned for a return to Italy's 'classical values' (*El País*, 11 October 1997).

As in both England and France, Italy is depicted as being a country with both passionate and inconsistent support: 'I have never seen a country as passionate about sport as Italy. . . . When they lost to North Korea, a cloud of unhappiness settled in the Italian soul. This was followed by a national day of mourning' (*ABC*, 24 July 1966). The more fickle nature of Italian support is also hinted at: 'The Italian manager went from a national hero to being wretched and loathed' (ibid.). Then in a similar fashion, 'Bearzot [Italy's manager] will have problems with the Italian fans if they get a poor result and will increase his popularity if they win [against Spain]' (*El País*, 24 January 1978). In common with English coverage of Italy, Spain's print media, then, often allude to the inconsistency of Italian support: Italy is quite simply 'a fickle country' (*El País*, 11 October 1997).

Finally, Italy is viewed as being more than European colleagues with Spain. Italians are 'our Mediterranean neighbours' (*ABC*, 22 July 1955) or 'our Latin friends' (*ABC*, 24 July 1966), though in football terms there appears to be relatively little to bind the two countries together. Spain, it appears, has been somewhat in awe of Italy's 'glorious football history' (ibid.) and often labels Italy as 'favourites', even when they play Spain (e.g. *El País*, 13 June 1980); 'Spain, [which] usually considers Italian football with too much respect' (*El País*, 10 July 1994). Most of all, Spain envies Italy's 'defined style of play' and the 'definite, clear structure' of its football: 'Spain has always approached matches against Italy with apprehension. The roots of this inferiority complex lie in the fact that Italy has made *calcio* its own: Italy has always been a recognizable team, with a defined style of play' (*El País*, 9 July 1994). This is reinforced time and time again and there are references to 'the Italy of old' (*El País*, 18 June 1998); to a nation 'that doesn't change its identity' (*El País*, 1 July 1998) or simply that 'Italy was Italy' (*El País*, 2 July 1998). In short, Italy has achieved that which Spain has coveted: a defined style of play.

The image of Italy portrayed in the Spanish print media shares much in common with that of the English press. Italy's reliance on defensive tactics is not how the Spanish perceive themselves. Italy's tactical awareness is again a self-confessed weakness of the Spanish and Italy's stylish confidence a far cry from Spain's own pessimism and almost desperate reliance on *furia* to which the present study now turns.

Chapter 6

Spain

Land of hope and fury

Though football has been popular in Spain since the end of the nineteenth century, with many clubs founded around the turn of the century (e.g. Club Recreativo de Huelva, 1889; Athletic de Bilbao, 1898; FC Barcelona, 1899; [Real] Madrid, 1902; Real Sociedad, 1909), the Spanish FA itself was not founded until 1913 and the National Spanish League (*La Liga de Fútbol Profesional*) did not begin until 1928–29. Since then, just nine clubs have been crowned League Champions, with Real Madrid and Barcelona dominating (winning 29 and 17 times respectively).

On the international scene, Spain first put together a national team (*selección*) to participate in the 1920 Olympic Games in Antwerp. Since then, Spain has contested over 500 international fixtures (over half of them 'friendlies') against 70 countries. Spain has competed in 11 World Cup final tournaments, its first being in 1934, including every tournament since 1978. Spain has also participated in seven of the nine European Championships, failing to qualify only in the first competition in 1960 and in 1992. However, Spain's success is less impressive. Spain's best achievement in the FIFA World Cup is fourth place (in 1950) and it managed to reach the quarter finals in 1986 and 1994. Spain's greatest achievement has been to win the European Championship in 1964, on home soil. It was runner-up to France in this competition 20 years later in 1984. This lack of success by the perennial underachievers is at the root of some of the themes discussed below.

The Spanish self-image

The notion of a single Spanish identity is not a concept that has strong roots in Spain. Spain is a relatively new state. It was constituted as such in the Cortes of Cádiz in 1812. The Spanish Constitution of the same year established that 'the Spanish Nation is the union of all Spanish people, in both hemispheres' (Article 1 of the 1812 Spanish Constitution). Here, the nation is defined, then, not as a territory but as the people who populated it. The political nation was yet to become a cultural entity, however, and this process is still evolving, to a greater or lesser extent throughout the territory. It is hardly surprising that Spanish football was not centrally organized until well into the twentieth century, or that Spain did not have a national team until three decades after the foundation of its first domestic club.

In Spain, now living under its seventh constitution since that of 1812, the debate over the nation has been a constant theme in political and social circles. In the nineteenth century, it was the focus of discussion for federalists and centralists 'but always from a shared understanding of Spain as the *patria* [mother country] held in common by all' (Pérez Garzón 2003: 47). It was towards the end of the nineteenth century, as football was emerging across Spain, when alternative nationalisms to the Castilian/Spanish centralist model emerged as a strong political challenge to the view of Spain as a single nation, especially in areas such as Catalunya, the Basque Country and Galicia. This will be discussed further in the chapter that focuses on football coverage in Catalunya and the Basque Country. Today, according to the Constitution of 1978, Spain is a nation of regions and nationalities. Since 1978, Spain has consisted of 17 *Comunidades Autónomas*, with strong regional and national identities. These *Comunidades Autónomas* enjoy differing and negotiable degrees of self-governance. In order to avoid the connotations that can arise with translations that approximate the Spanish concept but are not exact equivalents, we have chosen to keep the term *Comunidad Autónoma* throughout.

In this section, we shall discuss autotypification with respect to a single Spanish (centralist) nation-state and a Spanish national identity as portrayed in Spanish print media discourse on football. As noted above, coverage of football in Spain in the early part of the twentieth century was scant. Even though football was growing rapidly in popularity, few column inches were dedicated to it in the newspapers in our sample. For example, in 1915, match previews (where they existed) were limited to speculating over team selection (e.g. *ABC*, 30 October 1915) and the *Notas Deportivas* (Sporting Notes) generally devoted more space to *Toros y Toreros* (the bullfighting section) than to association football.

Another relevant feature of the general football press at this time is that there is little (national) coverage of football played outside the capital, Madrid. Our sample, which was largely drawn from *ABC* during this early period, though supposedly a national daily in coverage, focused tightly on football within Madrid. Typically, while it might include a match report on Madrid (not to become Real until 1920), there would only be results reported from other fixtures played in other parts of the country. Madrid dominates the football pages. One (unusually lengthy) report, for instance, covers a match involving FC Sabadell without actually naming their opponents until towards the end when the reader is informed that the match was played in Madrid, following which Madrid's performance is discussed (*ABC*, 2 January 1916). Such is the Madrid bias, that it is assumed from the start that the readership knows that it was Madrid playing Sabadell and that this did not need stating at the outset.

In order to analyse the extent to which Spanish identity was mediated via football writing, it is important to understand the situation Spanish football found itself in at the start of the twentieth century.

Early attempts to play football above the local level were really dominated by regional teams. The final of the Spanish Championship (*Campeonato de España*), Español de Madrid versus Club Ciclista de San Sebastián, held in Madrid on 18

April 1909, saw representatives from the two regions fielded, at the expense of some of the regular players (Club Ciclista won 3–1). Already, the sense of the football club's identification with city or region had emerged. *Gran Vida* praised the efforts of Madrid's players accordingly: 'All the players who represented Madrid should be praised, for the enthusiasm with which they defended the Castilian region' (*Gran Vida*, quoted in Martialay 2000: 60). This identification had not, though, extended to the national level.

Unsurprisingly, football did not emerge with a strong Spanish national team, or *selección*. Again, the term '*selección*' does not translate easily. Literally, the 'selection' or 'chosen players', it usually refers to a national team, but in the Spanish case it can refer to any team at 'supra-club' level. It might refer to the Spanish national team but it might also refer to a Basque, Catalan or Andalusian team. It does not necessarily imply that the team aspires to 'national' status. Hence, again we have chosen to keep the Spanish term *selección* rather than attempt a translation which would prove inadequate. Indeed, it took some time before a team that could be called a Spanish 'national' team evolved.

Though the Spanish FA (*Federación Española de Fútbol*) was founded in 1913, there was still a lack of 'national' organization in Spanish football. The professionalization of Spanish football was not formalized until 1926, though the period 1915–26 is often denominated a period of *amateurism marrón* (professionalism being more developed in some areas – namely, Barcelona and Bilbao – than others). In the early years of the twentieth century, football links were already being made between northern Spain and southern France and relations with the English were, of course, already firmly established. Yet a national Spanish team had not emerged.

The breakthrough for the formation of a Spanish *Selección* was the 1920 Olympic Games in Antwerp. By early 1920, though, not all the Regional Federations agreed to participate in preparation of the *Selección* for the 1920 Olympics. Notably, the Northern and the Guipuzcoan Federations refused to collaborate in the venture. These were significant omissions given that 57 per cent of Spain's footballers registered with the FA were in Catalunya, the Basque Country and Asturias, and just 9 per cent were accommodated in Madrid (Bahamonde 2002).

There were indeed considerable doubts in Spain over whether or not to take part in the 1920 Olympic Games (Martialay 2000: 56). Sport was not highly organized in Spain at the time, neither was it centralized. Football was one of the few sports to enjoy a certain level of organization but was going through a minor crisis in this respect. Nevertheless, one journalist, Federico Caro, in *Madrid Sport*, wrote that 'Everyone should put the interests of the Nation ('*Patria*') above other more trivial interests and remember that it is not about going [to Antwerp] as tourists but about going, as ambassadors, to show the world that there is more to Spain than bulls' (quoted in Martialay 2000: 163).

Let us now examine in more detail the ways in which 'Spanishness' has been represented in the Spanish football press. To what extent does there exist a Spanish identity mediated through the print media? What images are presented as being 'Spanish'? Are the images constant or evolving? In order to analyse these matters, we draw on examples taken throughout the twentieth century but focus on key periods such as the 1920s (when the Spanish *Selección* was established) and the 1950s (a particularly successful period for Spanish football at a domestic level).

The overwhelming feature present and consistent throughout the history of Spanish (national) football is that of the *furia española*. We have discussed the concept of *la furia española* elsewhere (Crolley and Hand 2002: 105–23), but the importance of *la furia española* in any discussion of Spanish football and the mediation of identity via the press cannot be overstated: 'Spanish fury deserves respect from Spanish football because it is part of its essence, its very lifeline. Past and future. Anyone would be wrong to ignore it' (Martialay 2000: 290). Martialay also claims that 'there is no doubt that the expression "la furia española", as a defining characteristic of the Spanish national style of play, was first coined during the Olympic Games in Antwerp' (ibid. 287). There is widespread consent that the term was first applied to football at this time: 'It was in the Antwerp Olympic Games that the term took root' (*ABC*, 17 March 1942).

After considerable polemic over whether or not the team should compete at all in the 1920 Olympics (the lack of experience at international level of Spanish football and poor facilities led to pessimism about the team's chances and many feared ridicule and embarrassment), the Spanish won the silver medal. The spirit in which the team performed led to the coinage of the term '*furia española*'. It is unclear who first used the term, however. Martialay believes that it is likely that a French journalist, Henri Desgrange, was the first to refer to the *furia española* in his article entitled 'Denmark was beaten by the *furia española*' (*L'Auto*, quoted in Martialay 2000). Then the famous Spanish sports journalist, Alberto Martín Fernández, known under the pseudonym 'Juan Deportista', popularized the term within Spain in his articles following the Olympic Games in Antwerp. Ball (2001: 214) elaborates on the context of the origins of the term following Spain's match against Sweden, and acknowledges the contribution of *ABC*'s 'Rubryk' (quoted in Martialay 2000: 287) in emphasizing the symbolic significance of Spain's performance and character.

The original interpretation of the term is also unclear. Elements include 'sheer determination bordering on savagery. A team of "mates" capable of destroying their rivals. A style of play that is crude, primitive, and consists of booting the ball up-field towards the opposition net . . . where the Herculean, gigantic forwards run in like bulls to head the ball . . . a style of play that is brave and virile.' But this is only half the story: 'la furia is above all essentially about the will to win' (Martialay 2000: 288). This was the spirit of Antwerp. This is the basis of *la furia española*.

Since the 1920s, according to Martialay, 'the great Spanish teams throughout history have been supported by "*la furia*"' (ibid.). What made the Spanish *furia* special in 1920 was the style of play: 'playing football at hurricane speed, total control of all faculties . . . an enormous love of the game, of football' (ibid. 289).

There was not just strength but also skill. This style of play was to become part of the Spanish football identity and this is an inclusive identity in the sense that it transcends regional boundaries.

The concept of *furia* has been a constant theme throughout Spanish football history since 1920 and an essential defining element of Spanish (football) identity. In a way, the Spanish football identity pre-dates a more general Spanish collective identity. In 1942, for instance, the Spanish style of play is described as being distinct from the rest of Europe: 'The Spanish formula is different . . . it consists of players who are strong, brave, intrepid, enthusiastic, determined' (*ABC*, 17 March). Even when the word *furia* is not employed, the concept is not far away: 'Spain had deep determination . . . and speed without style' (*ABC*, 19 May 1950). In the same game, Spain dominated 'when there was rapid, energetic movement but lacked intelligence' (ibid.) and opponents 'England were less passionate than the Spanish' (ibid.).

The notion of *furia* is not confined to the national *Selección*. In 1941, Valencia's *furia* won them the Copa del Generalísimo 3–1 (*ABC*, 1 July 1941). Later, an article previews a Real Madrid European Cup tie against an English club in 1968, a week after the Spanish national side was beaten by England. The crowd is defined as follows: 'high expectations, Spanish desire for revenge, passion, colourful crowd' (*ABC*, 17 May 1968). Here the inspiring elements of 'Spanishness' are summarized and combine the notions of optimism ('high expectations'), passion and colour – the last two also very much features of foreign images of the Spanish.

By 1950, words associated with the concept of *furia* were being readily employed: Spanish attackers were described (positively) as 'impulsive' and 'spectacular' (*ABC*, 1 July 1950); their goalkeeper 'dived bravely' (*ABC*, 4 July 1950) and a strong idea of the style of play valued by the Spanish along with the attributes deemed desirable is also provided: 'Perhaps the English style was more scientifically perfect but the Spanish were faster, more committed, and fought more valiantly' (ibid.). This is revealing. What the Spanish value in their football is not perfect technique but commitment, speed and bravery – yet again values associated with the concept of *furia*.

In recent times, the notion of *la furia española* remains as strong as ever in the minds of Spaniards and is closely associated with the essence of Spanishness in the football context. It could be argued that Spanish football has its own identity, one which unites Spain. This is a safe identity, one that can be seen to exist without risking other regional and national sensitivities in Spain, as long as it is firmly associated with football, or indeed sport. It is not unusual to link the notion of *furia* with sports other than football (for example, the headline 'Madrid won with no ammunition other than *furia*' refers to basketball [*El País*, 18 January 1980]).

González Ramallal (2003) argues that there was a decline of *furia* in favour of *espectáculo* (literally 'spectacle') in the 1980s and 1990s. He cites the 1982 World Cup hosted by Spain as the beginning of a process of change towards a more modern vision of Spanish football identity. Gradually, the traditional structures of football were giving way to a more modern character; González Ramallal (2003) claims that one of the key elements of this process was the substitution of the importance of *la furia española* in favour of *fútbol espectáculo* (which conveys a notion of 'entertainment' or 'show', implying that the rôle of fan shifts to that of spectator rather than participant observer).

The word *'espectáculo'* has, indeed, been employed increasingly in the print media to describe 'big' football events: 'Let the spectacle commence!' (*Marca*, 11 November 1992); 'Real Madrid begin their preseason with the intention of winning and providing *espectáculo*' (*Marca*, 17 July 1998); 'Barcelona-Atlético, a true *espectáculo* awaits' (*Marca*, 27 November 1998); and Johan Cruyff wanted to create *fútbol espectáculo* at Barcelona (e.g. 16 August 1989). However, contrary to the expectations that González Ramallal's evidence provides, the notion of *furia* remains important. There is evidence in our sample in the 1990s that the Spanish press perceive *fútbol espectáculo* to be a more advanced form of football than that which relies on *furia* and that Spain would very much like to be progressive. Ideally, the Spanish press would like Spain to display qualities of *furia* combined with skill and flair (e.g. ABC, 13 June 1998). Unfortunately, it appears, Spain is not yet able to be successful without resorting to its traditional *furia*, and it is to *furia* that the print media appeal when desperate for victory: 'The best tactic is the heart; the Spanish team reclaims the concept of *furia*' (*El País*, 23 June 1998). Over-reliance on *furia* is, however, portrayed as a national weakness (ABC, 20 June 1998; 26 June 1998).

The domination of the characteristics associated with *furia* is, then, overwhelmingly the main feature of Spanish autotypification. However, there are other features of Spanish writing which are culture-specific. The politicization of Spanish football, particularly by the media, has been a subject of much debate (e.g. Shaw 1987) and our sample provides an insight into the ways in which football might have been exploited for effective politicking.

When the success of the Spanish side in the 1920 Olympic Games came as a surprise to many, the joy was apparently extra-sweet given Spain's self-perception that it was viewed negatively from the outside. Football writing did not shy away from political comment: 'Spain, our Spain so scorned by others . . . but as great as anyone, has shown to the whole world what we are capable of when we make the effort. Those countries who looked at us with hypocritical indifference – although deep down they understood our worth – by the end of the Olympics applauded and waved Spanish flags' ('Don Sincero', *Madrid Sport*, quoted in Martialay 2000: 291). Football, it was claimed, was helping Spain to become accepted and respected by the rest of the world.

Another article written in 1920 covering the Olympic Games emphasized the ambassadorial nature of the victorious display in Antwerp. The writer claimed that the whole team should be invited to the 'Capital of the Nation, for whose honour and under whose flag they have fought on foreign soil' ('*Homenaje*', quoted in Martialay 2000: 290). Football is now, then, probably for the first time in Spain, being used as a unifying force to bring the whole nation together under one flag. This trait is another feature which will recur in later decades.

In 1941, a Portugal–Spain match was previewed as 'the Spanish *furia*' against 'the Portuguese soul' (*ABC*, 14 January 1941). Spain apparently failed to win this match, played 18 months after the end of the Civil War, because the team was 'brought from the trenches'. Here, we find evidence of an attempt to use football as a vehicle to prove that Spain was not ostracized from the rest of the world but that it did have friends: this particular match was 'a fraternal sporting fiesta' (ibid.). This report, written by Alberto Martín Fernández – alias 'Juan Deportista' – goes to some lengths to emphasize the close ties between Spain and neighbours Portugal. He states that this match 'revives the deepest emotions of those traditional battles which serve to reinforce the indestructible affectionate ties that unite the sportsmen of the two countries of the peninsula' (ibid.).

The period of the 1950s was an important one for Spanish football at club level (when Real Madrid dominated Europe by winning the European Cup in five consecutive years), for the political manipulation of football and for the reinforcement of a Spanish identity via football writing. The victories achieved in Spanish football (of Real Madrid and, less frequently, the national team) were closely linked to the success of the Franco regime (see Shaw 1987 for more in-depth discussion of this). During this period, Franco's personal endorsement of both the national team and, more importantly, Real Madrid was demonstrated via his public attendance at the stadium. His reported presence was often a feature of football writing and, in *ABC*, the reporter would invariably describe the generous applause he allegedly received by all who surrounded him in the VIP area and beyond (e.g. *ABC*, 31 May 1957).

There has been much discussion already about the extent to which Franco exploited football to create a feeling of national pride and identity but little specific research has been put forward to support exactly how this was done. It is certainly true that Franco attended football matches, many of Real Madrid, though by no means exclusively. It is also true that Franco manipulated football in many ways – as indeed his regime controlled every aspect of public life. Franco appointed officials to run football administration and clubs as he did other official organizations. However, an analysis of the football writing during this period provides an insight into the ways in which the discourse employed can contribute to shaping public opinion by presenting a biased view of reality. We see glorified impressions created, for example, by the use of certain adjectives or superlatives, by the commenting upon some aspects of the game and not others, and so on. Let us turn to some typical examples.

In a preview of a Spain–England fixture to be played in Madrid, one journalist notes, 'We know that the Madrid crowd – representative of people all over Spain – does not need lessons on how to support a team' (*ABC*, 18 May 1950). During the Franco period, many reports commented upon the presence of government officials or military figures at the stadium (e.g. *ABC*, 17 March 1942; 19 May 1950; 31 May 1957). The political connotations of football played at this time were sometimes discussed. Though Spain was ostracized in large parts of the football world, when they did participate the match was taken as a sign of support for the regime. Even when a match was played between Stuttgart and a Barcelona *selección*, 'the match demonstrated continued support for *the Spanish*' (*ABC*, 6 July 1941, emphasis added). The point was made that '*the Spanish* scored the winning goal after a few minutes' (ibid., our italics). There was a clear playing down of the Catalanism of the fixture while reinforcing the 'Spanishness'. On a similar note, when a Madrid *Selección* played a Paris XI in Paris, the reporter goes to some length to inform the reader of the welcoming greeting by French officials (*ABC*, 15 June 1949). It is clear that football commentary spreads beyond its strictly sporting parameters into political innuendo when it chooses.

When Spain knocked England out of the World Cup in 1950 by beating them 1–0, the reports were overflowing with language which overestimated the achievement and generally over-hyped the triumph: 'Our national *Selección* beat England brilliantly on Sunday in Rio de Janeiro and achieved one of the greatest triumphs in the history of Spanish football' ran one headline (*ABC*, 4 July 1950), while the victory was 'sensational', 'glorious', 'magnificent', 'inspired' and 'undoubtedly deserved' (ibid.). The Spanish were praised for 'keeping the pressure on' and for being 'brave'. The Spanish press was also careful to make it clear that the victory was 'not just luck', and that the manner of the triumph was honourable: 'Every player shone as they beat [England] fairly' (ibid.). It was important to encourage the Spanish people to believe in the success of their football, which reflected upon the success of the regime.

The process of glorification of Spanish achievements is commonplace. Attempts to exaggerate the good performances of Spain (and also Real Madrid) were not unusual and the use of superlative language such as 'the brilliant triumph of Spanish football' (*ABC*, 17 May 1949) or Real Madrid's 'sensational triumph . . . and magnificence' (*ABC*, 31 May 1957) were commonplace. Such linguistic features are particularly rife in the writing of 'Juan Deportista'. Indeed, this journalist seems to contribute much to the linking of football, national spirit and national identity. In one match he called on God to help Spain: 'God willing, the Spanish flags will be waving triumphantly' (*ABC*, 16 June 1949). It is also common at this time for the press to emphasize the support of the crowd. In this case, 'the crowd were all cheering, waving their white handkerchiefs' in approval and singing '*España! España!*' (*ABC*, 4 July 1950). The Spanish team became 'our team' and this flitting between first person and third person to refer to the Spanish *Selección* is a reliable indicator of its success or failure.

Slightly later, the reports of the renowned sports writer, Gilera, also contribute to the glorification of the Spanish national performances. He had a habit of creating notions of 'Spanishness' with apparent innocence by telling the reader what is 'typically Spanish'. For example, 'Sanchís scored a typically Spanish goal, the work of a brave effort. Sanchís – a typical Spaniard – with admirable intentions and willingness, intelligent, capable of getting stuck in, quick, with individual flair' (*ABC*, 16 July 1966). This is what the Spanish aspire to – the combination of elements of *furia* and individual talent, and we shall see these qualities over and over again in future decades

One of the ways in which national identities are constructed through the media coverage of sport is via the self-analysis of the failures (or more rarely the successes) of the national team. While this is probably true of most nations, it is particularly relevant in Spain's case as persistent underachievers. Certainly in the latter third of the twentieth century and beyond, the extent to which failure to achieve at national level in football is constructed in the Spanish print media as being down to national characteristics and weaknesses in the national psyche. A recurrent feature of Spanish football that we have discussed elsewhere (Crolley and Hand 2002: 117) is that the Spanish are purportedly temperamental and suffer from nerves, tending to under-perform in important matches when they are under pressure to win. In 1966, for example, Spain is portrayed as playing worse than expected because of nerves (*ABC*, 16 July 1966) and that inconsistency was a consequence of 'our temperamental team' (*ABC*, 14 July 1966). Similarly at Euro 96, 'huge expectations' weighed heavily on the shoulders of the players and the training camp was reportedly 'fraught with anxiety' in a 'tense atmosphere' (*El País*, 19 June).

Perhaps related to this, is the *victimismo* (feeling of being a victim) and pessimistic *fatalismo* prevalent in newspaper reports prior to major football tournaments. This element of the Spanish mentality was pervasive in the context of football towards the end of the twentieth century, notably in the 1996 European Championship and 1998 World Cup finals (Crolley and Hand 2002: 114–15): 'Few teams have such a fatalistic attitude to the World Cup as Spain' (*El País*, 6 June 1998).

The Spanish often attribute this characteristic to the Disaster of 1898 when the Spanish Empire finally disintegrated after years of colonial unrest and conflict. The ramifications of this collapse were widespread culturally as well as politically and the 'Generation of '98' writers kept the subject at the forefront of national consciousness. As a result, the crisis of confidence this brought about was prolonged and became part of the Spanish psyche. This was also the time when Spanish football writing was developing. Evidence in our data now indicates that fatalism and pessimism actually date back in football writing to the early part of the century:

> We are given such reasons for going to the Olympics and such compelling examples of why, that I, one of those who was convinced of our moral obligation to go, am increasingly believing that we should not.
>
> Our last Spanish Championships (athletics) brought the disappointing reality home to us that we are quite far from those great names . . . . The football team will do a better job, but it won't represent us with dignity. . . . Today we do not have, unfortunately, a strong team that could put up a fight against the great foreign teams. . . . Perhaps the future Champion of Spain could go to Antwerp, reinforced if necessary. *National* teams formed with players from here and there, no way.
>
> To go to these places with individuals with wimps, with no muscles, no great force of resistance, not being prepared in the heart, the lungs or the stomach would be a sad thing to do and we should not do it.
>
> (*ABC*, by Rubryk, quoted in Martialay 2000: 290)

This excerpt is interesting in that it outlines Spain's pessimism towards competing in an international competition but also because it implies very strongly that the idea of a *national* team is still fledgling and that Spain is not ready as a nation to participate. Spain was not comfortable entering the international arena at this politically delicate time when it was suffering a crisis in confidence.

Spain's inferiority complex in international politics is clearly reflected in its football writing and elements of feeling 'hard done by', cheated by referees or plain unlucky are all persistently recorded in our data throughout the century as explanations for Spain's underachievement. Examples abound from every tournament in which Spain has participated: in 1934, the referee 'cheated' Spain out of the World Cup (*ABC*, quoted in Ball 2001: 219); in 1984, Spain 'felt cheated' when they drew with Romania 1–1 (*El País*, 15 June 1984); Spain complained at 'outrageous' refereeing decisions in 2002 (*El País*, 23 June).

Another interesting point is highlighted by Martialay (2000: 290) in his analysis of one journalist's account of the Spanish team's silver medal in the 1920 Olympics. The reporter wrote (in *Madrid Sport*) that 'if we hadn't been so unlucky, we would have won the gold'. Martialay questions the nature of any possible bad luck, though. There was no evidence of any during the tournament and he suggests this is an indication of 'outrageous *victimismo*', a trait later to be identified in the sports writing of journalists covering football at the end of the twentieth century (see Crolley and Hand 2002). Ball (2001), who expounds on these themes in his deeply absorbing and perceptively astute account of the history of Spanish football, also questions the basis for Spain's outrage in some cases.

Thirty years on from the Antwerp Olympics, Spain entered a World Cup match against England with a newspaper bemoaning in its headline that 'A draw would end all our hopes' (*ABC*, 1 July 1950). The article itself was more balanced in its approach to the game, though, and it could be said that there exists a pattern throughout the second half of the twentieth century for the headline to present the glass as half-empty while the article itself justifies why it might be half-full. This tendency for Spaniards to see themselves as inevitable victims continues today and has been evident in every international competition in which Spain has participated since 1982. By now, the readers share an understanding of this element of self-definition. Pessimism and fatalism are part of a Spanish (sporting) national imagined identity.

Both the city of Madrid and the football club, Real Madrid, are central in the creation of a Spanish identity, at least in football terms. As we have seen, Real Madrid's victories, particularly in the 1950s when they dominated European football, were (not surprisingly) portrayed as Spanish success. 'We are the best . . . and now we have proven it' the reports proclaimed following Real Madrid's victory in the 1957 European Cup final against Fiorentina (*ABC*, 31 May 1957). Indeed, this report is interesting and in several ways illustrates succinctly some of the points highlighted in this discussion. Not only does the headline claim that Real Madrid are the best but that '*We* are the best', thus creating a close identification between the achievements of Real Madrid and the (supposedly national) readership. By employing the first person plural subject, the journalist manipulates the readers so that they become part of the event and part of the success (see León Solís 2003: 47 for further discussion of this 'experiential' feature of football writing in Spain). This is reinforced throughout the article: 'We have won', 'Our players have won' (the 'our' belongs to the nation). This nuance is not lost on the writer. His affirmation that 'We are the best, and though it might sound absurd, it benefits the Nation' is proof that he is not innocent in this process. Thus, the successes of Real Madrid are transferred to the nation: 'In this way, Real Madrid flies the flag for its country with their triumphs' (ABC, 31 May 1957). Just in case the point was missed by some readers, the writer reiterates: 'Real Madrid is more Spanish than anyone. . . . That is why 100,000 handkerchiefs are waving' (ibid.). This refers to the Spanish way of demonstrating strong emotions by waving white handkerchiefs at the match (or, indeed, any other event). The writer, then, deliberately transfers the joy and emotion of Real Madrid fans for their team's victory in the European Cup final to mean something quite different – a victory for Spain, and ultimately the approval and legitimacy of the Franco regime. The parallel between Real Madrid as football heroes and Real Madrid as national heroes is again made explicit: 'When those lads pull on their white champions' jerseys they feel like crusaders used to when they wore their coats of armour. That moral strength, the absurd inability to give up in the eyes of defeat is the secret weapon that Real Madrid have exploited in their international triumphs' (ibid.). Not only does this writer attribute the successes of Real Madrid to their crusading character (itself an interesting metaphor in a strongly Catholic country), but he also claims the moral high ground and hints that Real Madrid's international victories are attributed somehow to the club's moral superiority over others.

Spanish people are, therefore, encouraged to imagine Real Madrid as a symbol of Spanish identity and this process which equates the football success of Real Madrid with national triumph continues throughout the 1960s and beyond. Examples abound in our data of such manipulation of expression: 'Madrid is not parochial and local but is particularly national' (ABC, 8 May 1968). Real represents more than Madrid. It is a symbol of national identity. At the time, the Spanish Selección was based around the Real Madrid team and included many Real Madrid players. The reporter attempts to create a hierarchy within football where the national team is more important than domestic clubs by stating that, although Real Madrid were to play an English team in an important European Cup tie the following week, the forthcoming international match was more important. Indeed, so close was the relationship between Real Madrid and Spain that the following week, when the European Cup tie was played, Real Madrid and Spain were referred to synonymously: 'Real Madrid need to get last Wednesday's defeat out of their minds' (ABC, 16 May 1968). Furthermore, parallels between the two matches were drawn constantly; after all, both games involved Spain versus England and it seemed to be natural for the domestic clubs to mirror the styles of their national teams. There were lots of banners waved at the Spain–England match, 'displayed by the greatest national support there has ever been in Madrid' (*ABC*, 9 May 1968). It is just a pity that the reporter claims to have forgotten his glasses and was unable to see what was written on the banners.

Even before the Franco period, (Real) Madrid were built up as something special. They dominated the Madrid-based press and were portrayed as superior to other teams: 'Sevilla aren't good or important enough to play against Madrid' (*ABC*, 2 November 1915). Little wonder that Madrid gained a reputation for smug superiority by many outside the city. The glorification of Real Madrid was consistent throughout the 1950s: Madrid's victories were 'magnificent', 'sensational' or 'triumphant' (e.g. *ABC*, 31 May 1957). Its image as a club dedicated to entertaining was firmly established: 'Madrid is a team that is excessively dedicated to technical virtuosity' (*ABC*, 25 June 1957). It is good at 'art' and not so good at 'doing the donkey work' (ibid.). The same image of Real Madrid exists today. When Fabio Capello steered Real Madrid to the top of the League after six months in charge, many fans were not happy because the style of football lacked '*espectáculo*' (*El País*, 27 January 1997). Later, the 'supermen' were extolled for reclaiming this *espectáculo* with its team of *galácticos* (*El País*, 6 July 2004). Madrid are expected to entertain but are sloppy defensively.

As we have demonstrated, then, in some ways Spanish football writing has evolved over the last century in the way in which it presents Spanishness. Beginning with a weak, tenuous claim to a notion of collective identity, it has developed a clearly defined sense of a Spanish style of play, represented by characteristics which have come to symbolize Spanish inclusiveness: the *furia española* typifies these traits. Features such as pessimism and *victimismo*, which frequent the pages of the Spanish press at the end of the twentieth century, date back to the start of national coverage of Spanish football. However, Spain is keen to move on from what it perceives as over-reliance on rather crude, unsophisticated qualities and is attempting to create a new, more glamorous, facet to its identity. There is evidence that the Spanish print media discourse exploited football politically, in particular the successes of its newly formed *Selección* in 1920 and of Real Madrid in the 1950s, in order to promote a collective pride in Spain. The extent to which this has been achieved will be discussed further in the chapter on football in Catalunya and the Basque Country.

Spain viewed by England

Disappointingly, and despite extensive searches in our data, there are large gaps in coverage of Spanish football in the English print media in the early twentieth century. The attitude of the English to sport in Spain can perhaps be glimpsed via a letter to the editor of *The Times*. The contributor, writing from the Deanery, Durham, admits that 'it is not the habit of Englishmen to criticize the sport of other nations' before going on to do precisely that. He states that, to the English, 'bullfighting has never seemed a wholly legitimate sport' and then 'rejoices' that

Spain and England are meeting 'as friendly antagonists in so purely humanitarian a sport as football' (12 December 1931). Implicit in early references to sport in Spain is Spaniards' cultural inferiority.

Portraits of Spanish football and Spaniards in the English print media are not simple. Unusually, for large parts of the twentieth century at least, there is no clichéd shorthand to which journalists resort. As with early coverage of French football (see above, Chapter 3), the English portray the Spanish as 'Continental' (e.g. *The Times*, 9 December 1931), which means that they play a 'continental' style of football – they play short passes, with some individual flair, are reluctant to tackle, and resort to deceit and underhand methods of play.

Prior to the Second World War, English journalists admitted to being fairly ill-informed about Spanish football. *The Times* recognized that 'It is possible that there is not yet sufficient appreciation here of the development of the game on the Continent' (ibid.). Certainly, the journalist's assertion that one Spanish player 'is said to be able to run with the ball balanced on his head and so carry it to its required destination' suggests a level of naïvety about football 'on the Continent'. This lack of understanding (or interest?) in Spanish football continues even into previews of the 1984 European Championships where 'Spain are unknown quantities' (*The Times*, 12 June). This is partially because there was still relatively little coverage of Spanish domestic football in England but also to some extent because no one knew just what to expect from the Spanish. There was no strong stereotype in the way that there was for, say, France or Germany.

By 1955, several of the themes relating to Spanish football are emerging in the English print media discourse even though Spaniards are still 'Continental'. One report on England versus Spain, played in Charmartín Stadium, Madrid, does not actually state the result but focuses on the differences in styles between English and 'Continental' football (*The Times*, 19 May 1955). In one game, which England won 4–1, blame for Spain's lack of goals was attributed to the fact that 'Spain played the old type of football of the continent before its possibilities were developed and exploited by the devastating finish of the Hungarians. . . . They bunched, they over-elaborated their close passing, they overdid criss-cross scissors movements, and generally lost themselves in the maze of their own argument by becoming long-winded' (*The Times*, 1 December 1955). Some time between 1955 and 1960, the English print media drop the use of the 'Continental' label and decide that Spain is a distinct football nation.

Once we examine in more depth the content of some of the football writing surrounding Spain's performances, we can trace the roots of some of the themes which later emerge as constants. Some of these themes are, however, contradictory. The Spanish are optimists but at the same time fatalistic and believe themselves to be victims, either of conspiracies or simply bad luck. They can play with fire in their bellies or in an utterly lack-lustre way. There is no real chronological pattern to when these images occur and part of the enigma of Spanish underachievement in major competitions is often explained by their unpredictability and psychological fragility.

Our first detailed report of Spanish football followed England's visit to Spain, where Spain were beaten, 'surprisingly', 4–3. Early impressions mirror those of the Spanish print media in the 1920s in that *The Times* refers to Spain's 'enthusiasm' and 'terrific pace' and the fact that they 'never gave up trying' (16 May 1929). The fans, too, were 'enthusiastic', so much so that they invaded the pitch when Spain equalized to make the score 3–3. In contrast to the early images of Spanish football writing in Spain, however, which set the tone for the rest of the century, some of the early descriptions of Spanish football in the English press contrast sharply with later reports. In 1931, when Spain first played England on English soil, at Highbury, they were described in *The Times* as 'mostly light men, some of them almost frail' and therefore 'able to move quickly', with 'skill in dribbling . . . and tricking. They do not go in to tackle, being content merely to wait for the ball to be presented to them. They seemingly also did not expect to be tackled themselves' (10 December 1931). This lightweight style, hesitant to tackle or be tackled, is a far cry from Spain's self-depiction at the start of the decade when the team earned its reputation for *furia española*. It is more in keeping with the more general English image of 'Continental' footballers.

In a report in 1960 following England's home victory against Spain, we find *The Times* beginning to distinguish Spanish-specific references. This characterization is carried out in simple ways. First, the opening sentence of the report firmly establishes the opposition not only as Spanish but as failures: 'For the third time – in a football sense – a Spanish Armada came to grief on the rocks of England yesterday' (*The Times*, 27 October 1960). The metaphor is hardly obscure, and the battle theme continues throughout the article. Again, in reports of both fixtures between Spain and England in 1960, there is an acknowledgement that the Spanish have a different style of play from the English and the derision of the Spanish individualistic technique lurks close to the surface: 'The pirouetting Spaniards' lost control of the game and 'the tricks fell' (ibid.); 'Martínez, with a typical Latin flamboyance' (*The Times*, 16 May 1960); 'these football peacocks were able to strut proudly, spreading their colourful plumage to the unbounded joy of their admirers' (ibid.). These images are of a very different Spain from the image that existed within Spain itself. This heterotypification of Spain draws upon images of Latin colour, vibrancy and swagger and is, of course, reminiscent of flamenco dancers and bullfighters, cultural archetypes with which the English are undoubtedly familiar.

At the same time, however, 'the Spanish defensive cover was powerful, ruthless and tight' (ibid.). At odds again with the image of a slick, skilful team is the other facet of Spanish football: its 'quick, relentless tackling' (*The Times*, 30 November 1955). So how do these portraits square with the contrasting images above? It is apparent that there is no clear typecasting of Spanish football in the English print media in the 1950s and 1960s. While Spain are flamboyant and skilful, Martínez's goal was the result of 'an arrogant shot' (*The Times*, 16 May 1960) and 'England's goal unhinged the smooth, skilful Spanish game' (*The Times*, 30 November 1955).

The Spaniards' reported lack of psychological strength is a feature of football writing in English print media discourse. In our English data, as in our Spanish sample, we find evidence of this characteristic dating back to the 1950s: 'Spain's greatest enemy may be their temperament' (ibid.). This characteristic is not perceived as being Spanish at this time, though. Rather it is an element of the 'Continental' style of football: 'England got off to the flying start that counts so much against Continental temperament' (*The Times*, 1 December 1955). Later on, they are still temperamental, both on an individual level (e.g. 'the temperamental Juanito' [*The Times*, 10 June 1982]) and as a collective (e.g. 'Who was to know which Spain would turn up' [*The Guardian*, 23 June 2002]). The fact that Spain are 'regular underachievers' or 'a soft touch . . . with a tendency to punch below their weight' (*The Times*, 4 June 2000) is commented upon at every tournament. *The Guardian* provides a typical quotation in a review of the 2002 World Cup: 'For Spain it was the World Cup that might have been. . . . Here was a World Cup that Spain might have been able to win, yet confronted with ostensibly beatable opponents and an attractive path to the final they [too] reverted to type and fell apart' (30 June).

As we have already seen elsewhere (Crolley and Hand 2002: 21–4), the English press has a strong tendency to portray foreign footballers as deceitful and lacking in the sporting ethos espoused by the English: one preview of an England–Spain clash at Wembley, for example, questioned whether the Spaniards would 'resort to some of their questionable tactics' (*The Times*, 30 November 1955). Similarly, later, 'As is the tedious Latin custom, Camacho fell as though mortally wounded' (*The Times*, 6 July 1982). There are also many such examples within domestic football where Spanish footballers are accused of 'diving' or 'professionalism'.

Finally, the weather is a theme which we have identified elsewhere as being recurrent within later football writing in the 1990s and especially on match reports covering England–Spain fixtures (see Crolley *et al.* 1998). While discussion of the weather and the use of meteorological metaphor lack any great socio-political, historical or cultural significance, such is the frequency of occurrence within the English texts throughout the period examined that it would be inappropriate to ignore this theme entirely. Prior to the 1950s, we have noted the many references to the wind in our sample, but these references are not dependent on the teams participating in the match, rather they help explain the patterns of play on the pitch. By the 1950s, match reports begin to roll out what are later to become a cliché in reports about Spain: 'The sun is still shining in Charmartín' (*The Times*, 19 May 1955). In a later article, however, we see the theme of the weather emerge fully: 'The weather, no doubt, this day was an English ally. Dark clouds chased before a puffing wind, unloaded their cargoes. Belting rain beat down almost from the first to the last and on a pitch that left a trailing spray behind the ball, Wembley now might have been some paddy field' (*The Times*, 27 October 1960). One match in Madrid took place just after a storm, and the reporter enjoyed immensely the opportunity to relate how the weather was not hot, dry and sunny and 'the ground was spattered with puddles – ideal for Britons' but this glee was short-lived, the weather changed and England lost 3–0: 'now the sun was shining and Spain was happy again' (*The Times*, 16 May 1960).

Perhaps the starkest contrast journalists can think of when comparing England and Spain is the climate – Britain's old ally against the Spanish Armada in 1588 – and this explains the insistence on discussing the weather whenever the two countries meet: 'Madrid offered a passionate background and heat [when England played there in 1960]. Wembley yesterday was partly wrapped in the grey shawl of fog' (*The Times*, 1 December 1955) (floodlights were reported to be used at the end of this match for the first time in an England international at Wembley).

Though we reserve the discussion of Spanish regions and nationalities to the chapter on Catalunya and the Basque Country, it is appropriate to point out here that Spain is portrayed largely as a homogeneous unit in the English print media: 'The voices of the population of 35,000,000 will be as one as they attempt to spirit Spain through the various rounds until that ultimate glory in Madrid on July 11' (*The Times*, 10 June 1982). While the divisions of the Spanish nation are recognized, it is more of a nod of acknowledgement to the individual rivalries within the squad than an understanding of broader political and social issues: 'Nothing unites a country better than war. . . . The fierce regional rivalries and jealousies that fester beneath the skin of any Spanish squad could break out. . . . Internal feuding has destroyed them before' (ibid.). The article goes on to quote squabbling between individual players but nothing based on true national or regional hostilities.

There is surprisingly little political comment on the Spanish situation in the English sample. Even when a bomb exploded on the eve of the opening of the 1982 World Cup, the relevant article is scant and rather superficial, explaining that the bomb was probably planted by ETA, but detailing little in-depth political commentary (*The Times*, 15 June). Indeed, acknowledgement of a complex nation-state with its own special political context is rarely present. Prior to the 1980s at least, there are only very occasional references to regions or nations within Spain: 'The Spaniards, and particularly those from the north, are closer to the British style in their use of the shoulder and in strong tackling' (*The Times*, 30 November 1955). There was occasional demonstration earlier in the century of awareness of cultural and political complexities in Spain. For example, *The Times* understands that 'It is not hard to believe that the Basques (the race to which many of the Spanish players belong), with their instinctive skill with a ball, should be made masters [of football]' (9 December 1931). This even suggests that the Basques have a stronger, more defined identity than that of Spaniards at that time.

It is not until the late 1990s that we see any real evidence of an understanding of Spanish heterogeneity. This is largely because of developments in domestic football, partly explained by the rise in TV coverage of Spanish football (notably BSkyB's), followed by the exchange of high-profile players between England and Spain, and finally by the appointment of Rafael Benítez and his accompanying 'Spanish Armada' at Liverpool, which led to numerous articles on 'Spanishness' in the English print media. It is often quotations from the Spanish players (or manager) themselves which raises awareness: for example, Benítez is reported widely as protesting against accusations that Spanish midfielder, Xabi Alonso, might be unprepared to play against one of Liverpool's arch-rivals by retorting that 'Xabi is Basque and can cope with such rivalries easily' (*The Times*, 16 September 2004). Hence, there is an enhanced awareness of some of the current socio-political issues in Spain, though what is emerging might be more of a Europeanization of stereotypes and clichés than a greater understanding of different countries and nations.

The English print media, therefore, share many themes with their Spanish counterparts. Presentations of Spain as flamboyant, skilful, vibrant but mentally weak contrast with those of a tough, relentless nation. Some of these images date back to the 1950s at least when a true Spanish identity developed and Spain's image as Continental footballers began to fade. Many of the ingredients of the Spanish identity painted in the English print media are consistent with those offered in Spain. The balance, however, is not the same. While in Spain *furia* is emphasized, in England the fragility (of mental and physical strength) is key.

Spain viewed from France

With regard to French press coverage of Spain, a number of themes are developed, notably in reports of France–Spain matches. However, the first two matches ever played between the two countries received scant attention and reports of them tended to be short, factual and descriptive (see for instance *Le Matin*, 1 May 1922; 29 January 1923). It is, therefore, only in later match coverage that a recognizable Spanish identity emerges as journalists appreciate and interpret Spaniards' actions on the pitch as deriving from an increasingly familiar sense of Spanishness. Throughout the French press coverage, there is an awareness of the (stereo)typical passion of the Spanish and this was evident in one early report of an 8–1 defeat of France by Spain in Zaragoza in which it was said (tellingly in the light of the discussion of *furia* above) that 'the demoralized French put up only limited resistance to the "furia" of the Spaniards' (*Le Matin*, 15 April 1929), thereby utilizing a key item in the lexicon of Spanish football itself, that of *furia*, and establishing a theme that would enjoy considerable longevity in the French press. A subsequent report, for instance, commented on the typical passion of the Spanish football crowd with the aid of a simile that connects with the historical importance of Catholicism in Spain: 'this match was played in a full stadium, in the liveliest of atmospheres where everyone incessantly stood up and sat back down as if they were at mass' (*Le Matin*, 25 January 1935). The term 'Spanish furia' is used on numerous occasions as a shorthand for the supposed passion of the players that reflects the enthusiasm of their fans as it was in a match preview of 1955, for example, where it was also noted that 'Spanish footballers, being quick and impetuous, are always difficult to beat on their own soil' (*Le Monde*, 18 March 1955). The report of the game itself further conveyed the concept of Spanish passion with an extended metaphor of what was and still is for many Europeans a symbol of Spanish culture, bullfighting: 'The passionate atmosphere of the bullfight truly reigned here' as the stadium was occupied by 120,000 'fanatical spectators' who had come to witness 'the French team being put to death' (*Le Monde*, 19 March 1955; the technical bullfighting term *estocade*, meaning the death blow, is used by the article). However, as it was the French who won, 2–1, the metaphor has to be reversed: 'the death blow duly came but, for once, it was the matador who paid the price' (ibid.).

The purported passion and liveliness of the typical Spanish identity is regarded as admirable in France when it is translated into a particular style of play on the football pitch, as is evidenced by a number of match reports and related articles from the French press from the 1940s onwards. The first encounter between France and Spain after the Second World War, for example, was noteworthy for *Le Monde* for the characteristically 'effervescent' and 'attractive' way in which the Spaniards played the game: 'the Spanish attacked impetuously . . . jumped like lambs . . . flew like arrows . . . [and] were electric' in their demonstration of the 'dazzling qualities' of 'virtuosity and speed' (19 June 1949) that led to a 5–1 victory. Similarly, 10 years later, the same newspaper's appreciation of these traits had not diminished as the notion of Spanish liveliness was by now effectively cemented into French print media discourse: 'The Spanish team has a personality, a brio, a quality reminiscent of the best South American outfits' (17 December 1959).

Indeed, by the mid-twentieth century, the concept of Spanish brio is so dearly held and so firmly regarded as a given in media discourse that the sight of Spaniards not playing football in a lively, up-tempo way becomes a source of considerable consternation and much disappointment is registered in the French press whenever a Spanish national team fails to live up to expectations in this respect. An 'unexpected and unpredictable' French victory over Spain in 1959 provided one such occasion (*Le Monde*, 17 December 1959). Despite including 'the most expensive players in the world' such as Di Stefano, Suarez, Kubala and Gento, the 'stars' were 'off form' and allowed the French to snatch a 4–3 victory (ibid.). The reverse is almost inexplicable but the newspaper does imply that it is attributable to the suspect temperament of the Spaniards. The picture is depicted of a team of flashy superstars who lost interest in the game owing to the poor (un-Spanish?) weather and the state of the Parc des Princes pitch in Paris. Why did Spain fail? 'Thanks to [their] temperament . . . the rainy weather, the pitch upsetting them? Who knows?' Ultimately, though, they simply 'disappointed' all present (ibid.). Similar condemnation even followed a subsequent game that the Spanish team actually won. Despite a 2–0 home victory, *Le Monde* reported that the fans left 'disappointed and unhappy' and characterized the Spanish star players as 'having come down to the level of ordinary footballers' (2 April 1961). Clearly this is not good enough in the world of print media discourse where Spain is expected to put on a dazzling display and the newspaper duly laments 'the lack of improvisation that is usually the mark of a Spanish team' (ibid.). The return fixture in the same year, which resulted in a 1–1 draw, prompted similar comments. 'Excellent at club level, Del Sol, Di Stefano, Santamaria and others were disappointingly lacking in liveliness' (*Le Monde*, 10 December 1961) and, once again, there is more than an implication that Spaniards are incapable of adapting to difficult playing conditions given that 'the Spanish are *always* ill at ease on a heavy surface' (ibid., our empha-sis). The theme of the temperamental Spaniards who fail to live up to expectations is, of course, one that is developed at considerable length towards the end of the twentieth century across Europe and especially in Spain itself (see Crolley and Hand 2002, 2005; Hand 2002). As we have seen, it is also a theme prompting much comment in the French press since the 1950s at least.

Finally, it is worth noting that the complex and frequently changing political context in which football in Spain operated as the twentieth century unfolded is often commented on in French newspaper coverage. At times, the intrusion of politics into football is portrayed as unwelcome, whereas at others football is itself portrayed as an extension of the domestic and international political scenario of the day. Protests at one match in 1949, for instance, resurrecting the ghosts of the Spanish Civil War, were not well received by the *Le Monde* journalist covering the game. A group of fans unfurled the old red, yellow and purple flag of the Spanish Second Republic (overturned by Franco's nationalists in 1939) and booed the playing of the Spanish national anthem, prompting the reporter to state: 'It is regrettable that political passions should enter sport, from which they ought to be totally banned' (21 June 1949). In the post-Franco era, though, the difficulties posed for Spanish football by the political tensions between Spain's nations and regions tended to be commented upon in a more neutral and objective way. Prior to a meeting between France and Spain in 1978, for instance, *Le Monde* points out the extent to which the fierce rivalry between Real Madrid and Barcelona, itself a footballing manifestation of wider socio-political issues (see below, Chapter 7), affected the coach's selection policy as did the refusal of certain Basque players to join the national team, such as the Bilbao goalkeeper Iribar. The specificity of the Spanish case is not lost on the French journalist: 'More than anywhere else, the future of the national team depends on the good will of the big clubs' (8 No-vember 1978). Somewhat surprisingly, however, given the nature of the content of *Le Monde* (a quality newspaper focusing primarily on national and international current affairs and politics), on occasion, the paper simply ignored the political context surrounding matches involving Spain. Even when one game was played during a general strike in the Basque Country in protest against the death in prison of a suspected Basque terrorist, no mention was made of these events in the match report, which preferred instead to concentrate on the poor tactics employed by French manager Michel Hidalgo that led to a 1–0 defeat (18 February 1981).

The final of the 1984 European Championships between France and Spain was, however, portrayed at least in part as an extension of international politics. There is an 'interdependence' between sport and politics, *Le Monde* noted (29 June 1984) and this final, watched by 'the whole of Spain and France from tip to toe' was not simply 'a major international event', it was also 'the latest episode in the stop-start, bumpy, passionate and difficult relations between Paris and Ma-drid', particularly evident in what was then the run-up to Spain's entry into the European Community (ibid.). The links between football and politics were further emphasized by the newspaper's reporting of French President François Mitterrand's views on the game and by its noting that he would shortly be travelling to Madrid 'to console the Spanish [on their defeat] by promising them that their entry into the EC would still follow the agreed schedule' (ibid.).

As is the case in both Spain itself and in England, then, eventually a recognizably Spanish identity does emerge in the football writing of the French press, one which revolves around the notions of Spanish brio, passion and temperament and from which political complications are never entirely divorced.

Part II

Nations within states

Chapter 7

One nation, one team, one image

Catalunya and the Basque Country in Spain

Since the emergence of football in Spain towards the end of the nineteenth century, its organization on a local or regional basis has been strong. Regional football federations (of the *Comunidades Autónomas*, see Chapter 6) even today maintain a high level of control within the structures and organization of Spanish football. Football developed at different paces throughout the early quarter of the twentieth century and was particularly strong in the Basque Country and Catalunya where the cup competitions and championships were established earlier than in many other parts of Spain. These areas also had their own *selecciones*, teams who represented these regions. Because of Spain's politico-administrative organization (see previous chapter) the status of such *selecciones* is ambiguous and open to interpretation. They might be teams representing the regions, or they might be perceived to represent the nation, according to the political perspective of each individual. An analysis of the football writing of the Spanish print media during the twentieth century in the cases of Catalunya and the Basque Country is illuminating.

Catalunya

According to the Catalan Parliament, the Generalitat (2005), the roots of Catalunya (Catalonia) as a nation with its own territory and government date back to the early part of the Middle Ages. Throughout its history, Catalunya has enjoyed differing degrees of autonomy and even sovereignty. In modern times, interest in Catalan nationalism heightened towards the end of the nineteenth century as Catalunya industrialized with political and economic implications (Ramos Oliveira 1946: 79–122). Fragile ideological ties which might have bound the regions to the centre in Spain were weakened further by social and cultural movements which expressed pride in the Catalan nation (Solé Tura 1985).

Hence, football emerged as a sport as Catalunya was embracing symbols of national identity. FC Barcelona quickly became such a symbol. At the start of the twentieth century, FC Barcelona already represented (as its own slogan states) 'more than a club', not only as a symbol of Catalunya but also in its international outlook – embracing players from outside Spain – and in its opposition to local rivals Espanyol as well as, of course, those from Madrid. During General Franco's rule (1939–75), as mentioned above in Chapter 6, the regime controlled football as it did other social institutions. Football in Catalunya was no exception and Franco appointed state officials to run football clubs. The Catalan Generalitat, though, was restored in 1977 prior to the new Spanish Constitution of 1978 entering into force. The term 'restored' is used not only because the Generalitat had already existed in democratic Spain during the Second Republic (1931–39) but also because the name had historical and cultural meaning, having first been used for the executive body established by the *Corts Generals* of the Federation of the Catalan–Aragonese Crown in the fourteenth and fifteenth centuries. As León Solís reminds us in his analysis of competing discourses of Spanish and Catalan national identities in the Spanish media, 'The debate on national identity has, of course, political implications regarding conceptions of the structure of the State' (2003: 2). The post-Franco period has proven that different nationalities can co-exist, even with differing degrees of autonomy, within a Spanish state. Careful wording of the 1978 Constitution opened the path for various legal routes to different degrees of self-government. The 1979 Statute of Autonomy and the Catalan Generalitat are responsible for defining the present structures of political power in Catalunya. Despite this, discussion over regionalism/nationalism still thrives and was, indeed, the subject of many lengthy debates in 2005 and 2006 as the *Comunidades* of the Basque Country and Catalunya have been thrashing out their new constitutions (for an excellent, concise introduction to the regional question in Spain, see Lawlor and Rigby [1998: 33–8]).

In this section, we analyse three aspects of the press in order to try to ascertain the extent to which a Catalan identity is communicated via Spanish print media discourse on football. First, we examine the coverage of the Catalan *Selección* (or 'national' team). Second, we turn to clubs themselves which represent Catalunya, in particular FC Barcelona, and third, we look at ways in which individual players from Catalunya (regardless of club) might facilitate the mediation of a Catalan identity.

Attempts to organize football in Catalunya really began with the foundation of the Associació de Clubs de Futbol de Barcelona in 1900. This later became the Catalan FA (Federació Catalana de Futbol Associació) in 1916. The Catalan *Selección* was also founded in 1900, and has played many times over the last century (see Webdelcule 2006 for a complete list). In its early years the Catalan *Selección* played mainly against Basque or French *selecciones* (such as Euskadi, Vizcaya, France, Provence and Guipúzcoa). During this period, there is little coverage of these matches in our sample and where they are mentioned at all details are dry and factual, giving the score and sometimes team sheets. For example, *ABC* mention that a *selección* from the city of Barcelona played (and were convincingly beaten, 7–0) against a team representing the French League on 21 February 1912. There is no mention of Catalunya's match against Guipúzcoa in December 1915, but the existence of a Catalan *selección* is not ignored entirely: one of Sabadell's players, for instance, 'is good enough to play for the Catalan *Selección*' (*ABC*, 2 January 1916).

Following the Spanish Civil War, the Catalan *Selección* played under the name of the Barcelona *Selección* (between 1941 and 1958). After that, the Catalans played only twice between 1960 and 1993 (in 1968 and 1976). During the Franco period, when the regime suppressed any public demonstration of opposition to centralism, unsurprisingly, we find very little evidence of Catalan identity mediated via the national press. Reports on this Barcelona–Catalan *selección* during the Franco period are limited to a mention of the fixture, with even that much being unusual. When they played a fixture in March 1942, for example, *ABC*'s coverage was succinct: 'In Barcelona a match was played between the Catalan *Selección* and a *Selección* from Castilla. Cataluña won 4–2' (17 March. The Castilian Spanish version of the name for Catalonia is used and most certainly not the Catalan one). When the Catalan *Selección* play a team from Stuttgart, members of the team are referred to in the match report as both the *Selección catalana* and 'the Spanish' (*ABC*, 14 January 1941). The terms are not mutually exclusive. The fact that the *Selección* represents Catalunya does not imply that it is not Spanish. On the contrary, there is some suggestion of a certain reinforcement of Spanishness in these reports, which consistently refer to the Catalans as Spanish.

During the transition to liberal democracy in the post-Franco period, Catalan nationalism re-emerged. Football was sometimes a catalyst in the resurgence of Catalan identity. FC Barcelona began to use the Catalan language in its dealings. In 1972, football matches were transmitted in Catalan on Radio Barcelona, which was another important step for the Catalan linguistic normalization programme (*El País*, 6 September 1982). Football was one of the first aspects of Catalan culture that lobbied for its democratization and devolution from central control (*El País*, 5 June 1977). This was accompanied by the reassertion of the Catalan *Selección*. Catalan identity is at least partially determined by the structure of Catalan politics and the relationships between Catalunya and the central Spanish state. Dual identity is now not unusual. Catalan identity, even nationalism, is allowed within a broader framework of Spanish hegemony. Permitting Catalunya to be an outlet for Catalan nationalism rendered any serious challenge to the established political order meaningless.

There has been a recent revival of the fixtures involving the Catalan *Selección*. Since 1993, there has been an attempt to play annually and this match usually takes place in December (for example, Catalunya–Brazil, 25 December 2005; Catalunya–Argentina, 29 December 2004; Catalunya–Ecuador, 28 December 2003). These matches are well attended and can usually count on the presence of the leader of the Generalitat. Given the 'friendly' nature of these fixtures, we might expect little press coverage but towards the end of the twentieth century, when several columns are dedicated even to testimonial matches, we find suspiciously little coverage of matches played by the *selecciones*. Interestingly, *El País* talks of the tradition of the Autonomous Communities to field a *selección* around Christmas time (27 December 2002). Grouping the *selecciones* of Catalunya and the Basque Country along with teams fielded by *Comunidades Autónomas* such as Andalucía, Asturias and the Balearics awards them all the same status: no more than *selec-*

ciones of *Comunidades Autónomas.* This presumably does little to serve the aspirations of some Catalans and Basques who would like the status of their *selecciones* recognized (by the governing bodies UEFA and FIFA) as national teams eligible to play in international competitions. It is also worth noting that these fixtures are frequently described in *El País* as 'commercial ventures', the nationalist dimension being implicitly downgraded by omission as insignificant (e.g. 9 June 1976). On other occasions, recognition that the fixture forms part of a wider celebration of Catalan culture goes no further than that (9 June 1976; 25 April 1993; 24 June 1995; 29 December 2002). Nationalist aspirations are largely ignored.

The rôle of *selecciones* (other than the Spanish *Selección*) competing at international level has raised polemic recently. The existence of *selecciones* in other sports strengthens the identity of the Catalan nation and sport serves to reinforce political attempts at nation-building. The case of ice hockey is interesting. Towards the end of 2004, Francisco Antonio González, spokesman for the political opposition, Partido Popular, asked the (Spanish) government to clarify its position on the participation in international competitions of sports teams representing Spain's *Comunidades Autónomas.* This followed the visit to China of Pasqual Maragall (of the Partido Socialista Obrero Español [PSOE] and President of the Catalan Generalitat) to support Catalunya's hockey *Selección* (*El País*, 24 October 2004). While Catalunya was eager for the International Hockey Federation (IHF) to recognize Catalunya as a full member (rather than the existent Spain–Catalunya) the Spanish Ice Hockey Federation vehemently opposed such a ruling. The IHF voted against allowing the Catalans membership (by an overwhelming 114 votes to 8), the reason circulated to the media being that they did not feel they could allow the inclusion of a member who could not be recognized by the International Olympic Committee as it would threaten the inclusion of the sport in the Olympics. The Catalans, in true Catalan fashion, talk of political manoeuvres by the Spanish Federation which excluded them (*El País*, 27 November 2004).

Catalunya again called for the acceptance of its status as an international competitor, and as a nation, when football and ice hockey joined forces in a demonstration on 29 December 2004, on the occasion of the annual Catalan *Selección* football match (against Argentina): '*Una Nació, una Selecció*' ('One nation, one *Selección*') the banners read. Ivan Tibau, captain of the Catalan ice hockey team, read a statement prior to the match in favour of the recognition of Catalan national teams. In it, he defended freedom: 'Long live Freedom! Long live Catalunya! We want Catalan *selecciones*, now!' The crowd then joined in an 'emotional' rendition of '*Els Segadors*', the national anthem of Catalunya. Accompanying the call to award international status to sporting *selecciones* of the *comunidades* is the desire to modify the Sport Law, which does not permit *selecciones* of the *Comunidades Autónomas* to play against Spain. Needless to say, the Spanish FA would vehemently oppose such developments which would compromise the unity of Spain. In general, however, there is more press coverage in this period on political aspects of the Catalan *Selección* than coverage of the football event itself. What there is reveals little of significance within the reports of the matches played by the Catalan *Selección*.

Our second line of enquiry leads us to analyse coverage of domestic football and we turned to Catalan domestic clubs for our evidence. Here, the rôle of FC Barcelona stands out as being the catalyst for Catalan images. It is clear by the 1920s that a close identification had been built between FC Barcelona and nationalist ideology (Crolley 1997; Sobrequés i Callicó 1991). The club embraced modernization and social mobility, as did Athletic de Bilbao in the Basque County (Bahamonde 2000: 147). With this ideology, defeats were explained by *victimismo* (victim mentality) and by the 'external enemy' and permanent conspiracy theories, which litter the twentieth-century coverage of football in Catalunya. Defeats, therefore, became legitimized and justified.

In this sample in the Franco period, far from finding evidence of a Catalan identity (there is no evidence either to suggest a Catalan style of play in this period), the relatively few detailed reports on Catalan football teams – compared, pointedly, to those on football played by clubs in Madrid – actually seem to make a point of reinforcing the Spanishness of Catalan football by mentioning Franco's attendance (at the Cup final in 1957, for example) or the reception he received. Several editions of *ABC*, for instance, contain special articles of thanks to the *Generalísimo*, Franco, for bestowing the pleasure of his company on the city of Barcelona: one such article appears with the heading 'Barcelona Thanks the *Generalísimo*' in *ABC* on 14 June 1957. Then the following week, the Catalan Football Association thanked General Franco officially via the pages of *ABC* for attending the same Cup final in the city, when it was noted that, 'Enthusiastic ovations rang out while His Excellency handed the trophy to the champions' (20 June 1957). This is typical of coverage. There is no evidence within the football writing here of any anti-Francoism in Catalunya displayed in the football writing. On the contrary, much effort is made to give the appearance of full support for the regime. Since later football writing explains the intense animosity of large parts of the population of Catalunya in general and of FC Barcelona in particular by reference to the Franco regime, there is some incongruity here. Since Franco's 'politics of revenge' (Preston 1990) was responsible for a weakening of Catalunya's recorded culture, cultural history relies heavily on the oral transmission of events and memories. Either contemporary reports in the national press whitewashed political commentary or retrospective discussion evokes an imagined (or manipulated?) collective memory. Or perhaps a combination of both elements is responsible for the huge chasm between the reality of national coverage of football in Catalunya in the print media at the time and current perceptions of the relationship between football and politics.

To what extent is there evidence of a Catalan identity mediated in the Spanish print media coverage of Catalan football in the modern era, since Spain's transition to democracy when demonstrations of Catalan identity have been allowed to flourish? If Catalans perceive themselves as 'hardworking, moderate, responsible, thoughtful; that is, as characterized by an identity driven by reason and not by passion' (León Solís 2003: 2), then to what extent is this image either mediated via the Spanish national press, or indeed via the print media discourse abroad? Do the print media distinguish between Catalunya and the rest of Spain? Or are we presented with a homogeneous image which ignores more complex notions of identity? Several themes are evident which provide us with the outline of a Catalan stereotype in Spain.

There is some evidence of how the print media believe FC Barcelona should play and, to some extent, this ties in with the Catalan stereotype outlined by León Solís. While Catalans view themselves as hard-working and are more at ease with progressive, modern and mainstream European values rather than traditional Spanish ones (León Solís 2003), there is only limited evidence of this in our sample. FC Barcelona's style of play is often described as 'industrious' or 'diligent', reflecting the image of Catalans as hard-working. Teamwork is certainly a more salient characteristic than in descriptions of other teams: references to 'collective efforts' – such as '[Barcelona] plays well collectively' – are plentiful (e.g. *El País*, 10 November 1997; 23 February 1998; 10 April 2004). Former managers Louis Van Gaal and Johan Cruyff both recognized this collective mentality as a strength of the Barcelona way of functioning. Van Gaal explained that, in Barcelona, 'football is a team game not a sport for individuals' (*El País*, 14 September 1997). There are also disproportionate references (compared to coverage of other clubs) to money and to the business world when talking about FC Barcelona, either in terms of calling the club a 'business' or 'industry' (e.g. *El País*, 12 April 1985; 16 February 1998; 25 November 2003) or by prioritizing discussion of the business and financial side of the club (such as negotiations over contracts, transfers, commercial partners). One article in *El País*, which examines the nationalist aspirations of Catalunya and the links between FC Barcelona and Catalan identity (headed 'Warning: Cataluña is more than a club') summarizes several of the themes most closely linked with Catalan identity:

> Average Catalans, helpless when faced with the *old enemies*, and *hidden forces*, have the possibility . . . of defeating centralism. Sitting comfortably they have the opportunity to feel the greatest, in the biggest stadium and with the biggest club, and all for 1,000 pesetas and the effort of getting themselves to the stadium. . . . Generally speaking, Barça's great triumphs are down to this ability to feel part of a collective, an important collectivism . . . as on many Sundays millionaires [i.e. the players] sweat for their club . . . which tries to be an ambassador for the Catalan nation.
>
> (*El País*, 12 April 1985, italics in original)

Here, as well as the political commentary on the state of Catalanism, which is developed further in the piece, various facets of Catalan identity are mentioned and it appears that the readership is expected to share an assumed Catalan identity – one which involves *victimismo*, the paranoia that everyone is against them, respecting the value of money and rating collectivism highly.

More than the treatment of the style of play, however, the commentary surrounding the club reminds us of its identification with Catalunya. Indeed, it is the people talking from within the club who most reinforce the relationship between FC Barcelona and Catalunya and this political commentary is covered extensively in *El País*. For example, the club president, Joan Laporta, speaking at a conference in London claimed that 'Barça is a bit like the Catalan national team', before making the political point that 'Catalan is not recognized as an official language by the EU' (*El País*, 7 March 2005). Here, Laporta (speaking mainly in Catalan, we are told) is making the point that, since Catalans do not enjoy official recognition, then they must turn to FC Barcelona as an institution to represent them. Interestingly, it is the Barcelona board, players, fans or managers who make this point repeatedly in the print media. FC Barcelona made public in 1977 its support for the introduction of Catalan Statutes of Autonomy (*El País*, 15 April 1977). Another example comes from the fans themselves. *El País*'s coverage of FC Barcelona's victories is generally celebrated by referring to the team's victory in the name of Catalunya. This is made more explicit the more important the occasion: for example, when they won the Cup Winners' Cup in 1979, 'Barcelona fans have begun to show their extreme Catalanism again.' It was pointed out that the fans chanted, 'We've won the Cup. Barcelona has won for Catalunya and for our flag' (*El País*, 18 May 1979). Another example involves the reporting of an FC Barcelona–Real Madrid fixture on 20 November 2004, the weekend following a Spain–England 'friendly' match when Spanish fans in the Bernabéu in Madrid were heavily criticized for racist chanting. A mosaic around the Nou Camp pronounced '*Ja som 125,000*' ('Now there are 125,000 of us', in Catalan) while a banner proclaimed 'We are not Spain' (in English, the Catalans clearly distancing themselves from Spain and addressing an international audience). Such demonstrations led *El País*, for example, to brand the club as 'more than ever a nationalist insignia . . . playing for prestige and their own identity' (8 March 1999).

One of the articles quoted above (*El País*, 12 April 1985), however, issues a warning to Catalans who 'try to use symbols which have no economic power or political effectiveness.' Support for Barcelona, it is argued, can lead to simplistic nationalism and even engender racism and xenophobia. The journalist ends by declaring emphatically that 'the symbols [of Catalunya] are in our Statutes and they are the *senyera* [the Catalan flag], '*Els Segadors*' [the Catalan anthem] and the Generalitat, because Cataluña is more than a club.' While it might be uncomplicated to relate FC Barcelona to Catalanism, it would be simplistic to assume that Catalanism relies solely on its association with the football club.

There is some evidence, then, of a distinctive Catalan identity via football writing in terms of the prevalent themes which emerge in football print discourse, though quantitatively this evidence might not be strong. However, where Catalan identity is closely connected to football is via the politicization of FC Barcelona and it is the representatives of the club itself that promulgate the sense of Barça as 'more than a club'. Less remarkable was a search through football reports of other Catalan teams such as Espanyol, Sabadell or Lleida. Here, there were few images which would suggest the reflection of a Catalan identity. Perhaps the symbolism of FC Barcelona as Catalan means that other Catalan clubs are not stereotyped. They are, however, labelled frequently as Catalans, or 'the Catalan club'.

The ground was no more fruitful in terms of identifying characteristics and images of Catalunya when the attention turned to Catalan footballers playing at domestic level. While some players (such as Guardiola, Sergi, Nadal, Ferrer or Salinas) have clearly been renowned for their support of Catalanism – though we have not found evidence of any Catalan player refusing to play for the Spanish *Selección* on political grounds – there does not appear to be any clear association between being Catalan and playing in a particular style. Again, Catalan identity appears to be mediated in terms of strength of support for Catalunya rather than inventing stereotypical images of Catalans. This differs from our analysis of Basque football (see below).

There is undeniably an acknowledgement of diversity between Catalunya and the standard images of Spain – in particular regarding the strong work ethic, collective mentality and paranoia/*victimismo* of Catalans – but this appears to be more of a nod of recognition that Catalans have their own characteristics than it is any support for any stronger claims to a different nationality. The fact that Catalan and Spanish identities can contradict each other is no more commented upon than the fact that there exist contrasting images of Spanish mentality. However, the politicization of football writing is high. This commentary often promotes a Spain of a single unit, especially during the Franco period but also beyond, even though it acknowledges diversity within the existing legal and political framework.

The Basque Country

The Basque Government describes the Basque Country (Euskadi) on its Internet site as 'a European region with its own cultural, economic and industrial idiosyncrasies' (Euskadi 2005). There is no mention of Spain itself and the casual surfer would, therefore, be forgiven for believing that the Basque Country had no politico-administrative ties with Spain at all. Madrid even appears (along with Chile, Argentina and Brussels, for example) in a list of places where the Basque Government informs us that it has 'foreign delegations' based.

The oldest historical records of the Basques date back to Roman times and it is probable that Basques inhabited the area they do now for many years prior to then. The Roman conquest of Spain never managed to penetrate the hills occupied by many Basques. The Basques have enjoyed considerable autonomy and self-government, known since the feudal era as *fueros* (old laws). Even after the Basque Country became part of Spain, it was never fully integrated into its political and administrative systems. Elements of the *fueros* remained intact. The Basques' *fueros* were an important element of their self-identification. Though the *fueros* of individual provinces differed, they provided a symbol of Basque self-rule. Whether or not this represented real independence is debated today at length. The loss of these *fueros* became critical under General Franco and he also sought to take the integration of the different linguistic minorities in Spain one step further. He wanted total Castilianization: the Basque language was to be eradicated from public usage. After the death of Franco, when King Juan Carlos and the Spanish Parliament passed the 1978 Constitution, the system of *Comunidades Autónomas* restored the *fueros* in spirit, though not in every detail, via the approval of the Basque Statutes in 1979. Movements also began to revive the Basque language and football became part of this process.

The Basque Country presents a strong argument for its status as a distinct nation. The Spanish Constitution of 1978 recognizes that Spain consists of 'regions' and 'nationalities' and divides its territory into the *Comunidades Autónomas*. The Basque Country is one such entity – comprising the three regions of Alava, Vizcaya and Guipúzcoa – which has a population of something over 2 million on the Spanish side of the French border. Just as Catalunya claims kinship with Languedoc-Roussillon, the Basque Country extends into France as well. There are, therefore, also Basques to the north in France and some say in Navarre, too, since this was one of the seven provinces which made up the original Basque homeland. Our focus here in terms of the organization of football, however, concentrates on coverage in the Spanish print media. It should be borne in mind, though, that when we talk about Basques and in particular Basque footballers, we are inclusive in our definition. After all, any Basques are eligible to play for the Basque *Selección* (or 'national' team).

Although the Basque language is the key binding force of Basques (hence the movement to revive it following the Franco years which had stifled its use), other factors also define Basque identity relating to history, culture and an individual's place of birth. The Basque flag, the *ikurriña*, is a strong symbol of Basque identity. Díaz Noci (1999) explains the internal and external factors which have contributed to the construction of a Basque identity and identifies language, a particular vision of history, the *fueros* and the birth and defence of violence as a means to achieve a political goal as 'invented traditions' (Hobsbawm 1983). This rough, tough image of hard Basques is clearly prevalent in football writing. Durkheim's definition of a society involved individuals living within a defined territory, the things they use, but, most importantly, by the way in which they perceive themselves, and it is this element of the nation that it so elusive to pinpoint and yet so crucial in Basque political and social debate. The study of the impact of the past on the present has become a subject of interest for many academic disciplines, including social and political scientists and historians (Aguilar 2002), and this impact is strong in the Basque case.

Heiberg (1989) explains how deep social and political structural changes (industrialization and state centralization) within a short period of time explain the importance and rise of nationalism in the Basque Country in the twentieth century. As in the Catalan case (see above), nationalism in the Basque Country was rising as football emerged and became adopted by the indigenous population. Let us now examine the ways in which Basque identity has been formed or communicated via Spanish print media discourse on football. To what extent has the Basque Country been recognized as a nation with distinct characteristics? Does Basque football enjoy its own style or defining qualities? Has coverage changed during the political turmoil of the twentieth century? As in our Catalan sample, we analyse coverage of the Euskadi *Selección* and reports of Basque domestic teams.

In the early years of the twentieth century, footballing links were already being made between the Basque Country in Spain and southern France. *ABC* provides a few details of fixtures at this time, but coverage is limited to factual matters. A team representing the French League played a team representing the Basque Country in Irún on 13 June 1912 (the French were victorious and won 2–1). One important match in the early process of identity formation in Spanish football was that which took place between Real Sociedad and Athletic de Bilbao, the final of the Campeonato del Norte, which took place in Atocha, San Sebastián, on 17 February 1918 (denominated the 'historic match' by Martialay [2000: 168]). The match, which ended in a 2–2 draw, was described as 'violent, aggressive. A clash of two giants to see which was more Herculean.' This was a significant match for Basque and also for Spanish football. It was a dirty game and an incident between Belauste and Arrate resulted in the crowd invading the pitch and fights breaking out among players and fans alike. The match was abandoned with seven minutes remaining. The spirit of this game – reminiscent of the Spanish *furia* discussed above in Chapter 6 – was not to be forgotten in future coverage of Basque (and Spanish) football. In fact, the elements of Spanish *furia* are never far from the images of Basque football, which is depicted throughout the twentieth century as having a harsh, tough, direct style of play, contested by highly competitive, courageous, committed players in front of a fanatical crowd. It is perhaps ironic that Spanish and Basque football are so closely linked via the notion of *furia*. It appears to be Basque football that provides the basis of Spanish football identity. The reader is also reminded of the British roots of Basque football. These descriptions are extraordinarily consistent and perhaps represent the strongest images of a national identity within our entire sample in Spain.

The Basque *Selección* played its first match on 12 May 1915, against a Catalan *Selección*, in Madrid. The Basques won 1–0. The team was called the *Selección Norte*, but all the players were Basques and this is considered to be the antecedent to a real Basque *Selección*. In his comprehensive history of the Basque *Selección*, Gotzon (1998) identifies three phases in the development of the Basque *Selección*: the evolutionary phase (1915–31), the Civil War phase (1936–39) and the current phase (1979 – the present day).

In its evolutionary phase – when it was known as the *Selección Regional del Norte* (North Regional *Selección*), the *Selección del País Vasco* (1916) and then as Vasconia (1930–31) – the team played friendlies against Catalunya. A few encounters were played in the early 1930s (notably on 8 June 1930 in Montjuic, Barcelona, and on New Year's Day 1931, in San Mamés, Bilbao). Given the paucity of coverage of football in mainstream daily newspapers in general during this period in Spain, it is no surprise that coverage of Euskadi's efforts was almost non-existent at this time. Indeed, football coverage reflected heavily the Madrid bias of many of its reporters.

It was not until the second phase of the Basque *Selección*, during the Spanish Civil War (1936–39), that the *Selección* became known as Euskadi. Football was suspended in the Basque Country at the start of the Civil War in 1936 but, by early 1937, several 'friendly' matches were played in the Basque Country, organized by political groups, Acción Nacionalista Vasca and the Partido Nacionalista Vasca, then by *selecciones* from the regions of Guipúzcoa and Vizcaya. These matches provided the impetus for the re-creation of the Basque *Selección* (Gotzon, 1998: 37). The aim was to send the Basque *Selección*, Euskadi, on tour abroad.

So in April 1937, the Basque *Selección*, Euskadi, was formed, with money obtained from the matches previously mentioned and other sporting events. The idea that lay behind the creation of the *Selección* was twofold: propaganda and fundraising, both for the Basque cause. In short, the Basque *Selección* were intended to be Basque ambassadors abroad. In the 1937–38 season, the Euskadi *Selección* went on tour in Europe and Latin America to raise funds for (and awareness of) the Basque cause. They played matches in France, Poland, the Soviet Union, Norway, Denmark and Cuba. Matches in Argentina were cancelled because of intervention by FIFA. In 1938–39, Euskadi participated in the Mexican League (and actually won the championship). As the Spanish Civil War ended in 1939, the Euskadi *Selección* dissolved. Not surprisingly, since the purpose of the tour was to raise awareness of the Basque cause abroad, this tour received scant attention back in Spain, though Gotzon's comprehensive history of the Euskadi *Selección* gathers quotations from sources elsewhere during the Basque travels. The Russian press apparently reported that the Basque footballers were well organized and physically fit and strong (Gotzon 1998: 81–4).

Since there was little action for Euskadi in Spain during the Franco period (1939–75), we look elsewhere in our sample for evidence of a Basque identity within football writing. Though in the 1950s and 1960s many football match reports were still short and factual, there is plenty of evidence in some of the more descriptive passages of a Basque identity. When we turn to match reports of the Basque clubs and comments on Basque players, we do find strong clues to how the Basques are perceived. In our sample, the central characteristics denoted which were invariably employed to describe Basques were courage (via regular references to the 'brave Basques'), commitment and strength. As an example, Athletic de Bilbao are referred to as 'the brave Basque team' (*ABC*, 22 January 1955). Furthermore, 'the Basques try harder and have a higher work rate' than Real Madrid (*ABC*, 26 January 1957) and 'the power of the Basques showed through and they dominated the second half' (*ABC*, 12 April 1960).

By the end of the Franco period, football and Basque national identity were already closely linked at club level. Unlike in Catalunya where FC Barcelona became a unique symbol of the nation, in the Basque Country several teams represented the nation. Clubs tended to represent the city or region in which they were located rather than the Basque Country as a whole, though (notably, Athletic de Bilbao in Vizcaya and Real Sociedad in Guipúzcoa). From the outside, however, collectively, Basque clubs mediated a national image. For example: 'The Real and Athletic players have done as much as political parties have towards the recovery of the *ikurriña*. And football in the Basque Country has a different feel from that in other places' (*El País*, 31 May 1977). One commentator notes: 'Something unimaginable in England is the combination of implacable rivalry and fraternal cooperation which can be seen from time to time in the Basque Country' (Walton 2001: 25). An example of such Basque football rivalries being buried (temporarily, of course) for a greater cause was seen in 1998 on the occasion of the funeral of a Basque fan who was murdered in Madrid because he was Basque: 'Basque football formed a great family yesterday. Representatives of Real Sociedad, Athletic de Bilbao and Deportivo Alavés strengthened their relationships beyond rivalries on the pitch' (*El País*, 11 December 1998).

Basque football is frequently in touch with its political environment. By 1977, 'the *ikurriña* flies high at the San Mamés [home of Athletic de Bilbao]' (*El País*, 20 August 1977). It is not uncommon to hear of *ikurriña*-bearing team captains in the Basque Country leading their players onto the pitch at poignant moments in their nation's history, or in order to make a political statement. In 1976, for instance, at a derby between Real Sociedad and Athletic de Bilbao, the captains of the two clubs led the teams onto the field each carrying an *ikurriña* (*El País*, 9 December). Again, in 1977, poor previous refereeing decisions (that is, *victimismo*) were blamed in *El País* for the stance of the Athletic de Bilbao and FC Barcelona captains who entered the field carrying aloft the *ikurriña* and *senyera* respectively (20 February 1977).

It was not until 1979, four years after the death of the dictator General Franco, that the Basque *Selección* was finally re-established. A testimonial played for Basque footballer, José Eulogio Gárate, who played in Madrid, saw a Euskadi team fielded, though not yet under the name of Euskadi. The thought was expressed in *El País* that the (re)creation of a team that represented the whole of the Basque Country could serve to unite the Basques with a common cause (31 May 1977). The first few matches played by the Euskadi *Selección* during this period were in support of a campaign to promote the use of the Basque language, Euskera (*El País*, 13 December 1979). The Euskadi *Selección* was part of a broader cultural (and, for many, political) resurgence of Basque identity. After 36 years of dictatorship, when Franco prohibited any public displays of 'Basqueness', the newly established Basque government was keen to assist proactively in the revival of Basque culture. Foremost in this revival was the restoration of the Basque language and culture in primary schools. Funds from matches played by the Euskadi *Selección*, then, contributed to fund these cultural campaigns in Basque schools, known as *ikastolas*. 'Sport and culture went hand in hand, football and the Euskera language represented the same thing, a revindication of Basque identity' (Gotzon 1998: 129).

As the Basque *Selección* began to play football matches, albeit irregularly, the press did not eschew political comment. When Euskadi played against Ireland, at the San Mamés stadium, in Bilbao, on 16 August 1979, one article explained in detail the stance taken by Atlético Osasuna in prohibiting one of its players, Iriguíbel, from participating in the match. *El País* printed Osasuna's statement in which the club explained its decision for not releasing its player: 'Officially, the *Selección* that is playing against Ireland has been called the Euskadi *Selección*, and Osasuna's Board, in order to respect all opinions, believes that it should not act in any way that can be interpreted as political' (*El País*, 18 August 1979). Osasuna were, however, quick to qualify this statement by assuring their fans that they did, on the other hand, support the work of the *Real Academia de la Lengua Vasca* (Royal Academy for the Basque Language) to promote the Euskera language. Oddly, Osasuna claimed to view the language issue as cultural rather than political.

There is, in fact, more than a hint of a patronizing attitude towards the efforts of the Basques to strengthen their own national culture through football, as though humouring the Basques, and thus trivializing the political significance of their 'national' team. On occasions this is done through downplaying the political significance of the event. The report of the aforementioned match began thus: 'The Euskadi–Ireland match was a great fiesta. San Mamés was filled with an enthusiastic crowd, the great majority of whom came exclusively to enjoy the game, although there were a few political gestures and chants' (*El País*, 17 August 1979). The match was described as a 'cultural sporting event, in which politics remained on the margins' (*El País*, 16 August 1979). On other occasions, the attempt to trivialize the political overtones of the Euskadi *Selección* was greater: the match was 'a Basque fiesta – because above all that is what this fixture is about' (*El País*, 26 December 1979). In contradiction to what it had just stated, the same report went on to detail some of the politicized banners and chanting at that event, which proclaimed that Basque exiles wanted an 'amnesty' and to return to Euskadi. It was also noted that the Euskadi kit shared its colours with the Basque flag, the *ikurriña*, and admitted that 'for many the match played between Euskadi and Ireland was a nostalgic trip back in time to a glorious era in Basque football, when the Basque *Selección* went on an international tour in the middle of the Civil War' (*El País*, 16 August 1979). Finally, the post-match report mentioned the standing ovation received by goalkeeper, José Angel Iribar, as he was substituted after half an hour: what remains unsaid is the reason for such applause, 'the loudest ovation in the history of the San Mamés'. Iribar was one of the most respected figures ever in Basque football. His gesture of parading a Basque *ikurriña* at a time when it was still prohibited was to be remembered by Basques for years to come. Interesting, too, is that it was reported that the playing of the Basque, Irish and Spanish national anthems before kick-off was prohibited, 'presumably because of fears that the latter [the Spanish] would be booed' (*El País*, 17 August 1979).

The fanaticism of the Basques is never far from the surface: 'goals came to the cries of "Euskadi, Euskadi" and euphoria erupted on the terraces' (*El País*, 26 December 1979). The carnival atmosphere of Euskadi matches in the late 1970s and early 1980s is emphasized: 'there was an exciting atmosphere, thanks to the supporters of Navarra and the fanfares of Guipúzcoa' (*El País*, 17 August 1979). There is reference to 'the colour of the Basque fiesta' but also to the more political 'demands to restore their rights' (*El País*, 26 December 1979).

The Basque Football Federation was established in 1988 but really became effective in 1992. More recent developments in the contemporary history of the Euskadi *Selección* include the debate over its status as a national representative of the Basque Country and this has, therefore, raised questions regarding its rôle in world football. There was some talk of Euskadi presenting a side to compete in the 1982 World Cup (*El País*, 3 December 1978). This would have been legally permitted under the Spanish Constitution of 1978 but the drawback would be that Basque football clubs would then have to withdraw from Spanish 'national' competitions and form their own league. There are other administrative and political reasons why Euskadi cannot compete in official international competitions, though. FIFA is the only body that can rule on whether or not a nation can compete in official international fixtures. Article 10, paragraphs 1 and 6 of its statutes make it clear that Euskadi can apply for official status either if it is an independent nation or if the Spanish FA gives its consent for it to do so (FIFA 2004). In recent years, following the new passing of the Basque Sports Law in 1998, *El País* has covered the lobbying of the Spanish government on the part of the Basque Parliament to allow the Basque *Selección* to be recognized internationally (e.g. *El País*, 25 May 2002). (It is worth noting that UEFA's statutes were amended in September 2001 to state that new members of UEFA must be recognized as independent member states by the United Nations.)

There is relatively little in the football writing surrounding the Euskadi *Selección* that tells us about the Basque style of play. Coverage of the fixtures themselves are rather limited – after all they are 'friendly matches'. However, there is some evidence, most of which coincides with images of Basque players portrayed in other sources (and in particular in the Spanish press in other contexts). Far more common are simple announcements of fixtures involving the Euskadi *Selección* (e.g. *El País*, 2 March 1978) which sometimes include a list of squad members and the clubs they played for at that time. On 23 December 1979, Euskadi played Bulgaria, as with the previous match against Ireland, in an attempt to raise funds in support of the promotion of Euskera. While the reporting of this fixture focused more on the political situation that occasioned the event rather than the style of play, there were a few significant phrases which recur with frequency in match reports involving Euskadi: Euskadi 'moved with great speed, played good moves, and were a constant threat to the Bulgarian defence' (*El País*, 26 December 1979); Euskadi 'once again demonstrated how the old favourite of long balls is still the best' (*El País*, 2 June 1977). Much later, Euskadi's style of play is still said to rely on 'pressure and speed' (*El País*, 23 December 1993).

Apart from reporting on the Euskadi *Selección* itself, the print media can reinforce the links between football and Basque identity through coverage of domestic football and, in particular, reporting on Athletic de Bilbao and Real Sociedad. A few examples suffice to confirm a strong characterization. One match report when

Athletic played against Real Madrid in a league match in 1990 typifies the football writing about Basques in general: 'Real Madrid succumbed to the culture of trepidation, the way that Athletic usually face these big fixtures. . . . Athletic play a pressing style of football, putting the opposition under pressure, at a fast pace, in a style that is at times virulent' (*El País*, 18 March 1990). Similarly and previously, Basques had been noted to be 'intense', 'strong', have 'iron-like marking', play 'at pace' (e.g. *El País*, 15 October 1978; 29 October 1978). The typical Basque crowd, too, adheres to the image established at the start of the twentieth century and is 'enthusiastic' or 'fervent' (e.g. 17 August 1979). Segurola describes the Basques' 'Britishized' football as a 'dogma of faith' (Leguineche *et al.* 1998: 109) and this style of 'fast football, crosses from the wings for a big centre-forward to head, and little football in midfield' remains a stereotype of Basque football: 'Athletic wanted a passionate contest' (*El País*, 14 September 1997); they are 'tough' and 'physical' and play 'at a high pace in front of a passionate crowd' (ibid.). The notion communicated clearly and repeatedly to the reader is that Basque football relishes passionate matches, played with *furia* (e.g. *El País*, 23 March 2002; 12 November 2003). The Basque football stereotype is not equivocal. Readers are left in no doubt that Basque football clubs represent more than a sport. FC Barcelona's slogan *'més que un club'* ('more than a club') is no truer than in the Basque Country. Mario Onaindía, general secretary of Euskadiko Ezkerra, claimed that 'in Euskadi we all support Athletic, those that like football and those who never go. Athletic is a common cause, like Barcelona in Cataluña' (*El País*, 16 September 1980). Despite these words, the difference between Catalunya and the Basque Country is that in the Basque Country several clubs share the rôle of ambassadors for the territory. No single club enjoys the responsibility as representative of the Basque Country and, though in periods of their history relationships have not always been strong between these clubs (indeed there have been regional rivalries as well as political divisions among the Basque clubs), there is nonetheless a strong sense outside the Basque Country that all Basque clubs embody Basqueness. The notion that Basque clubs represent the Basque Country is reinforced almost on a weekly basis: 'the fact that [Athletic] would prefer Real [Sociedad] to win the League rather than [Real] Madrid escapes no one. . . . It would be very satisfying if the Bilbao club could help Real [Sociedad] to win the title' (*El País*, 17 May 1980). The club captain that day, Villar, admitted that 'There is no doubt that we would be happy to help Real [Sociedad] to bring the title to Euskadi' (ibid.). Apparently, in the ground in Bilbao there were chants of 'Athletic, Real, Real!' There exists, then, an overriding sense of Basqueness which, especially when faced with opposition from Madrid, overcomes any local rivalry.

The fact that Basque clubs are closely associated with Basqueness permeates football writing in many ways; even in the way it is reported that 'sales in Spanish flags rise when a Basque team comes to Madrid' and that there are fears of *'anti-vasquismo'* ('anti-Basque feeling') (*El País*, 16 September 1980). Hatred towards Basques has been highlighted on other occasions. For example, *El País* highlighted the abuse received by the Athletic de Bilbao goalkeeper, José Angel Iribar: 'there is a sector of the crowd who, when he plays away from home, whistles at him, and insults him throughout the game' (31 October 1979). On another occasion, stones were hurled at another Basque team, Erandio, when they played in Azagra apparently simply because they were Basques (*El País*, 12 May 1979).

So, symbols and characteristics of Basques pervade football writing in our sample of the Spanish print media. We find clear images of tough, spirited Basques. Their style of football reflects their national character and is direct and hard, relying on *furia*. The *ikurriña* holds a strong position in Basque football and is a clear symbol of Basque identity in football writing and political ties between Basques seem to be more powerful than football rivalries. Football is also linked to the other bastion of Basqueness, the Basque language. Press coverage draws heavily on political comment but eschews in-depth political debate in its sports pages.

Chapter 8

Beauty or the beast?

The Corsican question

Corsica became part of France in 1768 (ceded by Genoa). Situated some 200 km south-east of the mainland, the Mediterranean island has a distinctive and unique identity in French culture. Representations of Corsica are contrasting. Known as 'the Island of Beauty', it is renowned for its picturesque scenery and tourist attractions but the underdevelopment of its economy and the persistence of social problems also serve to fuel feelings of isolation from mainland France. Indeed, Corsican difference is a given. Half of the population speak the Corsican language (in addition to French) while a significant percentage of the island's 260,000 inhabitants retains separatist ambitions and, in the second half of the twentieth century, these were even expressed in terrorist campaigns, both on the island itself and on the mainland, led primarily by the Fronte di Liberazione Naziunale di a Corsica (FLNC), which has allegedly been responsible for thousands of attacks since its creation in 1976 including the assassination in 1998 of Claude Erignac, the Prefect of Corsica (the most senior representative of the French government on the island). Demands for independence or, at least, a form of autonomy punctuated the late twentieth century and kept 'the Corsican question' (Crettiez 1999) on the agenda of a country constantly searching for the best way to balance its political status as a unitary (and, until recently, highly centralized) state with its socio-cultural nature marked by the considerable regional diversity that is a legacy of its lengthy history.

France's history as a sovereign state dates back to the ninth century. Over the centuries since then, the country's frontiers have expanded (and contracted) before reaching the present borders which encompass a territory of over 550,000 km². Politically, France is defined in article 1 of its present constitution as '*une République indivisible*', a unitary state to be contrasted with the federal structures of some of its closest European neighbours (such as Germany, Spain and the United Kingdom). However, because of its geo-political dimensions and historical development, France displays considerable regional diversity within its borders. Regional diversity is not only admitted, it is increasingly positively celebrated insofar as it is not perceived as a threat to the unity of the nation. This makes the Corsican case somewhat different from the other French regions as, at times, the line between peacefully celebrating regional identity and aggressively pressing the case for independence appears to have been crossed with the result that 'the spectre of an increase in explosive events instigated by frustrated separatists continues to haunt this beautiful and profoundly paradoxical island' (Clout 2003).

Guy Michaud (Emeritus Professor at the University of Paris X) and Alain Kimmel (Professor at the *Centre international d'études pédagogiques*) reflect the official viewpoint in their best-selling introductory text book *Le Nouveau guide France* when they describe France as 'rich and diverse', 'a melting pot of civilization', the 'essential characteristic of which is diversity' (Michaud and Kimmel 1996: 9). Constitutionally, though, Corsica remains a region within a unitary and indivisible state and Corsicans cannot, therefore, be seen as a nation or a people in their own right. Indeed, the term 'Corsican people' was struck out of a proposed legislative text in 1991 by the Constitutional Council (France's supreme court) for this very reason (Conseil Constitutionnel 1991). At the end of the twentieth century, however, Prime Minister Lionel Jospin publicly acknowledged the existence of the Corsican people on national television (TF1, 4 May 1999), obtained a ceasefire from the FLNC and, in July 2000, put forward a proposal to reform French local government so that Corsica could benefit from a different system from the 21 other regions in France in that it would be governed by a single elected assembly with certain legislative powers relating to tourism and the environment exercised independently of Paris. (The proposal was ultimately narrowly rejected by Corsican voters in a referendum of 2003.) Although still unresolved, the Corsican question had forced France's politicians to finally catch up with what had certainly been prevalent in the popular imagination for some time: that there is a distinct and recognizable Corsican identity that merits special attention. Indeed, Corsica's uniqueness within France is often stressed with its identity partly deriving from its being 'a stage for a permanent ideological confrontation between state centralists and the proponents of autonomy' (Andreani and Ajchenbaum 2005: 8).

The feelings aroused in the rest of France by Corsican identity and its associated problematics are usually quite unequivocal. The island is, apparently, reputed for its population of 'hardy souls', 'tough', 'proud' people 'given to violence' and even a history of banditry and other criminal activity (Michaud and Kimmel 1996: 27, 92). The pen portraits provided by introductory guides to France such as Michaud and Kimmel's are revealing in this respect in that they supposedly focus on the essential summary characteristics of the cities and regions they describe and, in so doing, recycle rather than challenge traditional perceptions, perceptions that seem still to be informed by the historical and problematic stereotype of Corsicans as stormy, aggressive, violent, isolationist characters (Sinet 2000: 9–12). It will be interesting to discover whether or not the suspicion and even fear with which many in mainland France view Corsica are reinforced by football writing in the national daily press. In order to study the image of Corsica portrayed by the French press, two representatives of the island will be examined. First, the Corsican 'national' team will be studied with reference to the one and only time that it played an 'international' football match and, second, the island's most successful club side, Sporting Club de Bastia, will be considered, focusing in particular on their FA and UEFA cup exploits between 1972 and 2002.

The issue of ethnicity plays its part in the Corsican question. In football circles, then, it has not been unusual to hear pleas for clubs on the island to adopt a Corsican-only selection policy when recruiting players (for example, see *France Football*, 19 January 1999: 48) similar to the Basque-only policy followed in Spain by Athletic de Bilbao. These pleas are fuelled by nostalgic memories of the one and only time that a Corsican 'national' team played a match against a side representing a country. In 1967, France's new coach, the hero of the 1958 World Cup, Just Fontaine, invited football journalist Victor Sinet to select a team of Corsicans against whom the French national team could play a friendly, 'real Corsicans, mind you, not just the best players on the island' (Sinet 2000: 125). The match duly took place on 27 February at the Stade Vélodrome in Marseille and a crowd of some 25,000 saw the Corsican side win 2–0. Pierre Sinibaldi, Corsican coach for the day (alongside Sinet), apparently motivated his players before the game by telling them: 'What really matters is you all have the same blood flowing through your veins. You've been chosen because of your legendary qualities, your temperament, your ambition and your pride' (Sinet 2000: 126; see also *France Football*, 29 August 2000). The concepts of Corsican identity and ethnicity which were clearly very important features for Sinibaldi, Sinet and the Corsican players were, however, glossed over in the national press coverage of the match. *Le Monde*, which had established itself as France's main daily newspaper, carried a 60-line report of the game but refused to refer to France's opponents as Corsica, preferring instead the more anodyne terms 'Corsican selection' and 'Corsican 11' (2 March 1967), thereby discursively avoiding any suggestion that this might be a game between two 'national' teams. Moreover, the representative nature of Sinet's team and its potential implications were significantly downplayed by *Le Monde*: 'the only link the Corsican selection shared was their common origins' (ibid.). So, what for Sinet and many others was the major element binding the team's players together, their Corsican identity, their 'spiritual link' (Sinet 2000: 127) becomes for the most prestigious national daily paper in France little more than a minor curiosity. Furthermore, despite noting that the Corsicans played well and deserved their victory, the newspaper is keen to point out that this was only 'a training match' where 'the result is of little importance' (ibid.). In sporting terms, of course, the result was, indeed, of no significance but culturally, the presence of a Corsican football team representing the island-region for the first time ever might have been felt worthy of more attention than it was given by *Le Monde*. Or was the idea of a separate (and superior) Corsican 'national' team too much of a political hot potato to handle, a precedent that was not to be encouraged? Whatever the reasons, an opportunity to explore Corsican identity and its unique place in French culture had clearly been missed by the national newspaper in question. On the island of Corsica itself, however, the implications of the event were far-reaching and served the future development of Corsican football as a whole: 'However insignificant it might appear to those on the mainland, the victory of 27 February 1967 will remain engraved as a symbol in the history of the Corsican game. Its fallout in the island's sporting circles and beyond was huge. It had the indirect consequence of encouraging the clubs on the island to push on and to progress further' (Sinet 2000: 127).

To turn to Bastia, Duke and one of the present authors have explored the concept of a football club being seen as a regional ambassador (Duke and Crolley 1996a: 4, 25–6, 36–7, 40–3, 47–8) and this model may be duly applied to Corsica. According to this concept, a region's most successful football club is regarded as representative not only of the town or city in which it is based but also of its entire region, whether the region is defined in historical terms or in more modern po-litico-administrative ones (in Corsica's case, the two are identical). Furthermore, the notion of regional ambassador has added pertinence in France where the no-tions of place, community and locality are such significant features in the identity of a football club (see Mignon 1998: 209, 224, 257; Ravenel 1998: 122–8). Most importantly in the context of the present study, it will be interesting to note the ways in which these features are reflected by football writing in the daily press. To what extent is Bastia portrayed as an icon of Corsican identity?

Certainly Bastia already regards itself in this light. Originally founded in 1905, Bastia became the first Corsican club to play in a national French league in 1960 (the non-professional *Championnat de France Amateurs*) and turned professional in 1965, finishing fourth in Division 2. In 1968 promotion was achieved to the top flight of French football where, apart from a spell of seven seasons in the late 1980s and early 1990s, Bastia stayed for the remainder of the twentieth century (Berthou 1999: 60–4). A simple visit to the club's Internet site suffices to demonstrate the close links Bastia has established with Corsica as a whole and the status of island representative that it has taken on (a status much disputed by the other main club on the island, Ajaccio). A splash introduction page shows an outline of the island of Corsica and plays Corsican folk music while a number of text boxes fade into view above images of Corsican landmarks, architecture and scenery. The first text proclaims significantly that Bastia is 'A real football club in the image of Corsica' while the second states that this is 'The club for the whole community'. Just before entering the site proper, the visitor is reminded that Bastia is 'A different kind of club, an emblem of a region' (which is very reminiscent of FC Barcelona's slogan 'More than a club' – see above, Chapter 7) while, throughout the site itself, sil-houettes of the island and its historical crest of a Moor's head appear as graphics supporting the text and reinforcing the Corsican flavour of the site as a whole (SC Bastia 2005).

In terms of sports media discourse, the perception vaunted by the football club's Internet site that Bastia and Corsica are closely linked and inextricably identified with each other is reinforced in the French national daily press by a relatively simple discursive technique which, reflecting the importance placed by French football clubs on their symbolic, emotional and political links with their region of origin, describes the clubs in terms of the area in which they are based. Thus, Bastia is frequently qualified as 'Corsican' (e.g. *Le Monde*, 9 December 1977) and 'the Corsican club' (e.g. Le Monde, 14 April 1978; 2 April 2002) while its team members are 'the Corsican players' (e.g. Le Monde, 9 December 1977) or 'the Corsicans' (e.g. Le Monde, 17 March 1978; 11 May 1978; 12 February 2002; 11 May 2002; Libération, 14 September 1997). Bastia, as with many other football teams, then, may be read as an expression of place, an emanation of Corsica as a whole, symbolizing an island-territory whose real or imagined values it is felt to convey and in this sense French football clubs and their mediation contribute to the reinforcement and perpetuation of not just town- or city-based local identities but also regional ones (see also Ravenel 1998: 125).

The simple identification of Bastia with its region of origin is, however, not by any means the only mechanism at work in the French print media's representation of Corsican identity. Already in the early twentieth century, notions of distinct regional identities were being applied in French journalists' descriptions of football, contrasting teams from the Mediterranean, for example, as 'quick, but a little disorganized' and 'quick silver southerners' with 'the strong northern lads' and 'the rugged Bretons' (Wahl 1999). As we shall see, late twentieth-century print media discourse remains founded on such rather basic appreciations of French identities but, more interestingly, also goes on to extend and develop them in more specific ways, particularly with reference to Corsica as seen through the lens of its most successful football club.

The vocabulary and imagery employed in reports of Bastia's matches in the daily press serve to paint a picture of the island which is generally instantly recognizable and self-perpetuating in that it connects with widely held views in French culture at large by effectively recycling mainland perceptions of the imagined identity of Corsica. According to Ravenel, Corsica is already a special case in the football world anyway in that it has more in common with other European islands than with the rest of French football, which is largely based on urban population centres. Bastia fits into the same category, then, as Cagliari, Maritimo Funchal and Tenerife with its strongly partisan crowd, spartan stadium and facilities, and poor reputation in safety and security measures (Ravenel 1998: 40, 45. In May 1992, a temporary stand at Bastia's Furiani stadium collapsed before the French FA Cup semi-final against Olympique de Marseille resulting in the death of 17 spectators). Corsican difference is often reflected by print media discourse on football. The words 'passionate' and 'hot' frequently punctuate articles devoted to Bastia while the unwelcoming (almost bestial?) nature of the local crowd is conveyed by the Furiani stadium being referred to as a 'den' (e.g. Libération, 16 September 1997) in contrast to the arenas, theatres and stadia of other French clubs. Similarly, Corsican football is usually represented, in the common image of the island on which it is played, as aggressive, rough and ready. When Paris Saint-Germain beat Bastia 2–0 in one league game, for instance, they were said to have escaped 'the ambush' set for them by 'the Corsicans' (Libération, 14 September 1997). Again, the same newspaper affirmed that, in order to beat Benfica in a UEFA Cup tie, 'the Corsicans will have to count on their roughness to bring down an opponent of this stature' (16 September 1997); in the next round against Steaua Bucarest, we learn that Bastia 'showed its *usual* face, bustling energy to spare and that innate sense of solidarity passed on from generation to generation' (*Libération*, 6 November 1997, emphasis added). In this respect, we would agree with Gritti who notes that the stereotypical primitivism of Corsica is a pre-existing myth already in circulation outside the world of sport which media discourse is all too ready to acknowledge, to recycle and – supposedly – to present further evidence of (Gritti 1975: 144).

Bastia is undoubtedly Corsica's most successful football club having reached one UEFA Cup final (in 1978) and three French FA Cup finals (in 1972, 1981 and 2002), winning the trophy in 1981 (to add to the Division 2 title won in 1968). It will be instructive to consider in some detail the national daily press reports of Bastia's cup exploits in reaching the four finals in question with a view to understanding the mechanisms at work in the representation of Corsican identity. The 2002 FA Cup final is included here because, despite being outside the largely twentieth-century framework of the present study, the events surrounding the match generated much debate in the French press about the nature of the Corsican question itself and are, therefore, particularly relevant to any examination of the mediation of Corsican identity.

Bastia's first appearance in the French FA Cup final in 1972 in the newly renovated Parc des Princes in Paris resulted in a 2–1 defeat at the hands of Olympique de Marseille. The geographical origins of the two finalists allowed *Le Monde* to qualify this as 'the Mediterranean final' (6 June 1972) and the national daily went on to note that the Corsican monthly paper *Kyrn* had even dubbed it the 'Corsica versus France' match. However, *Le Monde* was swift to play down any implication of separatism or independence for the island being acceptable by condemning *Kyrn* and affirming that 'all reasonable minds will see this as an exaggeration' (ibid.). Having said this, there is considerable awareness demonstrated by the newspaper of the reputed qualities of the Corsican and, indeed, the wider Mediterranean identity (for an examination of Marseille in this respect, see Crolley and Hand 2002: 82–83). *Le Monde* notes, for instance, the 'enormous police presence' regarded as necessary to quell the possibility of Paris 'exploding' under 'raging' fans from the south arriving in the capital for this 'high-risk' match (ibid.). Indeed, the apprehension with which Corsica (and, for that matter, Marseille) is held in French culture is further indicated by the journalist's palpable discomfort on contemplating the crowd at the match itself. '[T]he virulence of word and banner' was noted as was the 'deafening racket' made by the fans. The best indication that the characteristically passionate style of fandom for which Corsica is well-known is treated with considerable suspicion comes in the remarkable statement that the 'atmosphere that reigned in the stands at the Parc des Princes was South American' (ibid.). So different are the Corsicans from what is perceived to be the French norm of the 1970s that they virtually cease to be French at all. In a sense, of course, the accentuation of Corsican difference to this extent actually contradicts the earlier statement in the report that this is absolutely not to be seen as a Corsica versus France match and thereby highlights not only the complexity of questions of national and regional identities in such a large and diverse country as

France but also some of the tensions that are generated in sports media discourse when it focuses on difference and diversity within a given state.

Bastia's UEFA Cup campaign of 1977–78 is regarded by many as having a political dimension at least in terms of its potential to portray a positive representation of Corsica at a time when the island was suffering economically and was bitterly divided by the activities of terrorist groups dedicated to independence. Through the vector of Bastia's progress all the way to the final of the competition, an image of a dignified Corsica, capable of uniting peacefully behind its successful footballers, was communicated; this also promoted a strong adherence to a truly unique and recognizable Corsican identity (see Rey 2003). However, the national daily press on the mainland initially gave scant consideration to Bastia's exploits. Notable victories over Sporting Lisbon and Newcastle United in the first two rounds were hardly accorded any coverage at all by *Le Monde* and it was only by the time of the second leg of the third round game against Torino that full match reports appeared. In a sense, Bastia's progress in the competition had forced the national press to take notice. *France Football*, the major weekly magazine, devoted a special article to Corsica immediately prior to Bastia's away leg in Turin which saw 15,000 Corsican fans travel to Italy for the match itself. The Corsican paper *Arritti* had already qualified the tie as 'Corsica versus Italy' in a front page headline when *Le Monde* confirmed Bastia's status as representative of the whole island-region of Corsica by the discourse employed in its subsequent article examining the 3–2 victory: 'the Corsicans', 'the Corsican players' (7 December 1977). Moreover, a reference is made to the rough and ready image Corsica enjoys as its 'surprising' and 'in no way exceptional' football team 'has booted out of the UEFA Cup other teams that are apparently better equipped' (ibid.). In many respects, the image of Corsican football communicated by the national daily *Le Monde* tallies with that offered by the Corsican press itself. *Kyrn*, for instance, declares the victory over Torino to be that of Corsican football as a whole with its characteristics of 'energy, speed and inspiration' to the fore, a style of football that exists, like the Corsican language, as a marker of identity and, like a language, a style of football that can be learned by players who arrive in Bastia and represent the island whatever their own origins (cited by Sinet 2000: 63–4).

In the report in *Le Monde* of the away leg of the quarter final, against Carl Zeiss Jena, further references to the stereotypical toughness of Corsicans are made as well as to their reputedly fiery or flashy nature: 'the collective brio of the Corsicans' was in evidence and 'their strength is based primarily on their attacking capabilities and their dynamism in demanding situations' (17 March 1978). Interestingly, when the typical qualities are absent from any given performance, consternation is expressed in the print media discourse. In the semi-final victory over Zurich, for instance, *Le Monde*'s reporter was concerned that, initially, Bastia were lacking their customary and 'somewhat frenzied dynamism' especially as their 'reserves of energy' are usually 'surprising' (14 April 1978). Normal service was resumed, though, once what would be the winning goal came as, 'All of a sudden, Bastia became once again the son et lumière Bastia of the big occasion' (ibid.). With the victory won and qualification for the final assured for 'the Corsican club', *Le Monde* once more further reinforced the links between football team and region by noting that 'the *whole of Corsica* will be very proud at the thought of SC Bastia becoming the third French side to earn the right to play in a European final' after Reims and Saint-Etienne (ibid., emphasis added). Qualification for the final was felt in Bastia itself as something of a welcome revenge over mainland France's often less than positive portrayals of Corsican identity. As Rey (2005) notes, 'Too often the island's teams were singled out for their brutal, rough game and the bad reputation of their crowds' but now a Corsican team had reached a major European final with seven consecutive victories to its name along the way.

The 1978 UEFA Cup final itself, 'the match of the century for Corsica' (Sinet 2000: 167), contested over two legs against Dutch outfit PSV Eindhoven, turned out to be a major disappointment not only for Bastia itself, beaten 3–0 on aggregate, but also for *Le Monde* covering the two games. The first leg at the Furiani Stadium went ahead, despite the protestations of both sides' managers, in atrocious weather conditions and was literally bogged down, resulting in a goalless draw. Possibly because the quality of the football on display was so poor, *Le Monde* chose to focus on issues surrounding the game and the discourse employed might be felt to connect with wider French assumptions about the less savoury aspects of the typical Corsican identity. The newspaper noted that the ground was full for the game, quoting the attendance as 8,000, but went on to state that 'as usual' several thousand more had 'crammed in' and the official figure was, therefore, to be read with some doubt. The gate receipts of over 1 million francs, though, would be added to the television rights and the money earned from previous rounds of the competition to generate an expected windfall of some 10 million francs for the club. However, the journalist notes, 'Corsican leaders can be very zealous at hiding their riches' (28 April 1978). Whatever the implication here and whether or not it is merely playful, suspicions of shady dealing, criminal activity and financial corruption never seem to be far away from depictions of Corsica. The second leg in Holland was primarily reported as an example of a football team failing to live up to its reputation, thereby deflating the image already preconceived for it both inside and outside the football context. 'What happened?' *Le Monde* was bemused. A 'European trophy might have been on its way to the Island of Beauty' but instead, there was a 'metamorphosis' and Bastia appeared as a 'shadow of a shadow', lacking 'energy and inspiration', 'In short, unrecognizable' (11 May 1978). To be unrecognizable necessarily presupposes that a recognizable Bastia/ Corsican identity had already existed up to this point and that that identity was clearly delineated and well-known. Furthermore, not only had Bastia failed to incarnate the typical and expected Corsican identity, but by 'going down without panache', 'unlike Reims and Saint-Etienne' (France's previous losing European finalists), they also failed to uphold the typical quality of stylish football for which France as a whole is renowned (see above, Chapter 3).

Bastia's passage to the 1981 French FA Cup final was largely ignored by *Le Monde* which rarely devoted any more than a line or two to the results and goalscorers of the matches played. However, the report of the final itself, a 2–1 victory over Saint-Etienne (one of France's top teams at the time who had, indeed, just recorded their tenth league championship), is noteworthy for the several references it makes to the notions of Corsican identity and difference as well as to the now familiar representative nature of Bastia.

That Bastia is Corsica's club is never doubted by *Le Monde*. On the contrary, it fulfils the 'rôle of standard bearer for a region that is very sensitive to its own identity' and its triumph here 'would be celebrated by Corsicans the length and breadth of the Island of Beauty' (16 June 1981). In order to leave no doubt about the significance of the victory, the newspaper reminds its readers that 'For the first time in 64 outings, the French FA Cup has left the mainland' (ibid.). It is not only Corsica's geographical separation from the rest of France that is foregrounded in the article in question as the distinctive nature of Corsican football is once again reiterated: 'With its Furiani Stadium worthy of a Dubout drawing, its crowds of 3,000, its budget five times smaller than Saint-Etienne's, Bastia is almost an anachronism in French football' (ibid. Albert Dubout was a celebrated Marseille sketch artist and cartoonist whose work portrays a caricatured version of a somewhat ramshackle Mediterranean world).

With respect to temperament, the match report also makes references to the stereotypical Corsican attributes. Indeed, the headline itself opposes the contrasting imagined identities of the two teams in the final: 'Bastia's enthusiasm stifles Saint-Etienne's organization' (ibid. Saint-Etienne, a metal working and textile town from the Rhône–Alpes region, has the reputation in French culture of being disciplined and industrious). The image is then extended throughout the article. Saint-Etienne failed to realize that a cup final requires 'more enthusiasm than class, more boldness than calculation, qualities that Bastia's maverick footballers demonstrate to the highest level on the big occasions.' Above all, Saint-Etienne failed to deal with 'the extraordinary temperament of this Bastia side that has clashed with and upset the élite of French football for over ten years' (ibid.). In short, in as clear a statement of Corsican difference as there could be, *Le Monde* declares Bastia to be such a good cup side because it can count on 'players who have Corsican temperament and Corsican blood' (ibid.).

As was the case over 20 years earlier, Bastia's route to the French FA Cup final of 2002 was given scant attention by *Le Monde*. Even the possible newsworthiness of a quarter final against an amateur team, Libourne, did not generate much copy and it was only after the semi-final victory over Sedan that the newspaper provided any substantial coverage at all. Once again, the representative nature of Bastia, 'the Corsican club', was highlighted (*Le Monde*, 2 April 2002). It was not until the ninety-fourth minute (in extra time) that the goal came 'that Corsica was waiting for' and, with victory achieved, 'From Bastia to Corte, Tallone to Fium Orbo, *the whole* of the Island of Beauty celebrated Bastia's third appearance in the FA Cup final' (ibid. emphasis added). *Le Monde* also quoted Bastia striker Tony Vairelles who declared himself 'happy for the Corsican people' (ibid.) thereby employing a term that had until lately been contentious, at least in official French public discourse.

The question of precisely what the term 'the Corsican people' means and the issues deriving from it exploded into full view because of the events immediately prior to the start of the cup final against Lorient. As the Marseillaise, the French national anthem, was being played with the teams lined up before kick-off, some of the 20,000 Bastia fans in the Stade de France booed and whistled, much to the ire of the guest of honour, the recently re-elected President Chirac, who somewhat theatrically (and only temporarily) left his seat in the stands prompting a delay of some 20 minutes to the start of the game itself, which Lorient would win and in which Bastia failed to display the qualities of 'inspiration [and] enthusiasm' expected of a Corsican team (*Le Monde*, 14 May 2002). The events received extensive coverage in the French daily press with many journalists reading the boos and whistles as a sign of Corsican separatism and anti-French sentiment displayed by a section of the Bastia support. *Libération* praised Chirac for his stance but noted that he would now have to deal properly with 'the Corsican question' rather than ignore it (13 May 2002). The rather more forthright *Le Figaro* stated that Chirac had taken laudable and refreshing action noting that 'That's how you should deal with Corsican separatist yobs' (13 May 2002). In addition to the report of the match itself, *Le Monde* devoted a front page article to the events, an editorial and five other articles spread over two inside pages of the domestic news section of the paper. It will be worth considering in some detail the focus of each of these pieces.

The front page headline was 'Chirac's Two Angry Outbursts' (one being over Israel, the other Corsica) and the article itself quoted the President describing the events as 'intolerable and unacceptable. . . . I will not tolerate or accept that the essential values of the Republic can be attacked in this way' (*Le Monde*, 14 May 2002). The national anthem, of course, symbolically represents the nation-state, the values of which, in the French case, are enshrined in the written constitution of 1958. Most notable in the present context is the unified and indivisible nature of the French Fifth Republic which is, therefore, a single, unitary state that does not allow subdivision into different components let alone countenance the notion that a federal organization might be possible. That France is composed of many recognizably different and diverse regional identities is not in doubt but, in official discourse, this is admitted only so long as the unity of the nation-state as a whole is never threatened or questioned. Corsicans whistling at the national anthem at a football match was perceived as just such a threat.

Le Monde's editorial (ibid.) explained the 'Corsican question' in more detail but ultimately noted that Chirac had done the right thing when presented with such a 'difficult case'. The action taken was typical of the man, impetuous and showy, but was also consistent with his respect for the symbols of the nation and his admiration for its values of unity and indivisibility. Moreover, Chirac had successfully distinguished himself from his former prime minister and political opponent, Lionel Jospin, who had literally quietly sat through similar 'anti-French' events at the France–Algeria international friendly of the previous autumn (see below, Chapter 9). With regard to the issue itself as opposed to the personalities involved,

Le Monde reported that a silent demonstration had been planned by some Bastia fans but that the whistling and booing were apparently spontaneous. In any case, the newspaper was of the opinion that any anti-French sentiment on display represented only 'a fraction' of the Corsican population as a whole.

The first article on the news pages exploring the events of the 2002 cup final (ibid.) was, however, somewhat less complimentary to President Chirac. Once Chirac had uttered the words 'Are they whistling? I'm off', it would seem he was able to dictate the sequence of events and turn them to his advantage. He instructed the embarrassed president of the French FA to take a microphone to explain what was happening to the crowd, summoned a television crew to give an interview, determined when he would go back to his seat to allow play to start and refused to go on to the pitch to greet the players. Chirac branded those whistling at the national anthem as 'a few irresponsible people' which, of course, allows little legitimacy to be given to any political point they might have wished to make, and then concentrated on maximizing the favourable publicity that he could derive from the affair.

President Chirac's claim that the affair was caused only by a few irresponsible people has to be qualified in the light of the interviews given to *Le Monde* and reported in the second news article devoted to it (ibid.). Dan Lodi, a member of a Corsican nationalist organization called the *Comité d'action contre la répression*, informed the paper that a demonstration had, indeed, been planned and that pamphlets had been distributed before the game calling for the release of Corsican prisoners held on terrorist charges. 'It's hard to respect the Marseillaise,' he said, 'because it's the national anthem of a colonizing country.' Other interviewees (whose political affiliations, if any, were not made clear) echoed the sentiment: 'We did it because nobody shows us any respect. And the Marseillaise isn't the Corsican anthem'; 'The whistling? I'm not French, sir. Me, I'm Corsican'; 'It was a demonstration by a people who have had enough of being treated by France as second-class citizens. It's our anthem as well but it would be even more so if France showed some consideration towards the Corsican people, their language and their culture'; 'it shows the exasperation and despair of the Corsican people'; 'it wasn't against the French people but against the State and the Parisian administrators'; 'It was the reaction of people who don't recognize themselves in the Marseillaise. It wasn't directed against the French people but against those people in the President's box.' Naturally, not all of the interviewees shared the same opinion. One Bastia fan noted that he was 'French through and through' and stated that 'It was a minority who were whistling' while another pointed out that 'Corsica is France. Sport should not be used for political ends and it's our own players who have suffered.' Finally, a Paris Saint-Germain fan summarized the affair thus: 'If they're not French, let them drop out of the French FA Cup.'

The third article reports other politicians' views of the events with particular focus on the grand gesture made by President Chirac. Unsurprisingly, Chirac's prime minister, Jean-Pierre Raffarin, and sports minister, Jean-François Lamour, were in total agreement with the President and used the same discourse of respect for national Republican values in support of him. Jean-Pierre Chevènement, leader of the Mouvement des Citoyens, called for a public inquiry into the events while the Mouvement national leader, Bruno Mégret, possibly demonstrating his limited appreciation of the nature of the game of football, declared that Chirac should have ordered the anthem to be replayed and, if the same result had ensued, cancelled the match. Leading figures in the Socialist Party such as Laurent Fabius and François Hollande were also quoted as lending their support to Chirac while the mayor of Bastia itself, Emile Zucarelli (Left Radical Party), claimed the protestors were in the minority and not representative of either Bastia or Corsica as a whole. What is possibly remarkable to an outside observer is the virtual unanimity of the French political class's reaction to President Chirac's handling of the events. Whatever their political affiliation, those quoted all represent a constitutionally and institutionally conservative viewpoint and, therefore, support the President's somewhat grandiose and theatrical defence of 'Republican values'. Only figures from the political wing of the ecology movement, which, of course, is itself positioned outside the mainstream of French politics, seem to express any doubts. Dominique Voynet, leader of Les Verts (the Greens), was of the opinion that Chirac had 'overplayed' his hand while Noël Mamère, spokesman for Génération écologie, pointed out that 'the identity problem is not solved. This old centralized France has got to learn to accept its differences.'

The fourth and fifth news articles in Le Monde attempt to explore some of the issues within Corsican nationalism and its possible links with the world of football. The fourth article reports on an interview with Jean-Guy Talamoni, a spokesman for Corsica Nazione, one of the island's leading political movements (ibid.). For Talamoni, who 'neither sang nor whistled at' the national anthem, Chirac's actions were no more than a party political gesture with an eye on the forthcoming parliamentary elections. The 'real political problem' was not and probably would not be addressed. The catalyst for the protest was Chirac's speech a month earlier in which he said 'there is no Corsican problem but there are problems in Corsica'. For Talamoni, though, 'the Corsicans have their own anthem and flag. . . . They are a society that is distinct from French society. . . . one cannot ask the Corsicans to respect the French Republic if, in turn, the Corsican people and their rights are not respected by it.' The tension and disillusionment felt by Corsicans had now been openly displayed and, Talamoni concluded, 'what happened on Saturday has to be seen as a major political event.'

In the fifth piece under consideration, Le Monde states that several members of SC Bastia's board have political affiliations but that these are quite wide ranging and do not only favour nationalist organizations such as A Cuncolta nazionalista and U Ribombu. For the newspaper, there is no question of Bastia being controlled or influenced by any group, nationalist or otherwise. Le Monde much prefers to cast the football club in the rôle of 'the most popular and the most frequently celebrated element in the island's identity and heritage' with its fans 'worshipping the region of Corsica' without any necessary nationalist or separatist agendas, which is a timely reminder, of course, that the Corsican question does not only revolve around the choice of France or independence but also involves issues of regional identity and difference within a diverse nation-state.

Overall, then, the picture painted by these articles is complex, complicated, but nonetheless vivid in its portrayal of the many issues surrounding Corsica, Corsican identity and what now has to be regarded as the Corsican question. What is of paramount importance to the present study is that it is within the football context and its mediation in the daily press that these issues are played out, demonstrating yet again the close links between football, the press and wider society. In this respect, SC Bastia, 'the standard bearer for the whole Island' (Sinet 2000: 46), might be regarded as a vector for the communication of notions of Corsican regional identity that are commonly held by the inhabitants of the island in question and serve, therefore, both to define that locality and to differentiate it from others in France. Football writing may also be seen to play a significant part in situating the concept of Corsican identity within the broader political debate over the governance of the island and its relationship with the mainland.

Part III

New (football) worlds

Chapter 9

The colonial shadow

Africans in the French imagination

The history of football in Africa is naturally linked to the political development of that continent and falls into two periods: before and after decolonization. It is, therefore, with one or two notable exceptions such as Egypt, only after the Second World War that independent African nations began competing on the international stage and that Africa became a prominent footballing continent in its own right. If the focus is placed on sub-Saharan Africa, rather than North Africa, then the involvement of black African nations in the global game is an even more recent phenomenon. Black Africa's first ever representatives at the World Cup finals, for instance, were Zaire in 1974 and they were followed in the twentieth century only by Cameroon (in 1982, 1990, 1994 and 1998), Nigeria (1994 and 1998) and South Africa (1998). By the end of the twentieth century, the *Confédération africaine de football* had become the largest governing body in the world with 52 member nations, most European leagues (especially the French) had recruited African players and the African Cup of Nations was being widely covered by the audio-visual and print media (see Armstrong and Giulianotti 2004; Darby 2002). However, sports media discourse on Africa tended not to differentiate between the sub-Saharan African nations themselves but rather to focus on the qualities that black Africans are reputedly said to share. These shared attributes generally fall into three categories, focusing on notions of physical power, indiscipline and naïvety (Hand 2002). It is the purpose of the first part of the present chapter to explore sports media texts drawn from the French daily press throughout the latter half of the twentieth century with a view to examining the evolution of portrayals of black Africans competing in world football.

Sub-Saharan Africa viewed from France

Among the earliest texts in the French press covering black African football in the post-colonial era would have been the two pieces in *Le Monde* in 1972 reporting on France's 2–0 victory over an African XI in the Independence Cup played in Maceio, Brazil. The preview of the game (16 June 1972) noted the rising popularity of football in Africa, the increased attention devoted to it by the media and the involvement in its financing of many political leaders who attached themselves to the sport as a means of promoting national pride (and their own careers) in the early days of independence from the colonial powers. The article also, however, drew attention to a facet of African football that would be a constant theme in the next 30 years of reporting: the 'stumbling and rough and ready way' in which Africans organize themselves and their football (ibid.). This overview is then directly transposed to the match report itself where we learn that 'the African team often dominated the game but could not organize itself well enough to take its chances' (17 June 1972). In terms of playing style, the preview also sets the scene for later portrayals of black Africans in this respect in that it describes African footballers as having 'brilliant individual qualities: consummate skill in controlling the ball, innate sense of how to dribble, fearsome striking of the ball, powerful shooting, suppleness, relaxed attitude and speed' (16 June 1972). Interestingly, the article explicitly links the social context of Africa to its expression on the football pitch. Social deprivation and economic underdevelopment often lead to a daily struggle to survive in Africa that breeds self-reliance and 'The spirit inherent to the social environment favours a highly individual style of play, a fairly selfish approach to the game. The ball is kept for oneself to display one's talents to all the onlookers. The crowd share the instincts, the attacking temperament of the players. If it's not methodical, African football is at least open and spontaneous' (ibid.).

It is not without interest, given this context, to consider *Le Monde*'s coverage of the first black African team to play in the World Cup finals, Zaire, in West Germany in 1974. Zaire is presented as a 'symbol of the growth of African football' and as a team 'of great potential' (20 June 1974) but the report of the heavy defeat against the former Yugoslavia tends to focus on a limited number of characteristics that are established as supposedly typical of black African football. First, the naïvety of the Zaire team, especially in defence, is commented upon and explicitly contrasted with the skill of the European team: 'the naïvety of the Zaire team led to their constantly being taken by surprise by their opponents' trickery and the Yugoslavs, experienced, battle-hardy professionals, were able to take full advantage' (ibid.). While attempting to defend one free kick, the Africans were, apparently, 'too busy saying good evening to their new keeper [the substitute Tubilantu]' to prevent a goal and the article continues in somewhat patronizing vein to note that, 'throughout the game, Zaire displayed a touching ingenuousness' before positing the given that 'defensive play is not part of their temperament at all' (ibid.). Finally, connecting with previous portrayals of African football, *Le Monde* sums up by saying 'obviously, it remains for order and rigour to be instilled into the whole system of play' (ibid.).

The 1990 World Cup finals provided a new decade, a new location (Italy) and a new sub-Saharan representative, Cameroon, and yet representations of black African football, in *Le Monde* at least, continued to evolve along now familiar lines. Throughout coverage of Cameroon's campaign, there are references to the spontaneity and lack of organization and method in the Africans' game. However, undoubtedly prompted by results on the pitch which included an opening match victory over World Cup holders Argentina and a defeat of Romania, these qualities are now viewed in a much more positive light than previously. Beating Argentina constituted the 'Miracle of Milan' in which Cameroon 'thumbed their noses at coaches everywhere', 'played for fun' and showed that 'there is still precisely some place for improvisation, heart and magic' as 'the savannah triumphed over the pampas' (10/11 June 1990).

By beating Romania, Cameroon became the first black African team to progress beyond the first phase of the World Cup finals and were eventually eliminated only after a narrow 3–2 defeat to England. *Le Monde* almost overflowed in its appreciation of the efforts of the Cameroon team in this 'historic' match: 'they brought a touch of magic that such a game needed' and the 'joyful upstarts' left fond memories behind by 'dribbling with logic, juggling with statistics and exposing the deficiencies of the calculating way in which the big teams play'; the Cameroon players may have arrived in Italy as 'exotic curiosities' but they left quite simply as 'heroes' (3 July 1990). It would seem, therefore, that Italia 90 marks an important turning point in French perceptions of black African football. What are regarded as the traditional qualities of Africans are still in evidence (as discursive givens, they could not be overturned) but success on the pitch has allowed these to be viewed in a more positive light. In turn, however, this allows French sports media discourse to resurrect a pre-colonial view of Africa as constituting a rich source of raw materials and labour for Europeans to draw upon. European interest in Africa in colonial times was, indeed, it might be argued, primarily economic and there is no doubt that the continent was exploited for its natural resources, raw materials and people, many of whom served as workers and slaves for Europeans. Such distasteful notions still linger in print media portrayals of African footballers. This perspective is all the more pertinent, of course, in the case of Cameroon which was colonized by the French (for more on the relationship between Cameroon and France, see Vidacs 2004). The Cameroon players, for instance, are described as if they are commodities, a potentially fine acquisition for European clubs, 'unequalled in terms of the ratio of quality to price' and highly attractive to European coaches who have come to Italy 'in search of rare pearls' such as these (*Le Monde*, 20 June 1990).

Cameroon also qualified for the World Cup finals in America in 1994 and, as they had appointed a French coach, Henri Michel, *Le Monde* took a particular interest in the African team as it prepared for its first match against Sweden. Images of indiscipline and disorder were to the fore: 'The Lions are here again and it's the same old mess' (19/20 June 1994. Cameroon's nickname is the Indomitable Lions). Rather than examine the squad itself, its strengths and weaknesses and Cameroon's tactics, the article preferred to focus on behind the scenes issues and accusations of financial wrong doing. The new coach had not been paid, there were disputes about hotel bills, and money from FIFA to support Cameroon's development had allegedly been diverted into private hands. *Le Monde* revealingly calls this 'the reality of Africa' as 'Cameroon is still Cameroon and crooks are still crooks'; this is 'the African way' (ibid.). When the newspaper finally gets around to commenting on the footballing aspects of Cameroon's participation in the World Cup, it does so by reinforcing previously established stereotypes of the black African player (see Orakwue 1998). The 2–2 draw against Sweden was a match played 'in the Cameroon tradition', that is by fun-loving, 'joyous troops' who 'smile all the time as they shake up the established order' (21 June 1994). This apparently typical African style is, though, presented in such a way as to appear endearing to a European readership but also, it must be said, not without a certain element of patronizing at work: 'The American fans have also taken to heart the challenge offered by the African game, adopting these jet black Cinderellas as they did one day in 1988 when they adopted the famous Jamaican bobsleigh team, stars of the Calgary winter Olympics' (ibid.). (Calgary is of course in Canada! The term Americans would appear to signify all North Americans, the USA and Canada together.)

Cameroon's third successive qualification for the World Cup finals in 1998 allowed images of African football in general to be recycled in the French daily press once again. The supposedly typical qualities of enthusiasm and naïvety were much in evidence in the media discourse. Enthusiasm is the 'prime' quality of the Cameroon team, its defining feature (11 June 1998), but it is invariably coupled with ingenuousness. Against Italy, for instance, 'the young Cameroon lions' assaults were flamboyant but often naïve' (Le Monde, 19 June 1998). In addition, although black Africans' physical strength is never in doubt, their psychological resolve is frequently called into question. 'Physically, their players are now equal to the best Europeans,' notes French coach Aimé Jacquet, 'but they lack a mental discipline that they need to acquire' (Le Monde, 25 June 1998). Interestingly, the accent placed on physical strength is by no means solely an element of heterotypification but one which also features in some black African self-definitions, too. Cameroon's Rigobert Song, for example, is quoted as saying, after a draw against Chile during which two players were sent off: 'Referees need to understand the African game. Us, we play hard, we fight in personal battles, it's tough, it's our temperament' (ibid.). Finally, images persist of Africa's richness in raw materials and, in one instance, the simple act of scouting for new players is portrayed via a metaphor that once again connects with wider perceptions of the continent's socio-economic past, as a source of valuable commodities for European explorers: 'Africa is an unexplored territory for big clubs' scouts. Le Roy and Mankouski [Cameroon's French coach and his assistant] thought that by going there themselves and lifting up the rocks on the river beds they might find some nuggets of gold' (Le Monde, 13 June 1998).

French images of black Africa at the World Cup in 1998 were further communicated by the former French international footballer turned television pundit, David Ginola, who noted on television that 'African players are very strong, normally' (BBC1 Austria vs Cameroon, 11 June 1998) and the theme is mirrored at some length by the English press as well. Descriptions in The Times of the Cameroon players who faced England in a pre-tournament friendly focused on their physique: they were 'powerful', 'big thighed', 'lithe of body', 'big', 'explosive' and like 'lightning', attributes that were to be contrasted with 'the know how that

England possess' (17 November 1997). Above all, the shorthand lexical item used to convey this accent on the body rather than the brain is 'athletic', an adjective that recurs very frequently in print media descriptions of black African footballers and which serves to recycle traditional notions of the congenitally athletic black male. Nigeria at France 98, for example, were said to have 'athletic power' (*The Times*, 8 June 1998) and 'loose-limbed athleticism' (*The Times*, 20 June 1998) while Cameroon were 'the athletic Africans' (*The Times*, 12 June 1998), the team of Omam Biyik, 'scorer of [an] athletic header' against Argentina that now has in its ranks Pierre Njanka who, in the game against Austria, 'galloped the length of the pitch' to provide proof 'of the Africans' extraordinary athleticism' (*The Times*, 13 June 1998). It is of note how many times media sports texts in France and England highlight and comment upon the physical prowess of black players. A clear research opportunity awaits to complete a thorough survey of the vocabulary used in the press to describe black African footballers. Such a study would complement the work of McCarthy *et al.* (1998) whose analysis of 100 hours of television coverage of football revealed that, in commentators' descriptions of black players' performances, emphasis tends to be placed upon the concept of physicality. There is definitely an impression from the press material studied here that certain items of vocabulary, such as the catchword 'athletic', are, indeed, used far more frequently to qualify black players than white. Moreover, the constant reduction of the black subject to his or her body in this way also plays an important part in the maintenance of perceived 'natural' differences between 'races' and of the social power relations between them, emphasizing as it does, the belief that blacks are closer to nature than the 'more intellectual' whites.

One of the last occasions on which black African football would have been reported in the twentieth century by the French daily press was the first ever meeting between France and Cameroon, in the Confederations Cup in Paris in 2000, a meeting that paired the reigning World and European champions with the Olympic and African champions. Whilst naturally the bulk of the match report in *Le Monde* concentrated upon the French performance, it is still noteworthy that, once again, accent is placed on the Africans' physique; it was 'thanks to their physical prowess' that Cameroon earned a 1–1 draw (6 October 2000). Indeed, apart from 'African' and 'indomitable' (as in the Indomitable Lions), the only adjectives used in the entire article to describe the Cameroon players are precisely 'physical' and 'spectacular' which, to an extent, provide a shorthand discursive summary of French perceptions of sub-Saharan football throughout the last quarter of the twentieth century.

The Maghreb seen from France

With the notable exception of Egypt, participants in the 1934 World Cup finals, North African nations' involvement with football on a global scale dates only from the latter half of the twentieth century given that, as with many black African countries, post-colonial independence arrived only after the Second World War.

The countries of the Maghreb that are of particular interest to the present study, because the colonial power there was France, affiliated to FIFA only in the early 1960s (Tunisia 1960, Morocco 1960 and Algeria 1963 [FIFA 2004]). To what extent are these former French colonies stereotyped by press coverage of football? What are the images of North Africa that are communicated by football media discourse in France?

Tunisia became a French protectorate in 1881 and, despite a degree of autonomy being granted in 1954, remained under French influence until its independence in 1956. Affiliation to FIFA followed in 1960 and qualification for the finals of the World Cup was achieved for the first time in 1978 in Argentina. As far as French press coverage of the Tunisian national football team is concerned, though, there is something of a void in this respect as scant attention has been paid to Tunisia in a football context. It was prior to the 1978 World Cup, for instance, that Tunisia and France played their first ever match against each other, in Villeneuve d'Ascq. *Le Monde*'s reporting of the 2–0 victory for the French was cursory to say the least. The win was noted as 'laboured' and attention not unnaturally paid to the fitness and performance of the French players but Tunisia rated no mention at all (21 May 1978). Similarly, despite creditable performances at the Argentina World Cup, Tunisia was, once again, passed over in the press coverage. Only the score was recorded by *Le Monde* when Tunisia beat Mexico 3–1 in their opening game while the defeat against Poland and the creditable draw against reigning champions West Germany received only a sentence each in global review articles (4 June, 8 June and 13 June 1978).

Tunisia suffers from an absence of image in France, a lack of identity that continues to obtain even by the end of the twentieth century. Tunisia's participation in the 1998 World Cup finals, for example, was given hardly any more regard than the Argentine campaign 20 years earlier. The only elements of an identity in the making derive from *Le Monde*'s qualification of the Tunisians as 'charming' in the game against Colombia (24 June 1998) and 'pleasant' in the draw against Romania (28/29 June 1998). Notions of North African footballers being attractive, skilful and æsthetically pleasing were, of course, coming to the fore at France 98 with the performances of France's own Zinedine Zidane, a French international of Algerian origins, being extolled by the media in France itself and abroad (see Crolley and Hand 2002: 65, 72–3) and it is not unreasonable to suggest, therefore, that the previously undefined Tunisians were to an extent benefiting in this respect from the Zidane effect.

Tunisia is largely bypassed by the processes of identity construction in which the French print media engage when covering football. Their fellow North Africans Morocco, however, would appear to be the focus of more activity in this respect. Like Tunisia, Morocco affiliated to FIFA in 1960 after independence was obtained in 1956 from the French protectorate established in 1912. Initially, little attention was paid to Moroccan football by the French press. The national team's games in the 1970 World Cup finals were ignored by *Le Monde*, for instance. By the 1980s, however, it would seem that elements of a Moroccan and, indeed, of a wider North African identity are already in the making. Morocco's draw with England at the 1986 World Cup finals attracted the attention of French journalists who saw the result as an indication of 'the progress of African football in general and of North African football in particular' (*Le Monde*, 4 June 1986). The Moroccans are described here as 'virtuosos rather than athletes', a fact that is linked by the newspaper under consideration with the socio-economic circumstances in which the game was developing at the time: 'African football, played on makeshift pitches and in public squares, has more in common with Brazil than with Europe, where it's taught in clubs and youth academies' (ibid.). The comparison between the North African and the traditional Brazilian style of play is one that will surface again in subsequent reports on the Maghreb (see below).

Morocco's 3–1 defeat of Portugal in the next game allowed them to progress unbeaten into the knock-out phase of the competition and the country's status as representative of an entire continent was sealed in the French print media discourse used to describe events on the pitch. Interestingly, this breakthrough in a sporting context is used to highlight wider social and political injustices in the world at large as *Le Monde* reminds its readers of Africa's isolation: 'A country is honoured, Morocco. A continent parties, Africa. A continent kept too long in the cold. . . . Football is not just football but a microcosm that perfectly reflects the state of the globe and its dynamics. Globe or ball, same shape, same conflicts' (13 June 1986). The perceived injustice of FIFA's allowing only two representatives from Africa to participate in the World Cup finals is portrayed as an extension of the world's dismissive stance towards Africa, as a symbol of the rest of the world closing its eyes to Africa and failing in its obligations to help the continent develop socially, politically and economically. Finally, Morocco's reaching the knock-out phase of a World Cup finals is portrayed metaphorically by *Le Monde* in an image that reconnects the country with its stereotypical North African desert landscape: 'A country from the African continent has at last found the unreachable oasis' (ibid.).

What the Moroccans found at that oasis was a meeting with West Germany. The game itself, a 1–0 victory for the Germans, offered an opportunity for contrasting portraits of the North African and the northern European styles of play to be elaborated in the French press, a process that is, perhaps, best summarized by the references to the Moroccans' 'virtuosity and liveliness' sitting alongside those to the Germans as 'battering rams' (*Le Monde*, 19 June 1986).

The theme of Moroccan sprightliness coupled with a lack of physical strength, established as a defining characteristic in the 1980s, was further developed during the 1998 World Cup finals held in France. The headline to one article previewing Morocco's chances is revealing in this respect: 'Morocco, lively but lacking power' (*Le Monde*, 10 June 1998). The article itself expanded on the point and, in so doing, highlighted a further distinction between North African and sub-Saharan African identities: 'The Moroccans are not noted for their athleticism, unlike other African teams such as Cameroon and Nigeria' (ibid.). The report of the opening match against Norway (which ended in a 2–2 draw) unfolded along similar lines. The Moroccans are described as 'the Brazilians of Africa', connecting with earlier print media discourse from the 1980s (see above), and are portrayed by means of a contrast in styles with their European opponents which, again, had already been previously established in the French press in its coverage of the 1986 World Cup: 'The Norwegians are known for their strength. The Moroccans were livelier but not as powerful' (*Le Monde*, 12 June 1998). The technique of conveying information about Moroccan identities by foregrounding contrasts of this nature continued to be used in subsequent reports. The 3–0 defeat of Scotland, for instance, was said to have been achieved largely because of the 'superior technique and more elaborate play of the Moroccans [overcoming] the legendary competitiveness of the Scots' (*Le Monde*, 25 June 1998). Finally, the typical and expected sprightliness of the Moroccan players is conveyed in the match report via a simile which, just like the metaphorical oasis of 1986 (see above), evokes the African landscape: 'the Chebabs, ponytails flopping in the wind, galloped around like arrogant gazelles' (ibid.).

By the end of the twentieth century, the principal characteristics of the Moroccan identity, in a football context at least, would then (unlike Tunisia) seem to have been clearly determined. When France played Morocco in a friendly in Marseille in 1999, for instance, *Le Monde* noted that this was a game pitting 'two technically gifted teams' against each other and remarked in particular on the 'strong tactical awareness' of the Moroccans which made them 'a charming North African team' to watch (22 January 1999).

Of all the countries of the Maghreb, Algeria is probably the most significant from the French perspective. Progressively occupied from the 1830s, Algeria underwent full-scale colonization from the 1870s. Fuelled by the so-called civilizing mission (*la mission civilisatrice*), France integrated its most important colony in Africa more and more into national life, with the province eventually being governed as part of France itself before an armed uprising in 1954 began a bloody war of independence that would cost many lives on all sides. It is not without relevance to the present study to note that, during the war, the revolutionary Algerian Front de libération nationale (FLN) ordered Arab sides to withdraw from the French colonial football leagues operating in Algeria and targeted several football stadia in the capital, Algiers, as part of its attacks on Europeans in the country. Assassinations of political opponents were also carried out by the FLN at high-profile football matches in mainland France itself, notably at the FA Cup final of 1957 in Paris (Dine 2002). The events of the late 1950s, then, inextricably linked football with the political tensions and conflicts that obtained between France and its colony, tensions that would resurface over 40 years later on the occasion of the first ever France–Algeria international match (see below). Independence itself was finally granted in 1962 and relations between France and Algeria since have tended to be tainted with suspicion and lingering bitterness. In particular, the presence in France since the 1960s of significant numbers of Algerian immigrants and their children, the second generation or *beurs*, has served to place on the socio-political agenda issues of immigration, integration and cultural and ethnic diversity (which came to the fore recently with the far-right Front national leader's progress into the second round of the 2002 presidential elections and the riots in the streets of Paris and other cities that took place in 2005 fuelled by social unrest among France's ethnic minorities).

In the context of football, Algeria's presence on the global stage dates to the 1982 World Cup finals, held in Spain (Algeria affiliated to FIFA in 1963, immediately after independence). Having said that, and despite the close historical links between Algeria and France, the French press largely ignored the Algerians' participation in the tournament. It was only really the remarkable 2–1 victory over the West Germans that grabbed French journalists' attention. This was a 'surprising Algerian team that combined technique and intelligence' (Le Monde, 18 June 1982) and relished its rôle as giant-killer, proving that the 'little' countries can still win in a sport increasingly dominated by the heavily financed big nations: with considerable irony but also connecting with images of Germany that were prevalent at the time (see above, Chapter 4), Le Monde describes the Germans as '11 Teutons . . . Goliaths . . . invincible giants' who were cut down by the 'North Africans' (ibid.) with goals from Lakhdar Belloumi, African player of the year of 1981, and Rabah Madjer, qualified by Dine (2002) as 'Algeria's first footballing superstar', who would go on to win the European Cup with Porto in 1987 and take over the Algerian national team in 1999.

By the time Algeria participated in the finals of the 1986 World Cup, however, elements other than admirable giant-killing had entered into the repertoire used to portray Algerian identities. On the one hand, Algeria were still being portrayed in France as something of an unknown quantity but one expected nonetheless to produce 'pretty football, full of finesse', whence the 'benevolent curiosity' awaiting their arrival (Le Monde, 5 June 1986). On the other hand, very well-known associations linking Algeria with violence and disorder were foregrounded by the match with Northern Ireland which brought together two countries whose histories had unfolded, to an extent, along parallel lines in that both had been colonized by a more powerful neighbour and both had recently experienced armed conflict involving independence movements. Did the troubled and violent recent histories of the two nations subconsciously influence the press reporting of the game itself? Certainly, the match report in Le Monde chose to focus on the conflictual aspects of the game, which was played out in 'a kind of madness' that, 'head to head, shin to shin, led to an encounter to be decided resolutely by the hard men of Belfast and Algiers . . . this was a contest for cloggers . . . a match between belligerents' (5 June 1986). Presenting this particular football match as a tough contest between 'belligerents' surely reinforces the imagery surrounding both Northern Ireland and Algeria in the wider social and political context outside football and thereby reiterates those countries' troubled natures historically.

By far the most significant press coverage in France of a match involving Algeria came in October 2001 on the occasion of the first full international meeting between Algeria and France. France was at the height of its powers, having won the World Cup, the European Championships and the Confederations Cup, and the

World Cup victory on home soil in 1998 in particular had served to forge a unity amongst French people of different generations and, most pertinently, amongst supporters from many different ethnic backgrounds. The victorious French team which, of course, included several players from France's ethnic minorities, most notably the iconic Zinedine Zidane (of Algerian descent), was portrayed as a metaphor for a supposed new racial harmony that was evolving in French society at large and the press coverage of this was euphoric and utopian, to say the least (Crolley and Hand 2002: 72–4). In this context, the French Football Association was only too keen to respond to overtures made to it by government ministers to arrange a friendly with Algeria which, it was hoped, would demonstrate even further how football in France operates as a federative force, bringing together in friendship people of different social and ethnic backgrounds. More particularly, it was expected that this historic match would symbolize the new, amicable and genuinely post-colonial relationship that France is now supposed to have with Algeria.

The full significance of the match against France's most important former colony and spiritual home to large numbers of Algerian immigrants in France itself was not lost on the French press. Le Monde, for instance, devoted no fewer than three articles over two days to a preview of the game and the special circumstances surrounding it.

The first article considered explained the origins of the match in that it arose after a visit to Algeria by the sports minister, Marie-Georges Buffet, in April 2000. The minister declared it 'an anomaly' that France had not yet played Algeria at top-flight level and set about encouraging the organization of a football match that, in her words, would act as 'a sign of renewed friendship between Algeria and France' (Le Monde, 7/8 October 2001). From the outset, then, even before a ball was kicked, the game was clearly politicized as it took on a significance that far exceeded its importance as a simple football match. The game was evidently viewed as an integral part of a wider project for France to come to a new and better post-colonial understanding with Algeria.

The two other previews in Le Monde, which both appeared on 6 October, also highlighted the political context in which the match would be played. A 'special political dimension' has been grafted onto the match, noted the first article which went on to quote Zinedine Zidane as saying: 'For the first time ever, I'll not be sad if France lose. The ideal result for me would be a draw.' The newspaper explained the comments as exemplifying the 'dual culture' foregrounded by this unique game of football, that of the beur generation, French by birth but North African by descent, and hoped that this match could be 'a festival of friendship' for all French and Algerian people, whatever their origin or status. Indeed, Zidane's coach, the national team manager Roger Lemerre, had already expressed such sentiments in the sports daily L'Equipe: 'It hardly matters whether Zidane's family is French or Algerian. He's lucky to live in France . . . but he has Algerian blood. Let him be proud of it! For him, this will be a match between friends, not one nation against another nation but brothers against brothers' (4 October 2001). The complexity of the issues raised by players such as Zidane, though, French by birth but of immigrant origins, leads to a wide diversity of opinion being expressed in print media discourse. For *Le Figaro*, for instance, the issue ought to be more clear cut: 'Yes, it would be preferable if Zinedine Zidane, who does not hide his fondness for his Algerian roots, stated clearly, that he is French and only French' (13/14 October 2001).

The wider, international context of the match served to complicate matters further as it became linked with the atmosphere of tension around the world following the terrorist attacks on the United States of 11 September and the American preparations for retaliatory action in Afghanistan. 'This friendly, already loaded with symbolism, has taken on a new dimension after the 9/11 attacks,' noted *Le Monde*, which went on to notify its readers that the game was now the object of special security measures that had been put in place, partially in response to threats that had been sent to the authorities (and subsequently leaked to the press). The other preview article appearing on the same day concentrated on the Algerian perspective on the game. The president of the Algerian Community Organization in Paris, Mohand Abdelkader Madi, explained that this was a 'huge event, a massive symbol for the two and a half million French-Algerians as well as for the Algerian people as a whole' and, with one eye on the poor image of Algerians circulating in France, stated that 'this will be a great festival . . . we're going to prove that Algerians aren't terrorists or vandals either'.

Regrettably, the fears surrounding the match which had been the focus of much of the previews' discourse were, to an extent, realized when the game itself was marred by crowd disorder. Before the kick-off, the French national anthem was whistled at by large parts of the Stade de France crowd, which seemed in the majority to be made up of Algerian supporters, and during the game, French players were systematically booed in their own national stadium, the scene, three years earlier, of their greatest ever triumph. Then, in the seventy-sixth minute of the match, with France leading 4–1, dozens of spectators from the Algerian sections of the ground started to pour onto the pitch. Although the pitch invasion did not appear to be either violent or coordinated, it was sufficiently extensive and disorderly for the referee to abandon the game (the first time a match involving France had ever been curtailed in this way) and, ultimately, 17 arrests were made for law and order offences.

As might have been expected, press coverage of these events was extensive. *Le Figaro* labelled the match a 'hysterical première' (7 October) and claimed it demonstrated that the burden of the troubled history of colonialism would still not allow 'normal' sporting relations to be established between France and Algeria. However, the events also coincided with the American air strikes on Afghanistan, the first action in the so-called war on terror and were, therefore, probably dislodged from what would otherwise have been a front page position. *Le Monde*, for example, devoted its first 19 pages to the situation in Afghanistan and referred to the France–Algeria football match on its front page only via a headline directing readers deep inside the paper, 'France–Algeria ends in disappointment' (9 October

2001). Once inside, though, readers interested in the events surrounding the football match were greeted by no fewer than four articles of commentary and interpretation, all of which shared a common theme.

The first article concentrated primarily on the disorder itself and demanded to know why the authorities, the police and the stewards had been so singularly powerless to prevent it even though they apparently knew in advance that the match was likely to be disrupted not by terrorists but by 'French youths of Algerian origin, youths from the inner cities, intent on disrupting the evening's entertainment' (ibid.). The article notes that this is the first time a match involving France has been abandoned and, on 'an evening that should have been historic . . . football ceased to be a festival' (ibid.).

The second article picked up this theme by providing an interview with the president of the French Football Association, Claude Simonet. Not unnaturally, Simonet's overriding emotion is described as one of 'disappointment' but the full impact of the events on the rôle of football in France is also recognized: 'My sadness is all the greater because this match could have shown, in difficult times, that football can bring people together' (ibid.).

The thrust of the third article on the events is similar. French player Marcel Desailly is quoted as saying, 'the party has been spoiled' and the Algerian ambassador to France, Mohammed Ghouli, remarked that the game 'was a victim of its own high passions'. The journalist agrees, noting the 'amazement and consternation' provoked by the game which had been signalled as one of 'reconciliation' but which was 'robbed of its dignity in the end by the wreckers' (ibid.).

Finally, the last article interviews two Algerian supporters for their perspective on the events. The first notes: 'It's a problem to do with our towns and cities. It's nothing to do with the attacks on America. It's nothing to do with Islam. Something happened tonight. Something real. It happened. Now we need to look to understand why.' The second supporter attempts to provide part of the answer: 'there are young people living in France who are adrift, who have been stuck between two stools for too long' (ibid.). Clearly what is being voiced in the press coverage here is the sense of disaffection felt by many *beurs* and the difficulties they face in establishing an identity and obtaining a full place in French society. On this occasion, that disaffection surfaced as crowd disorder at a football match. What is highly significant in this context, though, is the way in which the events of the France–Algeria friendly of 2001 are portrayed in the press as the direct antithesis of the events surrounding France's World Cup victory on home soil in 1998. The utopianism of the media coverage of 1998 has gone, to be replaced with a stark realization that the social and political problems surrounding immigration and the ethnic minorities are still as pressing as ever. The events surrounding one football match provided further opportunities in press discourse to portray once more 'the symbolic chasm existing between France and Algeria' (Gastaut 2005). It is, indeed, highly appropriate that, just as it was in the football context that the idealism of 1998 was first expressed, so too is it following a football match that a dose of realism enters French print media discourse on the subject or, as Dine notes (2002: 503), 'it was precisely . . . on the football field that [the] structurally flawed social analyses [of 1998] would be tested to destruction'.

In summary, a colonial shadow appears to loom over French sports media discourse on Africa in the second half of the twentieth century and beyond. Perceptions of both North and sub-Saharan African football nations are coloured by antiquated and often unacceptable yet lingering attitudes from the French colonial era that regarded Africa as the dark, unfathomable, indisciplined and dangerous continent that it was Europeans' duty to 'civilize' and privilege to exploit.

Chapter 10

Only in America

Representations of the USA national team

The United States Football Association (USFA, now US Soccer Federation) was founded in 1913 and the Americans affiliated to FIFA the following year. The history of international competition involving the USA, then, spans most of the twentieth century and, indeed, the American national team has a creditable record in the final stages of the World Cup. The USA participated in the inaugural competition in 1930, fielding a team of students that reached the semi-finals, and has been present at the final stages on six other occasions up to and including 2002, when they reached the quarter finals. By the dawn of the twenty-first century, the USA men's team had broken into the top 10 of the FIFA rankings and, therefore, constituted a force to be reckoned with, even if, somewhat paradoxically, for many Europeans there remains something incongruous about the sight of an American playing soccer, especially given the game's extensively documented subservience to gridiron (American football), baseball and basketball in American sport as a whole (see, for instance, Markovits and Hellerman 2001). It is the aim of this chapter to examine the portrayal of the USA in a sample of the European press with a view to understanding the mechanisms at work in depictions of Americans competing in the international football arena. To what extent are readily recognizable American stereotypes communicated by the sports pages of European daily newspapers throughout the twentieth century?

England on the USA

In the English print media it is unsurprising, given the paucity of writing on association football in the first half of the twentieth century, that there was little detailed coverage of football in the USA until football writing expanded in the final quarter of the century. In fact, early coverage is limited to Anglo-American connections within the football world. One article, for example, details (rather pompously for today's reader) how the USFA suspended players for 'unlawfully developing unsanctioned Association football, and attempting to suborn and intimidate affiliated clubs and players with the object and purpose of aiding and abetting them in such unlawful activities. The Football Association of England has been informed' (*The Times*, 22 November 1928). This article, though brief, tells us something about power within world football. Despite the establishment of the world governing body, FIFA, in 1904, the (English) FA still controls the global game, and 'unlawful' pursuit of the sport, wherever it might be in the world, should be reported to the English FA. The links between the USFA and England were close at that time: the first president, and co-founder, of the USFA was Dr G. Randolph, an Englishman (*The Times*, 2 December 1928).

In the 1920s, the only other references to football in the USA came in the form of brief reports of English football clubs, notably Preston North End, and their plans to tour the USA and Canada. These trips were sponsored by the US Football Association in an attempt to popularize the sport and improve the standard of play there (see, for example, *The Times*, 25 January 1929).

What does evolve in *The Times* as the football writing becomes more expansive in the 1960s and beyond is the perception of an American identity mediated via the sports pages. This is consistent, to some extent, with the one that emerges through other pages of the newspaper. Several themes reinforce an American identity via the sports pages: the hypothesis that American identity is strongly defined by sport; the belief that Americans are intensely patriotic; the idea that America is the land of the media-driven and money-obsessed entrepreneur; the assumption that Americans are driven by success; America's difficulties in becoming established in football's international arena are also prominent. Finally, commentary on the American style of play is less revealing but identifies some fairly consistent features. Let us examine these themes in turn.

First, football writing in our sample in *The Times* indicates that American identity is strongly defined by sporting factors. This is seen via the constant references to *American* sports in articles on football. Typical is the article in 1966 which covers the plans of the North American Soccer League to develop football in the USA and launch their own league when 'the north American continent with its baseball and own brand of American football, has no tradition for the Association code. This is the largest field of resistance that must be broken down' (1 November 1966). Football is not perceived as an American sport: 'Kids play football at school because it is a fun team sport for those of all abilities, but they follow baseball and gridiron because, to them, those sports have the emotional, historical and patriotic appeal football lacks' (12 January 2002). In the USA, football lacks these qualities, precisely those ingredients which give the sport strength in so many other nations across the world. Furthermore, 'There are plenty of "nay-sayers" who dismiss the chances of football ever diverting the Americans from the long list of sports at which their players excel: baseball, basketball, American football, ice hockey, tennis, golf, snowboarding, etc.' (18 June 2002). Football's competition is strong.

Added to this, the heightened sense of American patriotism which underpins many articles is an obstacle to football's increasing popularity in the USA. Whereas Americans are seen as intensely patriotic, they generally save their patriotism for other sports; Americans playing football 'in a strange soil' is somehow incongruous (*The Times*, 4 November 1968). There has been no close identification between the American people and its national team in a way that would be familiar to nationals of many other parts of the football world. Football, then, is excluded from the defining features of American identity. Indeed, not only is football un-American, it actually represents European and Latin American identities and, as such, is closely associated with the American immigrant population. Part of the reason for this distancing of football by the American public is suggested by a journalist in the *New York Times* (and quoted in *El País*, 25 June 2002): 'Football is perceived in the USA as a foreign sport, played by men who speak little English.' This reflects the fact that where (men's) football is most popular in the USA is among the immigrant (especially Hispanic) population. One commentator for the *Globe* claimed that, 'just like rock sounds better in English, football is better in Spanish or Italian' (quoted in *El País*, 25 June 2002). Indeed, Claudio Reyna, the USA's captain at the World Cup in 2002 and now of Manchester City, acknowledged that when the Americans played Mexico (the USA's greatest rival in football terms) in South Korea, it would be the first time, home or away, they would play Mexico without an openly hostile crowd' (*El País*, 17 June 2002), so accustomed was he to playing in front of Mexican partisans even within the USA. The *New York Times* headlined one eve-of-match story: 'Americans hope to show Hispanics that they can play,' further proof of the strong associations (and rivalry) with the immigrant population (quoted in *The Times*, 4 June 2002).

Another article articulates a similar understanding of the immigrant association with football in the USA: 'Anyone cheering for the US at an all-night bar is likely to be outnumbered by hyphenated Americans – particularly the numerous Mexican-Americans and Irish-Americans – traitorously supporting the "old country" over their adopted home' (*The Times*, 7 June 2002). When it comes to football, the ingredients of the great American 'melting pot' do not appear to have combined.

It is clear that the sport still suffers an image problem in the USA, which the English press covers with curiosity: 'A lot of Americans claim to like soccer just to be different, to appear hip and vaguely European. These are the same people who drink Orangina and snack on Toblerone bars' (*The Times*, 18 June 2002). Little wonder that football is finding it hard to penetrate deeply into mainstream 'middle America'. Football for many Americans, then, apparently contradicts the essence of 'Americanness' and, as such, it is unlikely to achieve status as a symbol of America, as a national sport.

The commercialized style of American society is another constant theme within football writing in the English print media. More specifically, some commentators found incongruous the application of this commercialism to sport and references to 'the materialistic and sometimes manic world of American sport' (*The Times*, 13 July 1984) are not unusual. America is the land of the entrepreneur and capitalist: 'The Greeks and the Romans may have competed for the feel of the wind in their face and all that, but this is modern-sport America and pure capitalism, not emperors, reigns' (*The Times*, 10 April 1985).

Associated with this capitalist society, several articles discussing the obstacles that stand in the way of the expansion of football in the USA allude to the entrepreneurial shrewdness of the Americans: 'With typical American "know how" in sales promotions they believe it can be done by means of television and the rest' (*The Times*, 1 November 1966). They recognize the importance of 'selling football to ethnic groups in America, drawn from nations already with a soccer background' (ibid.). Part of the promotion of football in the USA involved sponsoring English teams to tour (*The Times*, 8 November 1966) or appointing high-profile European coaches or players (e.g. *The Times*, 15 November 1966). Football writing on no other country in our sample focuses on the cost-effectiveness of football promotions, or whether or not football makes money.

The illustrious football reporter and writer, Geoffrey Green, one of the pioneering journalists to specialize in writing about sport in its broader context and who frequently offered thoughtful analyses of the state of the game in the 1950s and 1960s, commented upon the shape of football in the USA at the end of the 1960s. He identified several of the points referred to above. While North America was still 'virtually untapped', he claimed that 'professional football is on the way.' Green refers to the fierce competition of other American sports (namely baseball, basketball and American 'grid' football) and to the 'scramble to gain the loyalty and the cash of a nation' (*The Times*, 25 February 1967). Green, however, recognizes that football has been played 'in a semi-professional way since 1913', especially by ethnic minority groups. Again, football is portrayed as yet another product for sale in the American market. The ways in which promoters of the sport can persuade Americans to follow football are outlined in detail and include promotional fixes such as sponsoring famous European teams to tour the USA, grassroots development, media coverage, involvement of wealthy sponsors and huge merchandising efforts. At that time, talk of sponsorship, promotions, sales, products and marketing mixed with reference to football seemed inappropriate and more than a mild tone of cynicism could be detected: 'They [the Americans] may dabble in the world supermarket of football. But tradition cannot really be bought overnight' (ibid.). When we read articles which focus on the background of football in America (and there are many around the time of the 1994 World Cup hosted by the USA and during each subsequent World Cup final tournament), there are constant references to the 'football market' and football as a 'product' (e.g. *The Times*, 4 June 2002). This serves indirectly to reinforce the notion of football as a commercial enterprise in the mind of the reader, which makes football in the USA different from the notions of football associated with other nations.

Linked to the above is the emphasis on the media-driven nature of American society. The power of the media in shaping football is highlighted: 'This is America, the land of the sportcast, where so many super stations, cable channels and national networks compete to televize sport. . . . This is the country where a made-for-TV special like the United States Football League is drummed into being to fill a vacant slot in the Sunday afternoon screen' (*The Times*, 10 April 1985). Frequent mention in the English press of the priority of other sports over football, when it comes to broadcasting in prime time television slots and on main channels, serves to reinforce the idea that football's success is defined by viewing figures and programming schedules.

One further element of the American identity recognized in our sample is the view that Americans accept only winners. *The Times* suggests that, instead of going to all the efforts outlined above to promote football in the USA, 'Perhaps it might have more effect to tell the Americans that the United States once beat England in the World Cup. That might encourage them' (25 February 1967). This notion that Americans want to be associated only with success is echoed elsewhere and even coach Bruce Arena is quoted as saying: 'I would think a majority of people in the United States probably think we failed at the last World Cup because we're all about winning. . . . That's all they understand, that's the way it is in our country. We win in all the other sports. We are the world champions at American football because nobody else plays it and our NBA champions are the world champions at basketball. That's the way it is in the United States, you have to be a world champion' (*The Times*, 11 November 2005). Joel Stein backed this view, though tongue in cheek, in a satirical article for *Time* and said, 'We'll watch the World Cup when we win the thing, and not a second before' (quoted in *The Times*, 9 June 2002). So, it is not just the coverage of football or the way in which the Americans play that matter, but success or progress: 'Whether this tournament will prove a watershed for the American public, only time, *and the team's progress*, will tell' (*The Times*, 4 June 2002, our italics).

Finally, we noted an element of reluctance on the part of the English press to accept the USA as a credible force within football. On the eve of the 2002 World Cup, the Americans were very much portrayed as underdogs, 'with the United States unlikely to threaten' (*The Times*, 4 June 2002). Similarly, when they qualified for the 2006 World Cup finals in Germany, 'The US are supposedly the seventh-best team in the world, yet few would expect them to fare better next summer than Spain, Portugal, England and Italy, all of whom are inferior in Fifa's eyes' (*The Times*, 10 October 2005).

On the other hand, the progress of the USA football team has not gone entirely unnoticed in the English press and the team is beginning to shed its image as a bunch of naïve college graduates: 'The Americans have come a long way since 1950 when they were turning England over at the World Cup finals; these days, they are a genuine international power . . . no one really laughs at the United States now when it comes to football. . . . World order, natural order. Call it what you want, it has changed' (*The Times*, 14 November 2005). Their position in the top 10 in the FIFA rankings means that, according to some, the American national team were unlucky not to be seeded for the 2006 World Cup finals. The USA is not a football virgin any longer: 'Preaching to the converted may be overstating it slightly . . . but these days, Americans are not as ignorant of football as we like to think' (*The Times*, 9 June 2003). The current position of football in the USA is summarized thus, in an article worth quoting extensively, which covers several of the themes already delineated above:

The popular perception of the sport in the US remains that engendered by the ill-fated North American Soccer League (NASL) – of ageing mercenaries, half empty stadiums and the exaggerated hollering that would greet a long throw-in. The NASL collapsed in 1985, ten years after Pélé joined the New York Cosmos, but football is now enjoying a far deeper-rooted renaissance on the back of the success of the United States in last year's World Cup. Football in the US might never infiltrate the mainstream, which is dominated by baseball, basketball and American football, but it is establishing more than a mere cult following.

(ibid.)

As far as the style of play is concerned, there is undeniably more coverage in the English print media of the state of football in the USA in the early years than there is detail of the standard or style of play. What snippets there are prove unrevealing and do not form any pattern or appear to reinforce any national stereotype.

England's famous defeat by the US in the 1950 World Cup finals in Brazil came as a huge shock to the English nation (and indeed further afield too, as we see below). However, coverage of this event focused largely (and understandably) on the poor performance of the English and tells us little about the American style of play. Apparently, 'the close marking of the United States' seemed to upset England, who were surprised by the 'stubbornness' of the American defence (*The Times*, 30 June 1950).

The perceived lack of American roots in the global game means that there is (as yet?) no closely defined style of American football emerging. In short, there is no option for lazy football writers to resort to stereotypes. The early 'stubbornness' and 'close marking' mentioned in the 1950s are still features in the later reports (they are 'plucky' in 2002 [*The Times*, 7 June]). The American footballers 'lacked flair' when they were eliminated from the 2002 World Cup, and it was remarked that 'they do not play with enough style for their departure to be regretted and the side is hardly noble' (*The Times*, 22 June 2002). After beating (in football terms) closest rivals Mexico, one American player was quoted in *The Times* as saying that 'We are not always dominant in terms of possession or stylish play, but we are hard to beat' (*The Times*, 18 June 2002).

On the other hand, it is worth noting that 'they used their swiftness . . . were not lacking in enterprise and they . . . supplied as much entertainment as they could' (ibid.). We are no further enlightened three years later, however, when, 'there could be no doubt about the competitive nature of the football. The United States pressed like AC Milan in their heyday, under Arrigo Sacchi. . . . They kicked and held shirts as any European side, and dived with the subtlety of an Austrian or an Argentinian, while in Santino Quaranta, the substitute, they had a man with a Glaswegian hair-trigger temperament to rival James McFadden' (*The Times*, 14 November 2005). Here the writer desperately thrashes through a tangle of stereotypes in an effort to try to define the USA's style with reference to images that would be familiar to the readership.

So, the American style of play is overall difficult to define. There is a distinct lack of exclusive characteristics. As the Americans are portrayed as demonstrating some level of skill, defensive strengths, and, in short, qualities typical of both European and South American football, perhaps, after all, the American style of football does reflect the melting pot its society is supposed to represent.

The USA in France

With regard to French coverage of the Americans, the principal problem faced by any researcher in this domain is the relative paucity of material from the first half of the twentieth century. The Americans' matches in the inaugural World Cup of 1930, for instance, were covered but only in very perfunctory fashion. The opening victory over Belgium received no more than two sentences in *Le Temps* noting the result (3–0) and the crowd's discontent with the match officials (15/16 July 1930). Similarly, the defeat of Paraguay was noted without any further elaboration by the same paper (19 July 1930) and the semi-final was baldly reported as follows: 'In Montevideo, in the World Cup semi-final, Argentina yesterday beat the USA by 6–1' (28 July 1930). America's brief involvement with the World Cup finals in 1934 also received scant coverage from *Le Temps* ('Italy beat the USA 7–1' constituted the entirety of one match report [28 May 1934]).

To an extent, of course, the lack of coverage noted above merely reflects the way in which the World Cup as a whole was reported by the French press in its early years. Even by 1950, which saw the first post-war tournament, coverage had expanded only slightly. *Le Monde* provided a preview of the finals that filled no more than about 30 lines of copy explaining the format of the tournament and noting that the South American teams would be favourites (24 June 1950) and its reports of the games themselves were synopses of several matches on a round-by-round basis rather than dedicated coverage of any particular match itself. Within this context of limited coverage, it is hardly surprising that any given team, such as the USA, features so little. Even the Americans beating England (1–0) merited little by way of coverage. The result was, though, described as 'a sensational event' and 'a record-breaking surprise' by *Le Monde* (1 July 1950), which might be felt to provide an early indication of the way in which successive American teams would be portrayed in the rest of the twentieth century, and beyond, as a surprise package not expected to do well in major tournaments.

The United States failed to qualify for another World Cup until 1990 and it was only in 1979 that France played its first competitive games against the Americans. In these circumstances, then, American exposure in the French football press continued to remain very limited indeed. The 1979 encounters, however, are noteworthy for aspects of the portrayal of the USA in a football context, many of which reflect preoccupations already evident in the English press as described above. The first ever meeting of France and America took place in East Rutherford, New Jersey, on 2 May 1979 on the artificial turf of the Giants Stadium with some 20,000 spectators in attendance (Cazal *et al.* 1998: 257). Much can be gleaned about French expectations of America from the way in which the game, a 6–0 victory for France, was reported. *Le Monde*, for instance, registered surprise that there was 'no band nor any cheerleaders present to mark the game's high points' (4 May 1979). America is felt to be a land of show business and, when none is forthcoming, disappointment is duly registered. The journalist did, however, delight in covering the antics of the electronic scoreboard which played cavalry-like trumpet music and flashed up messages during the game such as 'Charge', 'Help' and 'Super Save', interventions that quite simply 'flabbergasted the French supporters' present, presumably because of their overtly brash American nature (ibid.). Indeed, so fascinating was this aspect of the match that coverage of it was greater than that of the actual events on the pitch itself. The final two paragraphs of the report covered the growth of football in the USA in general and painted a largely favourable portrait. With over 2 million players, a quarter of whom were under 18, the sport was 'making giant strides' (ibid.) in the USA and attracting increasing media and commercial interest.

The return friendly between France and the USA took place in Paris on 10 October 1979 and the French victory by 3–0 was duly reported by *Le Monde*. The article was somewhat scathing about the American performance, noting that this was 'an inexperienced team . . . technically lacking and in poor condition physically . . . that was never very dangerous' (12 October 1979). In condescending tones, the report even went on to suggest that the Americans are not worthy opponents for top European sides: 'Was it really necessary . . . to arrange a friendly with a side of such low importance as the United States?' (ibid.). Even by the latter part of the century, then, there was still the belief that there was something incongruous about the USA attempting to compete with European teams in the football arena and these notions were carried forward into the press coverage of America at the 1990 World Cup finals in Italy.

By the 1990s, the World Cup was receiving more extensive coverage in the French press than ever before and the Americans (among many others, of course) benefited from this increase in interest. Their match against hosts Italy in the 1990 finals, for example, was reported by a *Le Monde* article of over 200 lines, occupying three columns of space. The headline and sub-headline, however, firmly established the direction in which the report would go: 'American Tourists Out Of Place'; 'In the land of baseball, football has few disciples' (16 June 1990). The body of the article contains two views on American football that are hardly flattering. ABC correspondent Wolfgang Atchner describes America's participation in the finals as an 'anomaly' and the team as 'a group of tourists who should never have landed in Italy' while Giorgio Chinaglia of the *Gazetta dello Sport* speaks of the 'stupidity' of awarding the 1994 finals to the USA and of the fact that football 'is not part of American culture. . . . Throw a ball at a young European and, instinctively, he'll try to control it with his chest, head or foot. An American kid will catch it in both hands and set off on a basketball-like dribble' (ibid.). In other words, *Le Monde* has called up two overtly negative views of American football as a prelude to its own exploration of the game in the USA that firmly establishes in the discourse of the sports media the notion that football is simply not an American game and, therefore, the USA remains outside the mainstream of football in the international arena. The French paper continues with an explanation that American television networks favour gridiron, baseball and basketball, which, in turn, leads to a lack of sponsorship for football. The game is consequently underdeveloped and American internationals' burning desire is to come to Europe 'to peddle their mediocre talents to second and third division clubs' (ibid.). So, of the 14 paragraphs of the report, only four deal with events on the pitch (a 1–0 win for the Italians). The rest reconstruct the apparent weaknesses of American football and recycle the commonly held viewpoint that football is alien to the Americans. Rather than offer an encouraging and supportive appreciation of the potential of football in the USA (as the same newspaper had done in 1979), Le Monde in 1990 would seem to be somewhat patronizing and scathing in its coverage of the American team.

The staging of the 1994 World Cup finals in America itself, of course, presented the French press with many opportunities to develop further its appreciation of football in the USA. By and large, the coverage centred on two main issues: the place of football in American society and the stereotypical portrayal of Americans playing (and watching) football.

Initially, Le Monde continued with the now well established theme of America's indifference to football. 'Football is marginal in the United States', it claimed (17 June 1994), owing to the 'apathy of the general public' and 'the indifference of the media' (ibid.). Some 62 per cent of Americans know nothing about the World Cup at all, even though it is in their own country; despite there being some 16 million players, the game is largely relegated to the domain of children and is popular with adults really only in immigrant communities. The explanation given as to why football has not taken off in the USA depends largely upon an appreciation of what are felt to be typical traits of the American psyche. This is apparently a country that 'admits only winners' and is greeting the World Cup 'without any great enthusiasm' (ibid.). It is, therefore, difficult for football to gain a foothold in such inhospitable terrain. As the 1994 World Cup progressed, though, the American team's good performances became responsible for raising home fans' interest in the game. The victory over Colombia, for instance, according to Le Monde, 'provided the country with the success it needed for it finally to deign to take any interest in this sport' (24 June 1994). The team left the field 'carried by that patriotic fervour that Americans save for champions worthy of their affection' (ibid.), highlighting another aspect of American culture perceived as noteworthy by Europeans: its overt, combative patriotism, especially as displayed in a sporting contest. Once the American team had proved itself capable of competing on an equal footing with others in the tournament, the French press was able to re-present football in the USA as a commodity that was becoming more and more accepted. 'The USA team has navigated the ocean of puzzlement that surrounded it'; football has 'ventured into the cave of the sleeping giant that is the American public' and 'overcome its indifference' (Le Monde, 3/4 July 1994). A certain patronizing attitude towards the

Americans remained, though, in some of the reporting: 'The Americans may well still not fully understand football. It will be some time before they get to grips with the offside law' (*Le Monde*, 23 June 1994); they 'probably found it difficult to grasp the subtleties of the game's tactics' (6 July 1994). Still the image is presented of a game, football, that is essentially alien to American society.

Within this context, it is interesting to note the imagery employed by French journalists to report on the World Cup as a whole. 1994 is described as the 'World Cup of pioneers' and the teams participating are seen as 'missionaries' venturing into football's 'new frontier' (*Le Monde*, 17 June 1994). Similarly, when the Americans beat Colombia, the team was described as 'pioneers . . . conquering a land of indifference' (24 June 1994). The vocabulary would appear to be both inspired by and relating to wider events in American history in that it invokes the rôle of the European settlers who conquered the country and blazed a pioneering trail across it from sea to shining sea. Familiar themes in American history are, therefore, employed discursively to convey the impact of FIFA's decision to bring football's premier tournament to the New World. Additionally, portrayals of Americans playing and watching football might also be felt to connect with wider perceptions of American society. The players are described, for instance, as 'enthusiastic but naïve' (*Le Monde*, 18 June 1994) and the fans as fervent to the point of unseemliness: 'they detest not seeing their own come out on top' (28 June 1994). There is much in the way that Americans 'do' football that seems bizarre to European eyes, which is presumably why one French journalist could not resist commenting on the way the American fans prepared for their team's match against Brazil: 'They have prepared in their own special way. They have unfurled their star-spangled banners, got out their rockets and fireworks and stocked up their picnic baskets. . . . America has got dolled up like a schoolgirl at her first prom' (*Le Monde*, 6 July 1994). As the USA lost the match and were eliminated from the tournament, the cliché to use was obvious but, once again, typical of late twentieth-century media discourse's connecting with issues beyond sport itself: 'The American dream is over' (ibid.).

The USA in Spain

Though, as we have already mentioned, the USA enjoyed some early success on the international football scene, there is little coverage in the Spanish press. This is not surprising for two reasons: first, international football did not enjoy great coverage, or indeed prestige, in Spain at the time of the USA's emergence on the international football scene. The first World Cup finals (1930 and 1934) took place during a time of political turmoil in Spain and there was little coverage of the event at all in our sample. Second, the USA featured only once in the World Cup finals between 1934 and 1990, namely in 1950. We have, therefore, little data to work with. What we have is of interest, though, given that it tells us about the characterization of the (North) Americans as seen through Spanish eyes.

We are told that the USA team was 'one of the weakest, most improvised teams in Rio: a team that modestly turned up to learn' (*ABC*, 1 July 1950). However, despite a hint at the political situation (the newspaper debated the ostracism of Spain by the USA [*ABC*, 4 July 1950]), there is little evidence of the construction or reflection of national identity via Spanish football writing at this time.

There are, however, hints which suggest an emerging world order in football. In particular, the USA's victory over England was 'absurd given the huge difference in class between the football nations . . . England have proven many times their position as masters of football . . . the *Yanks* have ridiculed England, a team worth an estimated half a million pounds' (*ABC*, 1 July 1950). At a time when 'to beat England is the greatest glory American football can achieve', the report claimed that 'all roads are now open' for football in the USA and that 'the future looks good for American football' (ibid.). With hindsight, these optimistic statements might appear rash given that the USA failed to reach the World Cup finals for another 40 years.

By the 1980s, a number of themes are beginning to emerge within Spanish football writing on football in the USA: the obstacles football has to face in order to develop there; the concept that American identity is not allied in any way to football; that football is media-driven in a capitalist society; and the importance of success to the American psyche. Some of these themes are clearly shared with sports writers in England and France.

When the USA returned to the final stages of World Cup football in 1990, the tone of football writing is less positive than it was in 1950 when the future of football looked rosy and, indeed, a feature of the Spanish writing is this theme of lack of interest or poor development of football in the USA. *El País* acknowledged in 1980, for instance, that 'It will be a long time before the US will dominate the football world' (18 November 1980), despite a Kissinger-inspired boom for 'soccer' in America, and the USA 'will export their majorettes to Europe' (ibid.). In the run-up to hosting the 1994 World Cup numerous articles covered this supposed lack of interest in football (e.g. 'Football without a crowd' [*El País*, 26 December 1993]). While this theme is shared by football writing in England (as we have seen above), in the Spanish case, there are few of the counter-balancing arguments that were found in the English data to suggest that progress is being made in this period. Deeply engrained in the western European notion of 'American-ness' is the identification of the people with their own national sports: so many Spanish articles on the USA football team mention baseball, American football or basketball. 'American' sports, not football, are perceived as being an integral part of American identity.

The only evidence which suggests a more encouraging development of football in the USA comes not from coverage of the national football team but from coverage of pre-season tournaments played by Spanish teams in the USA. Real Madrid, for instance, crossed the Atlantic in the summer of 2005 'to bring passion to Los Angeles' (*El País*, 18 July 2005). According to reports in the Spanish press, Spain was surprised that Real Madrid enjoyed such passionate support since they had believed the Americans to be indifferent to football. It attributes this level of attention to the high-profile nature of the '*galácticos*' that would 'naturally' attract American interest. Little is said of the quality or style of football, except to reinforce the image of a naïve football nation: the Los Angeles Galaxy team was 'innocent' and their football was 'enthusiastic' (*El País*, 18 July 2005) – lexical items typically associated with football played by the 'emerging nations'.

The second theme to permeate Spanish football writing parallels closely that of the English press. Though there were very few articles that focused on football in the USA prior to the 1990s, those there were expressed surprise at the way in which football success in the USA was measured by marketing experts. Reports bubbled with rumours that Americans were about to reinvent the game to suit their market: 'There exists the possibility that next year in the US they will play with enlarged goals to make the sport more exciting and to give it a *more American feel*' (*El País*, 19 July 1993).

Third, following the USA's elimination from the 1994 World Cup, the eminent journalist, Verdú, recognizes how important it is to the Americans to win: 'the triumph of the home team would have meant progress for the interest in football in the US. Defeat has accentuated pre-existing hostilities' (*El País*, 6 July 1994) and then 'America buries football after the World Cup' (*El País*, 28 October 1994). The Spanish press, in accord with the English, perceived lack of success by the American public to mean that football was relegated once more in the USA to its position as a minority sport.

So, the importance of winning is essential to the status and popularity of football within the USA; we are told that 'The US victory has awoken a new interest . . . . This will attract the attention of many Americans' (*El País*, 6 June 2002). As the national team begins to win, the American media take an interest: '90 per cent of the population does not understand the rules, but patriotism is important to them. As are the superstars' (*El País*, 25 June 2002). Thus, we are told how the Americans value winning, are intensely patriotic, and the importance of the media in the positioning of the sport in American society cannot be understated. One journalist even introduces a religious perspective to the American character as an explanation for the importance of winning in their culture: 'Winning and losing is of great significance to the Americans, where in its Calvinist atmosphere success and defeat are directly related to God's esteem' (*El País*, 6 July 1994).

Reinforcing the power of the media in the USA, the popularity of football is frequently measured by viewing figures and by the yardstick of their other sports. A slight increase in television viewing figures, or the consideration of football in programming, is seen as a success story for football in the USA: 'The news is the increase in news. Last Monday the TV station ESPN preferred to transmit an ice hockey match instead of the Holland–Saudi Arabia match. Now it wouldn't dare. US interest in football has rocketed since the victory of its team against Colombia' (*El País*, 25 June 2002). This same article contrasts perceptively the differences in reporting styles of the American media and the European media, suggesting that the US media prefer to tell the personal stories of their stars rather than talk about collective performances. Perhaps this is a reflection on the American values which rate individualism highly in surveys on cross-cultural comparisons.

In terms of national characteristics that emerge in the Spanish reports on the American team, apart from those traits identified above (rather fickle, individualistic), it has been noted that there are several references to the 'arrogance', 'strong opinions' and yet 'naïvety' of some players who 'knew nothing about football' or were 'naïve when it came to football' (e.g. *El País*, 21 June 2002). This same article contrasts the styles of preparation of the American and the Italian teams during the 2002 World Cup finals (the latter, no doubt, representing a European stereotype). The Americans were based in the city centre, were 'laid back, and went shopping freely with their families, whilst the Italians camped out in isolation in order to focus their concentration.' The readers are left to interpret this according to their own thinking but perhaps the Americans do not take football seriously (enough?).

Spanish football writing on America, in fact, rarely goes beyond the stereotypes created in the discourse that we have outlined above. As with the English case, there is no defined style of play. Certain characteristics are sometimes attributed to the American players, though this is a relatively recent phenomenon, and is rare in our Spanish data. In 2002, it was reported that the American captain, Claudio Reyna, 'typifies the personality of the patriotic American stereotype . . . attitude, strength, determination, versatility' (*El País*, 22 June 2002), though this typecasting applies more to the imagined American national identity than to a specific football-related characteristic. Thus, as befits the inhabitants of the home of the brave, the American footballer is, first and foremost, all-American.

Chapter 11

Marshalling art
The portrayal of North East Asian football

Football in the Far East is dominated by two countries in particular, Japan and South Korea, who, of course, joined forces to host the 2002 World Cup finals (the first to be held in Asia and the first to be co-hosted). Football was introduced to the region by British merchants, traders and sailors in the 1870s and 1880s but, for different reasons, the subsequent history of the game at national level is somewhat chequered in both cases (see Horne and Manzenreiter 2002).

The Korean Football Association was established in 1928 but the country itself was under Japanese rule until independence after the Second World War. South Korea, more properly known as the Republic of Korea, then affiliated to FIFA in 1948 and has competed in seven World Cups, including all five since 1986, making its players 'the undisputed kings of Asian football' (Korea Football Association 2004). North Korea, however (or the Democratic People's Republic of Korea), despite affiliating to FIFA in 1958, has had only a brief flirtation with international football on the notable occasion of the World Cup finals of 1966 in England.

Japan's first international was the friendly against the Philippines in 1917 and affiliation to FIFA followed in 1929, eight years after the domestic championship was inaugurated. The Japanese were, however, excluded from the global game by its governing body owing to their participation in the Second World War and were not readmitted until 1950. Faced with the popularity of martial arts and another foreign import, baseball, football's rise to prominence in Japan has been neither easy nor swift and it is only since the 1990s, following the establishment of professionalism with the J-League (in 1993), that Japan has competed at the highest level of the world game, participating in the World Cup finals in 1998 and, of course, as co-hosts in 2002 (Japan Football Association 2004). It would appear that the idea behind the J-League was taken from Korea and that it was also part of the increasingly more open attitude of Japanese society, especially towards Western socio-cultural practices (Moffett 2003). Its rapid development, both economically and culturally, gave considerable impetus to the national team, which benefited from the improving standards of home-grown players such as Hidetoshi Nakata, as well as from the increasing media exposure of football itself.

It is the aim of the present chapter to consider print media portrayals of Japan and Korea in the football pages of quality European daily newspapers throughout the second half of the twentieth century with a view to identifying the principal characteristics of the Korean and Japanese identities. To what extent have readily identifiable identities been forged by Europeans of the twin powers of North East Asian football?

Japan viewed from England

Since Japan has been largely absent from the international, and indeed domestic, football scene until relatively recently, it is predictable that Japan does not figure in our sample from the English print media until the 1990s. The early 1990s saw minimal coverage of Japan's fixtures (results were noted and occasionally a few details on the team). There is, however, some degree of exposure as the J-League was founded in 1993 and developed between 1993 and 1996, notably when former England international turned media pundit Gary Lineker signed for Nagoya Grampus Eight to play out the end of his career on the pitch. Such was the iconic status of Lineker in England at the time that the media's rush to cover his move was inevitable and gave the J-League some valuable exposure. Yet the nature of this coverage, though informative at the time, was still rather limited in scope. It tended to focus on the development of football, attendances, and some elements of crowd behaviour – perhaps inevitably adopting an Anglo-centric approach and focusing on the differences in styles of support between Japan and England. These features are to recur throughout the 1990s and then become developed in a rather more sophisticated way by the time Japan co-host the World Cup in 2002.

The readers of *The Times*, for instance, are constantly updated about the progress of Japanese football, not only in terms of its standard of play but also apropos the rôle of football in society. Regarding the latter, there is a clear development as football matures from being considered 'trivial' to realizing a position of huge significance to the Japanese during the 2002 World Cup finals. It is only during the 2002 tournament, as Japan faced Belgium, that 'A nation [Japan] saw the point, understood what the mad spinning chaos of this game is all about' (5 June 2002). Even then, the different styles of support are emphasized with a slightly bewildered tone: 'The crowd begin to sing and chant, in an oddly orchestrated kind of way – most football club matches have a crowd leader, a self-appointed figure who directs the singing and the shouting through a megaphone. . . . There is a correct form, after all, to observe even when singing your heart out' (ibid.). In a sense, though the sport is new, some of the Japanese traditions have spilled over into their football styles of support. The importance of the 'correct form' to be followed is complemented by the overwhelming homogeneity of the fans' attire. The writer noted the uniformity of the blue shirts: 'I have never seen so many blue shirts in a stadium. Everyone wore the Japan blue team shirt. Absolutely everyone. Exceptions, with the Japanese passion for uniformity, were simply not permitted' (ibid.).

Indeed, 'traditional' Japanese values and traits of loyalty, politeness, obedience to higher authorities and efficiency permeate the discourse within the football writing of *The Times*: 'Japanese customs and traditions, which are marked by courtesy and extreme politeness, have remained relatively untainted by Western culture' (13 October 2002). These themes continue to resonate throughout the discourse within our sample. It does not take long to find examples to illustrate this point: 'The J-League began in an atmosphere of orderly politeness' (12 June 2002); 'Fans will have to cope with exorbitant prices, but they will at least find flawless organisation . . . and punctual public transport' (17 October 2001), and even a goal by the opposition, in this case Belgium, 'elicited respectful applause from the crowd of Japanese fans' (5 June 2002). The Japanese are respectfully efficient and polite, in the extreme to the Western observer. Footballers, at times, are portrayed as though to epitomize the characteristics of the population as a whole: FIFA officials famously inspected the Japanese dressing-room after their victory over Russia to find that 'These 21st century rebels had not only celebrated their triumph in a quiet dignified way – to avoid offending squad members who did not make the team, apparently – but tidied up after themselves' (*The Times*, 12 June 2002).

However, Simon Barnes of *The Times* explains the paradox that one of the features which sets football apart from other sports in Japan is precisely its association with values that are traditionally 'un-Japanese':

> When the J-League started, it had to compete with the bedrock Japanese sport of baseball. Baseball was also full of bedrock Japanese virtues: loyalty, hierarchy, obedience, short black haircuts. The J-League had not only flamboyant foreigners such as Dunga and Zico, it also had flamboyant Japanese players with long, chestnut hair and other rococo touches. . . . The rainbow-haired young want more from life than a salary for life. Fun is on the agenda and the early days of the J-League put football right into the whirligig of fashion and fun and youthfulness.
>
> (*The Times*, 28 May 2002)

Thus, the baseball–football dichotomy is presented as the old values versus the new and as symptomatic of societal changes within Japan itself. Also, this excerpt suggests that the rather staid character presented of the Japan of old is being replaced by a younger, more modern and high-spirited new generation. The message that is mediated via the football discourse is that football, imported from the West, is appreciated most by those who embrace new ideas and Western culture and is treated with caution by more traditional Japanese: 'Japan's following is young, young, young. . . . In a society governed by obedience and etiquette, football is making as great a mess of the traditional society. Now a football shirt might as well be a Hell's Angels jacket to traditional Japan' (*The Times*, 12 June 2002). Football, then, is a cultural import that, to the culturally biased English writers, represents Japanese progress and a less introverted outlook. Of the co-hosting of the World

Cup in 2002, *The Times* indicated that 'Japan has an opportunity to introduce the sport to a wider domestic audience and also open up its own society to diverse international influences' (5 June 2002).

The Japanese players and fanbase are described almost synonymously and adjectives are employed interchangeably to refer to either sector: they are 'fervent', 'frivolous', 'enthusiastic' and 'lively'. The national team, emulated by the youth of Japan, contains within it a strong element of flamboyance, epitomized by 'Philippe Troussier, their flamboyant French coach' (*The Times*, 1 March 2002) and 'personal flamboyance is something to be celebrated in modern Japan' (28 May 2002).

Also of interest in Barnes's views quoted above, since, perhaps surprisingly, it represents another theme throughout our data, is the (symbolic) mention of hairstyles. Consistent with the ideals of the fun-loving, rather extrovert, new generation of younger Japanese is the reported attraction for the overtly 'un-Japanese' trait of sporting outlandish hairstyles – in an attempt to redefine Japanese identity. It is no coincidence that Japan's favourite players have crazy hair – Hidetoshi Nakata's was usually yellow or orange, Kazuyuki Toda's Mohican style was red. Haircuts have come to symbolize in print media discourse the fun-loving nature of Japanese youth, rebelling against traditional societal boundaries. This is communicated explicitly in *The Times*: 'Kazuyuki Toda, cutting an imperial figure with his bright red Mohican haircut, was reduced to tears. An embodiment of the new Japan. A man so overcome with the emotion of defeat that he was not afraid to show it in public; not afraid to lose face' (19 June 2002).

According to our sample, Japanese football fans like what football represents – a relaxation of the old traditions: 'Japanese football is rock and roll' (12 June 2002). In some ways, Hidetoshi Nakata represents all this. He achieved his iconic status at least partly for his off-field stances: he 'had already broken the rules by refusing to address senior players as "San" (Mr) on the field of play and described the national anthem Kimayo (The Emperor's Reign) as boring. He needed a police escort and had to flee his apartment. The impact was colossal. Football was and still is revolution over here' (ibid.).

Despite these societal changes mediated via the football pages of *The Times*, change in Japan tends to be evolutionary rather than revolutionary. Strong characterizations remain and the Japanese are still described as 'the peace-loving people' who 'pick litter not fights' and live in 'clean, composed cities' (1 March 2002). They see 'supporters of the opposing teams as allies not enemies', and 'fans continue to sing about the Emperor and appreciate good play, even if it comes from the opposition' (12 June 2002). Tensions, however, remain: 'But the older generation do not appreciate that. They see only the outlandish hairstyles, foreign influence and excesses' (ibid.).

As though attempting to grasp an element of Japanese culture with which the reader might be only vaguely familiar, there are several references in the English press to Japanese martial arts and culture. For example, there is occasional allusion to aikido, a modern, non-aggressive form of martial art, developed in the early twentieth century by Morihei Ueshiba: Japan has 'a national team that is improving with the speed of an aikido manoeuvre' (*The Times*, 1 March 2002). This reference to martial arts in general and to aikido in particular fits in with other illustrations of Japanese style of play and culture found elsewhere in our sample. Aikido has evolved 'in the historic tradition of Japanese warrior arts. It is more than a science of tactics and self-defence; it is a discipline for perfecting the spirit' (Aikido Online 2005). This aikido spirit is reflected in the football writing in our data. Notably, Japanese football is not described in the same terms as Germany or England, for example, where military metaphor is rife. While the notion of team spirit and collectivism is present, so is that of 'great calm', 'peace and harmony' and 'serenity' (e.g. *The Times*, 4 June 2002; 5 June 2002), a somewhat odd blend in our lexis for describing football.

The explanation for this lack of militaristic jargon in football writing involving Japan relates, of course, to wider political, diplomatic and, indeed, cultural issues around Japan's development as a pacific nation since the end of the Second World War, and is offered in one article: 'There is national pride in abundance out there, but it is without the tribalism that traditional football powers go in for. The nationalism is in no way confrontational. It is quite without triumphalism' (*The Times*, 4 June 2002). Such is the 'conflict avoidance' and absence of aggression or overt hostility towards other nations that *The Times* refers to Japan as a 'quasi-neutral setting' (ibid.).

Perhaps the only familiarity with Japan that the average English readership will boast regards the martial arts and the odd cultural reference engendered by acquaintance with blockbuster films such as *The Last Samurai* (Akira Kurosawa's classic martial epic set in sixteenth-century Japan, produced in 1954 and lauded by many as the best film to hail from that country) and TV series such as *Shogun* (starring Richard Chamberlain in 1998). Unsurprisingly, then, we find references to both in our data. For example, 'Their star is Hidetoshi Nakata, who looks like one of the seven Samurai, the cool one who never speaks . . .' (*The Times*, 5 June 2002) and, 'Troussier, the self-styled "second shogun", has said that his role was to reawaken a samurai spirit in Japan that has been enfeebled by the rise of Hello, Kitty and Pokemon' (*The Times*, 19 June 2002).

It is rare for football discourse to delve into overt political comment about Japan. However, the chief sports writer for *The Times* in Yokohama, Simon Barnes, does attempt to explain the Japanese national characteristics depicted in print media discourse. The morning after the Japan–Russia fixture at the World Cup, for instance, Barnes explains the significance of the tie: 'This was a game from which Japan wanted a result . . . this was Russia. Japan has a long history of fear, suspicion and demonization of Russia. The two countries fought a war together a century back and such things always give a certain zing to a football match' (10 June 2002). The politico-historical theme continued in the match report: 'It was a great victory, and it had nothing to do with General Togo' (ibid.). Togo is most famous as the Imperial Japanese Navy Commander in the Russo-Japanese War who was responsible for the defeat of the Russian fleet at Port Arthur in 1904 and for his rôle in the Battle of Tsushima in 1905. This historical reference to General Togo is, however, unusual in a commentary that is more typically apolitical.

Some of the Japanese national characteristics already outlined above are transferred to the football milieu by the football press in England. The risk-averse, shame-based culture of the Japanese business community is translated into the football context as 'a home side so burdened by expectation that risk-bearing and individuality are strangled', and their play is 'characteristically understated' (*The Times*, 1 March 2002). Inamoto, then of Arsenal, was quoted in *The Times* as saying, 'Football is a very different sport in Japan from the rest of the world. . . . There is none of the aggression displayed' by either fans or players (17 October 2001).

However, there is no clear stereotypical style of Japanese football. The apparent reluctance to demonstrate individual flair is tempered by the emergence of the 'new' Japanese already mentioned above. Thus, the Japanese 'have developed an engaging capacity for cultured and penetrative approach play', which, as yet, 'lacks incisiveness in front of goal' (*The Times*, 1 March 2002). During the World Cup finals in 2002, they 'played with urgency' and 'passion'; their 'quick-witted, quick-footed game' beat Russia (*The Times*, 10 June 2002). Despite budding strengths, though, we are not allowed to forget that Japan is still an emerging football nation. Though our sample highlights stereotypes of the extremely polite, efficient and organized Japanese, the boundaries are extended to include a new, frivolous and dynamic younger generation emerging. Indeed, the coverage of Japan and football affords much more than a shallow impression of Japanese culture, history and society.

Japan in France

Japan's absence, until recently, from the highest levels of the global game means that, as is the case in England, significant French press coverage of the Japanese national team dates again only from the 1990s. Indeed, the first ever meeting between France and Japan took place in Tokyo only in 1994 during the annual Kirin Cup. Despite what might have been seen as the historic nature of this occasion, though, the reporting of the match itself, a 4–1 victory for the French, was sparse indeed. *Le Monde*, for instance, provided no more than nine lines of text, recording the score, the scorers and the fact that France had won the three-way competition, which also involved Australia. Japanese football was evidently still, even at this late stage of the twentieth century, an unknown and unremarkable entity.

The 1998 World Cup, held in France, with its extensive coverage in the press, saw the first signs emerge of a Japanese identity in construction in French print media discourse. For example, to prepare a preview article on Japan, a reporter from *Le Monde* visited the Japanese FA's palatial, hi-tech training centre, the J-Village, established in 1997, and returned impressed by 'the keen sense of perfection that inhabits the Japanese whenever they decide to throw themselves into an activity they don't know much about, in this instance football' (20 June 1998). Stemming undoubtedly from expectations arising out of the wider context of Japan's highly successful involvement with the automobile, telecommunications and electronics industries, the Japanese are expected also to be technically minded perfectionists in the football context. It is, therefore, a source of some consternation in the French press when the reality does not match the image: 'Unbelievable Japanese Inefficiency' ran the headline to one match report on the defeat against Jamaica at France 98 (*Le Monde*, 28/29 June 1998). The Japanese are not supposed to be sloppy and the concept is indicated in the discourse by the simple use of the adjective 'unbelievable'. Indeed, Japan's legendary tidiness was a feature of the 1998 World Cup that was displayed more by the Japanese fans themselves than their team and, as such, was the subject of much interest in the French press. The sight of Japanese supporters putting their own litter into bags and removing it at the end of matches prompted one reporter to note that such tidiness is, after all, 'one of their traditions' (*Le Monde*, 23 June 1998). Allied to notions of tidiness and efficiency are those of enthusiasm and fervour which, in the print media discourse examined, would also appear to be expected traits of the Japanese. The Japanese fans were qualified as 'the most fervent' in the World Cup (ibid.) while the team's performances were said to have been characterized by 'liveliness' (ibid.), 'audacity' (*Le Monde*, 16 June 1998), 'enthusiasm and candour' (*Le Monde*, 28/29 June 1998). Again, when the expected traits are not in evidence, surprise is registered: in defeat against Argentina, for instance, the Japanese were 'surprisingly defensive' and 'did not play with their *usual* qualities of liveliness and boldness' (*Le Monde*, 16 June 1998, emphasis added).

The 1998 World Cup, with Japan's elimination at the first hurdle following three successive defeats, might not have elevated expectations of the Japanese in terms of performance but clearly a Japanese identity in the wider sense is taking shape at this stage. By the 2001 Confederations Cup, held in Japan and South Korea as a dry run for the following year's co-hosted World Cup finals, certain aspects of that identity appear cemented (and are contrasted with that of neighbours Korea). *Le Monde*'s report of France's victory over Japan in the final, for example, whilst naturally focusing on the French performance, noted that 'As far as organization goes, the Japanese and Koreans have been perfect. That was expected of the former, the nice surprise has come from the latter' (12 June 2001).

The 2002 World Cup finals, extensively covered by *Le Monde* in daily supplements, provided plenty of scope for further analysis of the Japanese identity both on and off the football pitch. First, the established characteristics of perfectionism, organizational ability, technical skills and committed enthusiasm are much in evidence. Second, though, *Le Monde*'s coverage also extended to examinations of two interrelated political aspects involving Japanese identity, one deriving from the relationship with the former colony of Korea, the tournament's co-hosts, the other relating to Japan's militaristic past in general.

From the first category, reiterations of the expected attributes of the Japanese, examples may be quoted from *Le Monde*'s preview of Japan's game against Tunisia in the first round of the tournament. Japan, we are informed, 'play the football of purists'; this is 'a country that prides itself on its organizational abilities' and one 'that values above all else commitment to the cause' (14 June 2002). Furthermore, the Japanese are apparently 'disciplined, hard workers but lacking in personality' (ibid.). The fact that enthusiasm and technical ability have not guaranteed success on the football pitch for the Japanese national team is further portrayed by the newspaper under consideration here as an extension of Japanese culture at large, leading to football being perceived as a metaphor for the traditional values of society as a whole. Commenting on the good reception afforded to the Japanese players on their elimination by Turkey, *Le Monde* explained: 'Japanese culture traditionally accords greater weight to effort than to success and a certain dignity is conferred upon defeat which is elevated to an art form. This sympathy for the defeated hero who engaged in a desperate cause with a pure heart is anchored in the Japanese mentality' (20 June 2002).

Finally, with regard to French press coverage of Japan in 2002, the political aspects surrounding the World Cup's co-hosts were also very much to the fore. Initially, *Le Monde* was concerned with the potential impact of the World Cup on the joint hosts' own relations with each other. For much of the first half of the twentieth century, Korea was under Japanese colonial rule, and for much of the second half Japan had dominated the region's economy. 'Korea, therefore,' explains the newspaper, 'has always been distrustful of its Japanese neighbour . . . and anger and disputes subsist' while the Japanese themselves 'have ambivalent feelings of both guilt and superiority towards the Koreans' (1 June 2002). The World Cup is presented as an opportunity to break down the barriers between the two countries, to 'aid the rapprochement between . . . these cultural cousins but in many respects profoundly different neighbours . . . . The World Cup should accelerate the normalization of relations between the two countries, marked even now by a distinct animosity'; in short, 'Can football do better than the diplomats?' *Le Monde* asked, somewhat pointedly (ibid.).

In terms of Japan's relationship with itself and with its own past, *Le Monde* believed it detected a change in this respect as the tournament unfolded. Birchall (2001) analyses how the Japanese reluctance to engage in overt displays of patriotism had muted the development of national pride in sporting contexts and *Le Monde* duly provides confirmation of this analysis. Displays of patriotic fervour are infrequent in Japan, according to our newspaper, for fear of resurrecting images from the nationalistic past of the colonial era and the Second World War: 'the Japanese prefer to keep a low profile in this respect' (6 June 2002). The 2–2 draw with Belgium, however, which secured Japan's first ever point at the World Cup finals, was met with 'a well behaved patriotism that it is rare to see expressed so openly here' (ibid.). The theme continued with coverage of Japan's victory over Russia which gave football 'a place in the heart of the whole nation' (11 June 2002) and the competition as a whole was summed up as being responsible for the 'emancipation of [Japanese] nationalism, freed from the inhibitions of the past and its associations with militarism' (2 July 2002). It is, however, not without considerable irony, therefore, that, even if the Japanese themselves seem to have closed a chapter on their militaristic past, French newspaper journalists seem incapable of avoiding references linking the Japanese to militarism in general and to the Second World War in particular. One shot by Nakata in the match against Russia, for instance, was described as 'a missile fired at the crossbar' (11 June 2002) while celebrating fans diving into the river at Osaka after the victory over Tunisia were qualified as 'joyful kamikazes leaping into the water' (16/17 June 2002).

Japan in Spain

Given that Japanese football is still in its infancy as a professional sport, it is with relative ease that we can trace the development of the notions of national identity within writing in the Spanish press. While a few articles draw on clichés connected to notions of Japanese identity, these are less common than those found in relation to many other nations. The Spanish press outlines some of the key differences between football in Japan and Europe but prefers to examine the nature of football as a sport. Clearly, football is not presented as a 'national' sport in Japan, nor as one which connects strongly to the notion of Japanese identity. In this sense it shares something in common with coverage of American football in our data. Several Spanish journalists prefer to contrast the very essence of football culture in Japan with that of other, more 'traditional', footballing countries.

The Spanish print media draw parallels between football cultures in the USA and Japan: 'Japan, with no tradition in western sports, follows a purely economic model, in the North American way' (El País, 30 November 1998). The same article highlights the need for the support of sponsors in order for Japanese clubs to survive (and explicates the fluid nature of clubs who disappear and reappear either merged with another – often rival – club or under a new name following the whims of sponsors), and presents this as something extraneous to football – again more akin to the American style of organization of professional sport. Thus the economic model of the sport, the reliance on sponsors for the existence of clubs and organization of the professional game, and the broader sporting context (in which baseball is more attractive than football), all lead Spanish writers to conclude that football in Japan is run more along an American model than a traditional European (or indeed Latin American) one.

A report on the Toyota Cup, when Real Madrid played Vasco de Gama in Tokyo in 1998, for example, gives a hint of what to expect in later coverage of Japanese football: 'The crowd was silent during the game, and only made noise after certain moves, preferably long balls, free kicks, dribbling and shots at goal. The crowd didn't take sides in the match, but did seem to enjoy it. They even took pleasure in shots off target, displaying no recrimination' (El País, 4 December 1998). There are several points of interest in this report which will be developed in later articles, in particular during the 2002 World Cup: that the 'normal' state for the Japanese is silence; that they are polite to the extreme (not jeering at shots off target or criticizing poor performance) and easily pleased (taking pleasure in simple things). There is an implicit criticism of the naïvety of the Japanese appreciation of football, too; they cheer long balls (presumably because they are not used to seeing players able to kick a ball accurately over distance?). That the Japanese also lack passion for the game is also implicit – though arguably the description of the crowd's passive behaviour could be that of any crowd watching a match involving two teams from other parts of the world, for whom they felt no special affection and with whom they did not identify in the slightest. There is also evidence of relying on stereotypes: as players went to take corners, 'thousands of *flashes* came from the stands around (you see, thousands of Japanese mean thousands of cameras)' (*El País*, 4 December 1998).

There is relatively little coverage in the Spanish data of Japan's performances in France 98. This perhaps reflected the fact that they were an 'unfancied' team, with few stars (that is, few that played in Europe) and no World Cup history. What was written reflected 'the distance that remained between Old Europe and the new football world' (*El País*, 20 June 1998). There are, however, indications that there are exceptions to the rule and there is evidence of some skill: Nakata, for instance, 'is a mathematical, geometric midfielder' while the goalkeeper, Kawaguchi, is 'acrobatic and ever-smiling' (ibid.).

As far as the style of play is concerned, after Japan played Croatia, though the team played 'at a fast pace, and enthusiastically' (*El País*, 21 June 1998), the weaknesses of the Japanese were 'fundamentally defensive' and included 'their low levels of skills and technical ability' (ibid.). Rather patronizingly, one writer added that, on a positive note, every Japanese player did at least 'try to imitate a successful European or Latin American player' (ibid.).

When playing Jamaica, however, 'Japan showed more order, more control in midfield, and dominated the game', though they did 'keep losing possession' (*El País*, 27 June 1998). They had 29 shots at goal, but this appears merely to confirm their naïvety in the eyes of the journalists since this implied they were 'wildly optimistic', tried to shoot from anywhere on the pitch with only seven of these shots actually on target. The reaction of western Europe to the Japanese performance in the 1998 World Cup was summed up later by the ever-perceptive Santiago Segurola as 'kind curiosity towards the exotic' (*El País*, 10 June 2002). The analysis was simple: 'Their fans filled the grounds and the team lost. They were like a footnote to top-level football' (ibid.).

The national characteristics, and indeed stereotypes, of the Japanese are never far away from complementing match reports: when playing for Feyenoord, 'Ono earned the affection of the Dutch fans, who were astounded when he was sent off during a match and went round apologizing to all his team-mates and management team' (*El País*, 18 June 2002). The cleanliness of fans and teams alike is also, famously, commented upon (as it was across the European media): 'the changing rooms are left spotless, the cleanliness only rivalled by their supporters, who arrive at the stadium with a plastic bag in which to deposit their wrappers, plastic bottles and even cigarette ash' (*El País*, 21 June 1998).

It is interesting to note how the characterization of the Japanese has been subject to change, in football terms at least. In 1998, the Japanese were 'football virgins', 'enthusiastic' but 'naïve'; in fact, the portrayal was rather childlike. Their feelings towards the sport were on a par with how Americans were perceived to feel about football: of some (limited) interest, but lacking in passion and true understanding of the game. The portrayal of the Japanese identity and concomitant football culture changes significantly, though, during the 2002 World Cup.

When Japan co-hosted the 2002 World Cup with South Korea, this presented the Spanish print media with an excuse to delve much more deeply into the culture of Japanese (and, as we shall see, to a lesser extent Korean) football and it also provided the opportunity for journalists to explore the culture, politics, economy and society of these two countries with fresh impetus and in a more comprehensive way. The relationship between football and the Japanese was inevitably the subject of much discussion in the Spanish media, as it was all over western Europe. In many of these articles, Japanese and Korean characteristics and the cultural differences between Japan/Korea and the West were highlighted. The predominant traits as far as Japan is concerned were the quiet passivity of the people, their precise, careful organization and their 'excessive' politeness. Hence, despite the fact that they must have been 'frustrated' and 'bored' by the foreigners' queries, the volunteers who helped organize the tournament were 'extraordinarily polite at all times, and never showed their frustration' (*El País*, 1 July); there was 'almost excessive politeness' (ibid.) and the Japanese were 'exquisitely formal in their treatment of others' (*El País*, 5 June). Furthermore, 'Everything was always organized' (*El País*, 1 June).

The Japanese are also portrayed as good at absorbing the ideas of others: 'The Japanese have a remarkable way of assimilating everything that is going on in the world around them' (*El País*, 19 June 2002). Thus their increasing affection for football is justified as a logical result of improving communications in a 'global village' (ibid.). A further reason for the explosion in interest in football in Japan is explained by 'its links with European football' triggered by the signings of Nakata (then of Parma), Ono (Feyenoord) and Inamoto (Arsenal). Japanese players in Europe served to bring the two regions of the world closer.

At the start of the competition, Spanish football writing covered notions of Japanese football culture in much the same way as it did during the 1998 World Cup in France. Football is described as a form of cultural consumerism: 'Football's global diffusion couldn't pass by unnoticed in the very strong Japanese market. Another reason for its growth lies in the fact that it has established links with European football, which is equally interested in exploring new territories, principally for economic reasons' (*El País*, 10 June 2002).

The Japanese are also perceived as being rather odd in the eyes of European football writers in that they support the player rather than the club: 'the fans follow the fashionable player of the moment, as long as he is Japanese . . . but not the team' (*El País*, 30 November 1998). The main 'stars' of Japanese football during the 2002 World Cup (namely Inamoto, Ono and Nakata) became true idols, or 'messiahs' (*El País*, 18 June 2002).

In his article entitled 'Japanese Schizophrenia', John Carlin explains how apparently 'Japan is suffering from an attack of collective schizophrenia' (*El País*, 16 June 2002). It is worth discussing this exposé in some detail since it draws out some of the themes and characteristics which recur in other articles which make reference to a Japanese identity and football culture. Carlin goes on to clarify: 'On the one hand is the Japanese way of being: politeness and formality taken to the most exquisitely extreme expression. On the other, there are millions and millions of Japanese behaving like chimpanzees on heat, or a layer beneath the chimpanzees on the evolutionary scale, like English football fans.' Carlin highlights the cultural differences between the Japanese and the West by describing a simple event: a short train journey – where unwritten rules meant that silence reigned, even though the train was packed, and people only ventured to talk in low voices 'in order not to annoy others' (ibid.). The use of mobile phones is prohibited. Most passengers sleep, because they work such long hours they are always tired. However, when the train arrives at Kobe station, hundreds of football fans are waiting. 'Within the traditional Japanese culture, this is like a lunatic asylum, a dantesque vision. And worse, most are Japanese. Young, and almost all with dyed hair, many imitating the "Beckham look", jumping about, shouting, chanting songs in English, that many probably don't even understand (but who cares?)' (ibid.). They are singing along with groups of English fans. The journalist explains how disturbing it must be for Japanese traditionalists 'who want things to remain just as they are in Japan' to see the young Japanese taking on the English *hooligans* as their rôle models.

This leads onto another characteristic emphasized in this article in that 'the Japanese are the great imitators of the world' (ibid.): 'They don't invent things, they perfect them . . . . Now the Japanese youth are copying the English fans . . . . They imitate songs and chants, dances, hairstyles. And they do it so well these days that if you close your eyes when Japan plays, you could imagine that you are in not the Yokohama or Miyagi stadiums, but at Old Trafford.' Perhaps a slight indication of cultural superiority creeps into the article when Carlin explains how the Japanese choose to copy the English, firstly because they are there in great numbers, but secondly, and most interestingly, because they are doing what the Japanese really want to do: make noise. The implication is clear: the Japanese are a quiet people, but the silence is culturally imposed and given the opportunity to break out of their oppression they will do. The English 'are all around, making lots of noise, and noise is what the Japanese youth wants to make, after so many years obliged into silence' (ibid.). It is 'time for them to break free from their chains' (ibid.) in 'the most strict, most repressed society in the world' (*El País*, 30 June 2004). A Japanese national newspaper is quoted as saying that 'The indefatigable fighting spirit of these young people – with their hair dyed red, gold and silver – showed us a vision of the future in which this country will become diverse and full of vitality' (ibid.). At that time, though, the contrast between the shirt-and-tie brigade quietly sleeping on the commuter train and those who have caught 'football fever' is total.

The reluctance of the Japanese to display patriotic or passionate emotions overtly (that is, in a way, recognized as such by Westerners) is explained by one reporter who suggests that political events following the fall of Nazi Germany in 1945, the invasion of China and other Asian neighbours, waging war against the USA and its allies, led to an embarrassment in demonstrating patriotism and a reluctance to wave the Japanese flag. It was not until the World Cup in 2002 that it became socially acceptable to display elements of patriotism (ibid.).

So, to what extent did the characteristics drawn of the Japanese people transfer to the description of the playing style of the Japan football team? Many accounts of the Japanese style of play are unflattering and emphasize their naïvety and low levels of skill. The team has 'multiple deficiencies' (*El País*, 19 June 2002); 'The team tries to play at 100 miles an hour when only three or four players have that level of skill. The rest try to do at top speed that which they can't even do slowly. So the game slips away from them, beyond their control, because the ball is given away time and time again' (ibid.). The forwards are 'incapable of getting a shot at goal, no matter how off target it might be' (ibid.). Koji Nakata is described as giving away a stupid corner 'because of his technical clumsiness' (*El País*, 18 June 2002). In short, the poor quality of Japanese football is taken as read: 'the best of Japan is nothing great, of course' (ibid.). On a more positive note, Inamoto characterized the best qualities of the Japanese squad: he was 'hard-working, brave, the most accurate passer and goalscorer' (*El País*, 10 June 2002). Note that the qualities of 'hard work' and 'accuracy' are those associated with the Japanese in general in other articles. Following one of Japan's stronger performances, while there is still talk of their 'enthusiasm' there is now a 'freedom' in their style (*El País*, 15 June 2002).

By mid-June 2002, the Spanish media are clearly differentiating between Japan and the USA as World Cup hosts (2002 and 1994 respectively): 'This World Cup is not like the one in the US in 1994. A circus, a curiosity that came and went. Football, a sport with no tradition in Japan, in which 10 years ago there was no interest at all compared to baseball, has arrived and will remain forever' (*El País*, 10 June 2002); 'There is no doubt: Japan has become part of the great fraternity of nations in the world who worship the pagan religion of football. There is no going back. The exuberant passion of the people on the streets, on trains . . . proves it' (ibid.). By the time Japan won its first match, the press were talking of 'the awakening of football in Japan' (ibid.) and of 'Japan's happiest night since they won the war against Russia in 1905' (ibid.).

Japan's love of football is no longer portrayed as a fickle fashion accessory: 'From the Japanese national anthem – tragic, awful, profoundly depressing – to 90 minutes of tribal festivities, to the levels of hysteria that great triumphs bring in football in Spain, Brazil, England and other parts of the world. And now, in Japan too' (ibid.). Now, football is loved as passionately in Japan as it is in the rest of the 'traditional' football world, a far cry from the descriptors of 1998. The atmosphere in the Sapporo stadium during Japan's match against Belgium was 'an atmosphere of pure football. The tension, the happiness, the fear and the ecstasy . . . were identical to those felt in Spain or any other country with a fairly strong football tradition' (*El País*, 5 June 2002). The ultimate sign of acceptance into the football world follows: 'The Japanese crowd was a true football crowd' (ibid.).

The Japanese are no longer quiet, once 'blue fever' (*El País*, 15 June 2002) takes a grip. This change is recognized by one journalist who concludes: 'The whole of Japan has transformed as they have watched their team play. It is as though the inhabitants, or the vast majority of them, had drunk some magic potion that removed the sufferings of the last decade of economic stagnation, and got rid of the inhibitions that always seemed to define the Japanese character' (ibid.).

Korea in England

Despite South Korean participation in World Cup final tournaments in 1954 and 1970, Koreans are largely absent from the English print media discourse prior to the 1980s. One noteworthy exception to this was the coverage of North Korea during the 1966 World Cup finals held in England. In particular the unexpected 1–0 triumph over Italy drew the attention of *The Times*: 'North Koreans achieve startling victory' and 'We came expecting the inevitable. We left having witnessed the impossible' (29 July 1966). Yet, even here we are told little about a Korean style of play and there is no elucidation on notions of a Korean identity.

The salient characteristic of the Koreans in 1966 is apparently their size. They are 'little men' – indeed throughout the article individual players are described as 'little' and Pak Seung Zin, from 'the land of the morning calm', was 'little even by Korean standards' (ibid.). By the time South Korea co-host the World Cup finals in 2002, journalism appears to have gone beyond such superficial observations on physique and is attempting to delve a little further into the national psyche.

The themes which come to light via such writing on the sports pages of *The Times* include the naïvety and innocence of the nation (both in football terms and in terms of their global outlook); politeness and tolerance as part of the national character; and the gregarious nature of the Koreans.

The naïvety typical of coverage of North East Asian teams in general (on Japan and China too) is present in writing on Korean football: the football innocence of 1966 recurs throughout the later period: 'To their credit, the Koreans did not sit on their lead, though I believe they would not have known how' (ibid.) and then 'South Koreans revel in their age of innocence' (20 June 2002) – this could equally refer to their football or to Korean society generally.

While fearing the effect of invading foreigners on the Koreans, who are 'generally a polite and reserved nation' (*The Times*, 8 October 2001), the tolerant patience of the Koreans is not fully comprehensible to the Western journalists covering the 2002 World Cup. The tone of bewilderment is clear when one writer describes the behaviour of the fans when South Korea were losing to Italy: 'the mood did not waver and no player needed to be afraid that an error would bring the frustrated anger of the crowd pounding down' (*The Times*, 20 June 2002). In an attempt to understand the Korean tolerance, the journalist explains that 'This is an untainted audience . . . Koreans are yet to experience disappointment or resentment. They are only experiencing delight' (*The Times*, 20 June 2002). The Western perspective is imposed to explain the Korean behaviour. It is presented, rather patronizingly perhaps, as only a matter of time before the Koreans, once they are more familiar with the world of football, become disillusioned and frustrated. Then they will behave in a manner to which we (in the West) are more accustomed. Implicitly, this cultural variance is covered under a shroud of innocence.

Evidence of Koreans' apparent 'generosity' figures in many pages of the reporting during the 2002 World Cup by journalists who are experiencing Korean hospitality on a daily basis – the Koreans shared their cakes, their time, their food, their drink, often much to the surprise of the English observer. There is also a reported 'devotion to procedure' – usually followed by amusing anecdotes of how journalists have been stumped by the Korean logic of following procedures and instructions to the letter, no matter how illogical they might appear to the Western participant in the events.

Several articles also report on the stereotypically vivacious nature of the Koreans: 'Their rituals are high-spirited . . . gregarious . . . uncorrupted partisanship . . . young people are beginners in revelry' (ibid.). With the Koreans having no shorthand stereotype of their own, the writer resorts to borrowing one, attributing the comparison to an anonymous Other: the Koreans are 'sometimes referred to as the Irish of Asia . . . because they have a habit for hard work and hard drinking' (ibid.). Furthermore, there is a lack of 'violence that characterises the more grizzled football nations' (ibid.). The Korean identity created is one which is fun-loving and which does not take life too seriously.

There is, however, some recognition that Korean society is changing, as are other Far Eastern cultures: 'The country is changing and the youngsters are not simply unlined versions of their parents' (ibid.). Rather than look to internal changes within Korean society, cultural changes are attributed by the sports writers of *The Times* to the process of globalization. For example, the fact that many display shirts of European stars and that their idols are media-created icons leads the journalist to conclude that 'globalisation has shaped them [the South Koreans]' (ibid.). This is undoubtedly one of the strong forces of change in the Far East but is it not simplistic to explain all changes by putative global forces? Internal political and economic developments are also, for example, playing a huge part in the progress and development of Far Eastern countries.

The Korean style of play is portrayed as a reflection of the character of the South Koreans: they play football with 'ardour' and, as we have seen with the people and fans, they are characteristically 'ebullient' and 'lively' (*The Times*, 11 June 2002). The team also shares the 'hardworking' nature of the population at large (*The Times*, 31 May 2002). The innocence and naïvety of the fans is also understood to be part of the style of play: despite overwhelming pressures on the pitch, they 'refused to be demoralised' (*The Times*, 11 June 2002). The synergy between the character of Koreans depicted in the print media and that of the South Korean national football team is, then, unmistakeable.

Korea seen from France

With regard to portrayals of Korean identity in France, despite South Korea's qualifying for the World Cup finals as far back as 1954, Koreans are largely absent from the print media discourse examined until the mid-1980s with South Korea's World Cup campaigns in Switzerland in 1954 and in Mexico in 1970 rating hardly a passing mention in *Le Monde*, for example. However, North Korea's only appearance at a World Cup finals, in England in 1966, did generate sufficient media interest to warrant inclusion in the present study and, notwithstanding the significant geo-political elements distinguishing North Koreans from their neighbours in the South, it might be felt that the first traits in what would become a widely accepted vision of pan-Korean identity were posited in *Le Monde*'s coverage at the time. Initially, *Le Monde* appeared somewhat disconcerted by the North Koreans, 'about whom absolutely nothing is known' (14 July 1966) but, as the tournament progressed, the newspaper's journalists came to agree on the principal quality that would serve to define Koreans throughout the rest of the twentieth century and beyond: the Korean players were 'busy and energetic' (ibid.), they exhibited a 'beguiling liveliness', 'pleasantly surprised everyone with their enthusiasm and courage' (21 July 1966) and 'displayed unexpected determination and boldness' (23 July 1966), particularly in defeating Italy 1–0 in what was one of the most unexpected results in international football history. The qualities of being a livewire, unexpected package that burst onto the scene with such impact in 1966 via the North Koreans would be further developed in subsequent reporting in *Le Monde* in the last quarter of the twentieth century where they are attributed to South Koreans also.

In the 1986 World Cup finals, for instance, even in defeat against Argentina, the South Koreans were said to have 'charmed everyone with their simple game plan based on liveliness, skill and, above all, enthusiastically mounted attacking play' (4 June 1986). Similarly, a creditable draw was achieved against Bulgaria because the Koreans were able to counter the Europeans' greater experience with their own 'enthusiasm and liveliness' (7 June 1986). This explicit contrast between European know-how and North East Asian endeavour is one that would reappear in French print media discourse in both the 1998 and 2002 World Cups. Finally with regard to 1986, though, it must be noted that the report of the match between South Korea and Italy, which resulted in a narrow Italian victory, 3–2, contains a worrying example of sloppy journalism as the reporter remarked that the Italians had not learned the lessons of 1966 when they were knocked out by 'the South Koreans' (12 June 1986); of course, it was North Korea that won that day. Is this a simple typing and proofreading error or a symptom of a wider lack of awareness of the distinctions between North and South Korea? Indeed, as has already been seen, in terms of identity construction, there is little if any difference in European perceptions between North and South Korean identities, both of which appear to be founded upon the same notions of lively enthusiasm and courageous boldness.

South Korea's most noteworthy performances at the 1994 World Cup finals in the USA came in the draw against Bolivia and the narrow defeat against Germany where, once again, familiar qualities were perceived by Le Monde in the Koreans' style of play. Doubtless prompted by the team's nickname of the Red Devils, the word 'devil' itself is employed to describe the Korean players (29 June 1994) who displayed 'disconcerting speed', 'spontaneity' and 'stubborn attacking qualities' in scoring twice against the Germans before eventually losing 3–2 (ibid.). Similarly, at France 98, defeat at the hands of the 'more pragmatic and knowledgeable' Dutch came despite the Koreans' 'direct, swift, skilful play' (23 June 1998) while the draw against Belgium was attributed to the South Koreans' 'attacking spirit, liveliness and willingness' (27 June 1998). The word 'lively' (and its cognates or close synonyms) functions as a leitmotif, an item in the lexis of print media sports reporting that connects many portrayals of Korean identity with each other across different time periods, thereby providing a thematic continuity between them which serves to anchor the portrayal of the typical Korean identity over time itself. The theme would be developed almost to the point of apotheosis in the coverage of the 2002 World Cup finals, jointly hosted by South Korea itself, of course.

Korean qualities were increasingly extolled by Le Monde as the team progressed throughout the tournament all the way to the semi-final but they were also readily apparent from the outset. The preview of the group game against Poland, for instance, noted that South Korea would utilize a 'quick, technical, attacking' style favouring 'a lively approach' because 'Evidently, this is what suits them best' (4 June 2002). The potential of Koreans to cause an upset was also visible in the reporting at this early stage of the tournament: 'Koreans are naturally optimistic . . . why would an upset not be possible?' (ibid.). The traditional North East Asian interest in martial arts is then evoked to provide an explanation of how such a football upset might arise as the Koreans would 'adapt the philosophy of the martial arts to football' and learn their opponents' weaknesses to turn these against them (ibid.). When Korea duly won the game, 2–0, the subsequent match report focused heavily on the typical Korean attributes. The adjectives employed to describe the Korean fans were 'electric', 'striking' and 'intoxicating' and these were mirrored in the adjectives qualifying the players: 'keen', 'intrepid', 'quick', 'alert', 'excellent', 'creative', 'unbridled' and 'inspired' (6 June 2002). The only other adjectives used in the article to describe Korea are 'scarlet' and 'red', which relate to the national colours displayed by the fans and worn by the team. A semantic field is, therefore, generated around the Koreans that foregrounds the qualities of liveliness, creativity and enthusiasm, attributes that had already been established in previous competitions as integral to the portrayal of Korean identity and which would continue to be developed by the French newspaper under consideration. Indeed, Le Monde's articles add a further element to the depiction in that the South Koreans' participation in the World Cup finals in their own country is presented as a quest which is, in turn, linked to wider aspects of Korean identity. 'Korea would be plunged into shame' if the team does not qualify for the knock-out phase of the tournament, notes one report (4 June 2002), reminding its readers of the traditional oriental approach to honour and social conduct. The terms employed in the report of the victory over Poland are revealing: this is the start of 'an odyssey . . . a mission . . . a dream' (6 June 2002). This quest takes on a quasi-mystical aura in the preview of the match against the USA, which might be felt to further reflect images of North East Asian identity as we learn that the players enjoyed 'a Buddhist-like tranquillity in their preparations for the game' at their mountain base of Kyongiu, capital of the nation until the tenth century.

As Korea progressed further and further in the tournament, defeating Portugal, Italy and Spain along the way, the familiar attributes of Korean identity (to be lively and capable of the unexpected) continued to be displayed in the French print media discourse examined: Portugal were 'swept away by a tide of enthusiasm' (Le Monde, 16/17 June 2002) and Spain met 'quick, persistent, tireless opponents [who] have surprised all of those who were not expecting them to be able to compete physically with the Europeans' (Le Monde, 22 June 2002).

Given the highly charged vocabulary used to describe the Koreans' progress, it was inevitable that defeat against Germany in the semi-final would lead to the use of cliché: 'the adventure is over . . . the Germans have ended the dream' (Le Monde, 27 June 2002). Reaching the semi-final is, though, still classified as a 'miracle' and one which served to announce the arrival in the élite of world football of a new continent. 'Korea has lost but Asia has won' notes one article, and 'Westerners must now accept that Asia exists' (ibid.). South Korea had naturally enhanced its own reputation as a football country but its success is also extrapolated in the media to extend to the continent as a whole.

As with Japan, coverage of South Korea in the French press also concentrated on political aspects as part of the process of representing cultural identities. In particular, Le Monde covered South Korea's relationships with Japan, the United States and, most importantly, North Korea.

We have already noted the tension inherent to Korean–Japanese relations and the hopes expressed in the French print media that co-hosting the World Cup finals would go some way to easing those tensions. From the Korean perspective, resentment against colonial oppression by Japan in the past is the dominant emotion and, for Le Monde, South Korea's football team becomes a vector for the expression of patriotism and the establishment of an independent, self-confident national identity. 'The identification of a people with its football team and the nationalism engendered by it have reached indescribable levels,' notes the report of the victory over Spain in the knock-out phase (23/24 June 2002). The article further explains that a key element in this patriotism is the fact that Korea did better than Japan: 'The Red Devils have restored pride to the Korean people, bowed and divided by war then stifled by military regimes. The elimination of Japan worked wonders for the Koreans, who are still mistrustful of a neighbour History has rightly taught them to fear' (ibid.). As so often with football writing in the European press, performances on the pitch are seen as expressions and extensions of wider social and political issues within and around the countries involved. Ultimately, the World Cup's impact was 'primarily to consolidate South Korea's national identity' (*Le Monde*, 27 June 2002) but *Le Monde* remained unsure whether the enthusiastic expressions of patriotism throughout the tournament derived from football or football was merely a pretext: 'did the Koreans discover an unexpected passion for football or did they rather find in it a pretext for the expression of a heightened form of patriotism?' (2 July 2002). Whatever the answer, the reporter would seem to be somewhat disconcerted by the fervent manner in which that patriotism had been displayed, revealing that, while Korean fervour on the pitch is laudable, its expression in the stands is, to European eyes, slightly suspect: 'The Koreans gave full vent to an almost tribal passion' (ibid.).

Another geo-political element entered into the portrayal of South Korean identity with the group game against the United States. *Le Monde*'s report of the match, which ended in a 1–1 draw, ran to five paragraphs and yet, significantly, the first three were entirely devoted to the political and diplomatic context in which the game took place. Thirty-seven thousand American soldiers remain in the region monitoring the frontier with the Democratic People's Republic in the north as a legacy of the post-war conflict that led to the division of Korea into North and South. The continued presence of the American military, though, is apparently largely resented by the Korean population as a whole and the French newspaper took considerable pains to explain the security measures put in place for the potentially hazardous football match. Korean president Kim Dae-Jung appealed for calm before the game and then ordered 7,600 police officers to patrol the match and anti-aircraft missiles to be stationed on the stadium roof. In the circumstances, the fact that the match passed off peacefully without incident is seen as somewhat surprising by *Le Monde* which still feels the need to report on events that did not actually take place: 'There was no demonstration against the American military presence in Korea . . . the American anthem was not booed . . . the Korean fans did not turn their backs on the American team' (12 June 2002). Negative reporting in this vein merely serves to perpetuate the climate of fear and hostility that exists historically between Korea and the USA and an opportunity to report on a football match in a way that would diffuse tensions between the uneasy allies was, therefore, lost. Even in the absence of anti-American sentiment in reality, the spectre of it is still evoked in the imaginative world of print media discourse.

Finally, with respect to the 2002 World Cup, it was inevitable that a newspaper such as *Le Monde*, with its strong orientation towards global political issues, would also employ football writing to discuss relationships between North and South Korea. The principal prompt was provided by the South Koreans' victory over Italy who, of course, had been beaten by North Korea in the 1966 tournament: 'Thirty-six years later, the South has finally done as well as its neighbour with whom it is still technically at war' (20 June 2002). The article, which has the form of a match report but content that goes far beyond purely sporting issues, then employs a metaphor to describe the Italians' style of play that directly evokes the diplomatic conflict between North and South Korea: 'the double defensive wall of the Italians is to football what the 38th parallel is to the Korean peninsula' (ibid.). Having done this, the newspaper proceeds to portray football as a possible catalyst of a more harmonious future for the two Koreas: 'the World Cup obviously cannot overturn the geo-political order inherited from the Cold War . . . but it might nonetheless serve to bring young Koreans together' (ibid.). Even if this project is unlikely, football will still have served the purpose of regenerating pride and patriotism in South Korea itself, paradoxically symbolized by extensive use in fans' wardrobes of the colour red (matching the shirts of their heroes) which 'although historically the colour of the whole peninsula, has for too long been associated with the Stalinist regime of the North but which has now been reappropriated by the South' (ibid.).

Korea viewed from Spain

As in the English and French samples, Spanish coverage of Korean football prior to the 1980s was limited almost exclusively to the triumph of North Korea against Italy in the 1966 World Cup finals. In Spain, the victory was described as 'not luck, but it was because we were unaware that the country could play half-decent football' (ABC, 22 July 1966). At that time, the commentary acknowledged the limitations of the existing scope and knowledge of sports journalists in Spain. The nuance changed slightly two days later when an awareness of the emergence of a new football nation was declared: 'a new country, without sporting tradition . . . just realized that the ball is round and not square' (ABC, 24 July 1966).

However, not all is praise for the North Koreans; there are strong suggestions that their success could not be explained by football-related factors alone. After all, we are reminded that Korea had no professional football and that the team were paid military wages. The Spanish press question whether or not the Koreans would pass an anti-doping test (ABC, 23 July 1966). When the Koreans ('Asians'), 'who base their football on incessant running at top speed, were winning 3–0' against Brazil there were more questions about alleged drug-taking among the squad (ABC, 24 July 1966).

By the time Korea and Japan co-host the World Cup finals in 2002, the Spanish print media are talking about the 'traditional' football cultures of Europe and South America visiting a nascent football world, Asia. One report contrasts these worlds as one in which football is 'uncontaminated', 'pure' and 'innocent' and one where it is played in 'an immoral . . . cynical . . . and artificial climate' (El País, 5 June 2002). However, the traditional football nations have 'sort of class-conscious ideas that prevent them from valuing their [Asian] opponents because of their lack of football tradition' (ibid.).

At this point, the Spanish newspapers, in common with others across the world, carried articles and editorials on various aspects of South Korea, football-related and not. The fact that South Korea was probably relatively unknown to a large proportion of the general readership in Spain allowed the sports writers to fill this knowledge gap with snippets of information vis-à-vis Korean history, economy, politics and culture. The tournament put under an intense spotlight a country that would otherwise have remained in the background for the world's media. Generally speaking, the print media liked what it saw and Korea's success in the 2002 World Cup led to a new vision of South Korea: 'Football has allowed Korea to reveal itself as a young, dynamic and festive country' (*El País*, 1 July 2002).

If a stereotype exists for South Koreans in the Spanish press, then it is one of a humble population that works hard: 'The South Koreans are used to looking at their powerful Japanese neighbours, but in the land of Hiddink [South Korea's Dutch manager at the time of the 2002 World Cup] they hoped that the small and hard-working countries would have their chance' (*El País*, 5 June 2002).

As the Koreans progress in the tournament, the 'collective hysteria' of the country is noted on many occasions. Football became '*un espectáculo*'. The notion of Korea as a 'small, hard-working' nation spills over into the portrayal of the Korean style of play: 'The Koreans are more than little engines that don't stop. They also work hard, like to attack, defend more than reasonably well and fear no one. . . . They fulfil their obligation perfectly' (*El País*, 20 June 2002). Perhaps this 'lack of fear' might surprise a casual reader. South Korea 'are aggressive . . . organized . . . no longer timid . . . and take the initiative' (*El País*, 5 June 2002). Stereotypical features of the Korean identity portrayed by the Spanish press are, therefore, replicated in the discourse regarding the Korean style of play.

Bibliography

Aguilar, P. (2002) 'The Basque Memory of the Civil War', in P. Heywood (ed.) *Politics and Policy in Democratic Spain*, London: Frank Cass.

Aikido Online (2005) *The Principles and History of Aikido*. Available online at <http://www.aikidoonline.com> (accessed October 2005).

Albert, P. (1974) *Histoire de la presse*, Paris: PUF.

—— (1979) *Documents pour l'histoire de la presse nationale aux XIXe et XXe siècles*, Paris: CNRS.

—— (1990) *La Presse française*, Paris: Documentation Française.

Altabella, J. (1987) 'Historia de la prensa deportiva', in R. Zabalza Ramos (ed.) *Orígenes del deporte madrileño*, Madrid: Dirección General de Deportes de la Comunidad Autónoma de Madrid.

Anderson, B. (1983) *Imagined Communities: Reflections on the Origin and Spread of Nationalism*, London: Verso.

Andreani, J.-L. and Ajchenbaum, Y.-M. (2005) *La Corse: Histoire d'une insularité*, Paris: Librio Document.

Archetti, E. (1996) 'In Search of National Identity: Argentinian Football and Europe', in J. A. Mangan (ed.) *Tribal Identities: Nationalism, Europe, Sport*, London: Frank Cass.

Armstrong, G. and Giulianotti, R. (eds) (2004) *Football in Africa: Conflict, Conciliation and Community*, London: Palgrave.

Armstrong, G. and Harris, R. (1991) 'Football Hooligans: Theory and Evidence', *Sociological Review*, 39 (3): 427–58.

Bahamonde, A. (2002) *El Real Madrid en la historia de España*, Madrid: Santillana Ediciones Generales, Taurus Historia.

Bale, J. (1998) 'Virtual Fandoms, Futurescapes of Football', *Lecturas de Educación y Física, Revista Digital*. Available online at <http://www.efdeportes.com/efd10/jbale.htm> (accessed 8 March 2006).

Ball, P. (2001) *Morbo: The Story of Spanish Football*, London: WSC Books.

Berthou, T. (ed.) (1999) *Dictionnaire historique des clubs de football français*, Créteil: Pages de foot.

Birchall, J. (2001) *Ultra Nippon: How Japan Reinvented Football*, London: Headline.

Blain, N. and Boyle, R. (1998) 'Sport as Real Life: Media Sport and Culture', in A. Briggs and P. Cobley (eds) *The Media: An Introduction*, London: Longman.

Blain, N., Boyle, R. and O'Donnell, H. (1993) *Sport and National Identity in the Media*, Leicester: Leicester University Press.

Blumler, J., McLeod, J. and Rosengren, K. (1992) 'Comparison, Yes, But – The Case of

Technological and Cultural Change', in J. Blumler, J. McLeod and K. Rosengren (eds) *Comparatively Speaking: Communications and Culture across Space and Time*, London: Sage.

Boniface, P. (ed.) (1998) *Géopolitique du football*, Brussels: Editions complexe.

Bowen, W. (2000) *Spaniards and Nazi Germany: Collaboration in the New Order*, Columbia, MO: University of Missouri Press.

Boyle, R. and Haynes, R. (2000) *Power Play: Sport, the Media and Popular Culture*, Harlow: Pearson Education.

Cazal, J.-M., Cazal, P. and Oreggia, M. (1998) *L'Intégrale de l'équipe de France de football*, Paris: Editions Générales First.

Charle, C. (2004) *Le Siècle de la presse (1830–1939): la presse entre histoire sociale, culturelle et politique*, Paris: Seuil.

Clout, H. (2003) 'Corsica: island of paradox', *Modern & Contemporary France*, 11 (4): 475–7.

Conseil Constitutionnel (1991) Website. Available online at <www.conseil-constitutionnel.fr/n/91290dc.htm> (accessed 1 October 1998).

Crettiez, X. (1999) *La Question corse*, Paris: Complexe.

Crolley, L. (1997) 'Real Madrid v Barcelona: The State against a Nation?', *International Journal of Iberian Studies*, 10 (1): 33–43.

Crolley, L. and Hand, D. (2001) 'France and the English Other: The Mediation of National Identities in Post-War Football Journalism', *The Web Journal of French Media Studies*, 4 (1). Available online at <http://wjfms.ncl.ac.uk/footpress.htm>.

—— (2002) *Football, Europe and the Press*, London: Frank Cass.

—— (2005) 'Spanish Identities in the European Press: The Case of Football Writing', *The International Journal of the History of Sport*, 22 (2): 298–313.

Crolley, L., Hand, D. and Jeutter, R. (1998) 'National Obsessions and Identities in Football Match Reports', in A. Brown (ed.) *Fanatics*, London: Routledge.

Daninos, P. (1954) *Les Carnets du Major Thompson*, Paris: Hachette.

Darby, P. (2002) *Africa, Football and FIFA: Politics, Colonialism and Resistance*, London: Frank Cass.

Dauncey, H. and Hare, G. (1999) *France and the 1998 World Cup: The National Impact of a World Sporting Event*, London: Frank Cass.

Deutscher Fußball-Bund (2005) Website. Available online at <http://www.dfb.de/dfb-team/nationalteam/geschichte/index.html> (accessed 1 March 2005).

Díaz Noci, J. (1999) 'The Creation of Basque Identity through Cultural Symbols in Modern Times', paper presented to the Seminar on Southern Europe, University of Oxford. Available online at <http://www.ehu.es/diaz-noci/Conf/C17.pdf> (accessed 8 March 2006).

Dietschy, P. (2005) *L'Invention des styles nationaux*. Available online at <http://www.weare-football.org/a-la-source/8/lire/l-invention-des-styles-nationaux/> (accessed 14 October 2005).

Dine, P. (2002) 'France, Algeria and sport: from colonisation to globalisation', *Modern & Contemporary France*, 10 (4): 495–505.

Duffy, M. (2001) *England: The Making of the Myth: From Stonehenge to Albert*, London: Fourth Estate.

Duke, V. and Crolley, L. (1996) *Football, Nationality and the State*, London: Longman.

Eisenberg, C. (1990) 'Vom Arbeiter zum Angestelltenfussball? Zur Sozialstruktur des deutschen Fußballsports 1890–1950', *Sozial und Zeitgeschichte des Sports*, 4 (3): 20–46.

—— (1999) 'Histoire du football professionnel en Allemagne', in H. Hélal and P. Mignon (eds) *Football: jeu et société*, Paris: INSEP.

Euskadi (2005) Website. Available online at <http://www.euskadi.net> (accessed 31 March 2005).

FIFA (2004) Website. Available online at < http://www.fifa.com> (accessed 12 November 2004).

Gallie, D. (1997) *Employment, Unemployment and the Quality of Life: The Employment in Europe Survey 1996*, Report prepared for the European Commission. Available online at <http://europa.eu.int/comm/public_opinion/archives/eb/ebs_098_en.pdf> (accessed 8 March 2006).

Garland, J. and Rowe, M. (1997) *War minus the Shooting? Jingoism, the English Press and Euro 96*, Leicester: Scarman Centre, Crime, Order and Policing Series Occasional Paper no. 7.

Gastaut, Y. (2005) *Les Footballeurs algériens en France à l'épreuve des identités nationales*. Available online at <http://www.wearefootball.org/PDF/les-footballeurs-algeriens-en–France.pdf> (accessed 18 October 2005).

Gebauer, G. (1999) 'Les Trois dates de l'équipe d'Allemagne de football', in H. Hélal and P. Mignon (eds) *Football: jeu et société*, Paris: INSEP.

Generalitat de Catalunya (2005) Website. Available online at <http://www.gencat.net/ generalitat/cat/guia/antecedents/index.htm> (accessed September 2005).

Giulianotti, R. (1999) *Football: A Sociology of the Global Game*, Cambridge: Polity.

González Ramallal, M. (2003) 'La configuración del fútbol español como deporte espectáculo', *Revista Digital*, 66. Available online at <http://www.efdeportes.com/efd66/espect. htm> (accessed 8 March 2006).

Gotzon, J. (1998) *Historia de la selección de Euskadi de fútbol*, Bilbao: Ediciones Beitia.

Gritti, J. (1975) *Sport à la une*, Paris: Armand Colin.

Hall, S. (1980) 'Encoding/Decoding', in S. Hall, D. Hobson, A. Lowe and P. Willis (eds) *Culture, Media, Language*, London: Hutchinson.

Hand, D. (1998) 'Footix: The History behind a Modern Mascot', *French Cultural Studies*, 9 (2): 239–47.

—— (2002) *Football, Cultural Identities and the Media*. Available online at <http://www. leisuretourism.com> (accessed 27 June 2002).

Hare, G. (2003) *Football in France: A Cultural History*, Oxford: Berg.

Heiberg, M. (1989) *The Making of Basque Identity*, Cambridge: Cambridge University Press.

Hesse-Lichtenberger, U. (2002) *Tor: The Story of German Football*, London: WSC Books.

Hobsbawm, E. (1983) 'Introduction: Inventing Traditions', in E. Hobsbawm and T. Ranger (eds) *The Invention of Tradition*, Cambridge: Cambridge University Press.

—— (1990) *Nations and Nationalism since 1780*, Cambridge: Cambridge University Press.

Holt, R. (1989) *Sport and the British: A Modern History*, Oxford: Clarendon Press.

Horne, J. and Manzenreiter, W. (eds) (2002) *Japan, Korea and the 2002 World Cup*, London: Routledge.

Japan Football Association (2004) Website. Available online at <http://www.jfa.or.jp/e/ guide/guide7.html> (accessed 10 December 2004).

Jones, D. and Baró i Queralt, J. (1996) 'La prensa', in D. Jones (ed.) *Sport i mitjans de comunicació a Catalunya*, Barcelona: Generalitat de Catalunya.

Keating, M. (2000) 'The Minority Nations of Spain and European Integration: A New Framework for Autonomy?', *Journal of Spanish Cultural Studies*, 1 (1): 29–42.

Kedourie, E. (1960) *Nationalisms*, London: Hutchinson.

Kelly, S. (1996) *Back Page Football: A Century of Newspaper Coverage*, Harpenden: Aurora/ Queen Anne Press.

Korea Football Association (2004) Website. Available online at <http://en.kfa.or.kr/kfa_ history/history.asp> (accessed 10 December 2004).

Lanfranchi, P. (2002) 'Football, cosmopolitisme et nationalisme', *Pouvoirs*, 101: 15–25.   X

Langford, P. (2001) *Englishness Identified: Manners and Character 1650–1850*, Oxford: Oxford University Press.

Larsen, O. (2001) 'Charles Reep: A Major Influence on British and Norwegian Football', *Soccer and Society*, 2 (3): 58–78.

Lawlor, T. and Rigby, M. (1998) *Contemporary Spain: Essays and Texts on Politics, Economics, Education and Employment, and Society*, Harlow: Longman.

Leguineche, M., Unzueta, P. and Segurola, S. (1998) *Athletic 100: Conversaciones en la catedral*, Madrid: El País Aguilar.

Leitz, C. (1996) *Economic Relations between Germany and Spain 1936–39*, Oxford: Clarendon Press.

León Solís, F. (2003) *Negotiating Spain and Catalonia: Competing Narratives of National Identity*, Bristol: Intellect Books.

Livingstone, S. (2003) 'On the Challenges of Cross-National Comparative Media Research', *European Journal of Communication*, 18 (4): 477–500.

McCarthy, D., Jones, R. and Armour, K. (1998) 'Constructing Images and Interpreting Realities: The Case of the Black Soccer Player on Television', paper presented to the British Sociological Association conference, Making Sense of the Body, Edinburgh, 6–7 April.

McKeever, L. (1999) 'Reporting the World Cup: Old and New Media', in H. Dauncey and G. Hare (eds) *France and the 1998 World Cup: The National Impact of a World Sporting Event*, London: Frank Cass.

Martialay, F. (2000) *Amberes: Allí nació la furia española*, Madrid: Real Federación Española de Fútbol.

Mason, T. (1980) *Association Football and English Society 1863–1915*, London: Duckworth.

Markovits, A. S. and Hellerman, S. L. (2001) *Offside: Soccer and American Exceptionalism*, Princeton, NJ: Princeton University Press.

Marks, J. (1999) 'The French National Team and National Identity: "Cette France d'un bleu métis"', in H. Dauncey and G. Hare (eds) *France and the 1998 World Cup: The National Impact of a World Sporting Event*, London: Frank Cass.

Merkel, U. (1994) 'Germany and the World Cup: Solid, Reliable, Often Undramatic but Successful', in J. Sugden and A. Tomlinson (eds) *Hosts and Champions: Soccer Cultures, National Identities and the USA World Cup*, Ashgate: Arena.

Michaud, G. and Kimmel, A. (1996) *Le Nouveau guide France*, Paris: Hachette.

Mignon, P. (1998) *La Passion du football*, Paris: Odile Jacob.

Moffett, S. (2003) *Japanese Rules: Why the Japanese Needed Football and How They Got It*, London: Yellow Jersey Press.

Mourlane, S. (2003) 'Platini et l'Italie: les origines en question', *Migrance*, second semester: 111–18.

Nicholson, M. and Stewart, B. (2003) 'The Media's Use of Interpretive Frames during Football Club Relocations and Mergers', *Football Studies*, 6 (2): 66–78.

OJD (2005) *Chiffres: Presse payante grand public*. Available online at <http://www.ojd.

com/fr/adhchif/adhe_list.php?mode=chif&cat=1771&subcat=353> (accessed 29 November 2005).

Orakwue, S. (1998) *Pitch Invaders. The Modern Black Football Revolution*, London: Victor Gollancz/Cassell.

Paxman, J. (1998) *The English: A Portrait of a Nation*, Harlow: Penguin Books.

Pérez Garzón, J. S. (2003) 'State Nationalism: Cultural Nationalism and Political Alternatives', *Journal of Spanish Cultural Studies*, 4 (1): 47–64.

Perryman, M. (1999) *The Ingerland Factor: Home Truths from Football*, Edinburgh: Mainstream.

Pickering, M. (2001) *Stereotyping: The Politics of Representation*, New York: Palgrave Macmillan.

Poulton, E. (1999) 'Fighting Talk from the Press Corps', in M. Perryman (ed.) *The Ingerland Factor: Home Truths from Football*, Edinburgh: Mainstream.

Preston, P. (1990) *The Politics of Revenge*, London: Unwin Hyman.

Ramos Oliveira, A. (1946) *Politics, Economics and Men of Modern Spain, 1808–1946*, London: Victor Gollancz.

Ravenel, L. (1998) *La Géographie du football en France*, Paris: PUF.

Reid, G. (2000) *Football and War*, Wilmslow: Sigma Press.

Renan, E. (1882) *Qu'est-ce qu'une nation? Conférence faite en Sorbonne, le 11 mars 1882*, Paris: C. Lévy (repr. Paris: Imprimerie nationale 1996).

Rey, D. (2003) *La Corse et son football 1905–2000*, Ajaccio: Editions Albiana.

—— (2005) *Bastia–Eindhoven*. Available online at <http://www.wearefootball.org/un-jour-un-match/29/lire/bastia-eindhoven/> (accessed 14 October 2005).

Russell, D. (1997) *Football and the English*, Preston: Carnegie Publishing.

Saccomano, E. (ed.) (1998) *Larousse du football*, Paris: Larousse/Bordas.

SC Bastia (2005) Website. Available online at <http://www.sc-bastia.com> (accessed 29 June 2005).

Scruton, R. (2000) *England: An Elegy*, London: Pimlico.

Segurola (1999) *Fútbol y pasiones políticas*, Barcelona: Temas de debate.

Seidler, E. (1964) *Le Sport et la presse*, Paris: A. Colin.

Shaw, D. (1987) *Fútbol y franquismo*, Madrid: Alianza Editorial.

Sinet, V. (2000) *La Fabuleuse histoire du football corse*, Ajaccio: Editions Albiana.

Sobrequés i Callicó, J. (1991) *Un club al servei de Catalunya*, Barcelona: Editorial Labor.

Solé Tura, J. (1985) *Nacionalidades y nacionalismos en España*, Madrid: Alianza Editorial.

Tomlinson, A. (1999) *Globalisation and Culture*, Chicago: University of Chicago Press.

Tournon, P. (2000) 'The Right Man: Aimé Jacquet', in C. Rühn (ed.) *Le Foot: The Legends of French Football*, London: Abacus.

Vidacs, B. (2004) 'France in the Cameroonian Football Imagination', in G. Armstrong and R. Giulianotti (eds) *Football in Africa: Conflict, Conciliation and Community*, London: Palgrave.

Wagg, S. (ed.) (1995) *Giving the Game Away: Football, Culture and Politics on Five Continents*, Leicester: Leicester University Press.

Wahl, A. (1989) *Les Archives du football. Sport et société en France (1880–1980)*, Paris: Gallimard/Julliard.

—— (1999) 'Pour une histoire du jeu', in H. Hélal and P. Mignon (eds) *Football, jeu et société*, Paris: INSEP.

Walton, J. (2001) 'Football and Identities: England and Spain', in F. Caspitegui and J. Walton (eds) *Guerras danzadas. Fútbol e identidades locales y regionales en Europa*, Pamplona: EUNSA.

Walvin, J. (1994) *The People's Game*, Edinburgh: Mainstream.

Webdelcule (2006) Website. Available online at <http://www.webdelcule.com> (accessed 9 March 2006).

Wellings, B. (2002) 'Empire-Nation: National and Imperial Discourses in England', *Nations and Nationalism*, 8 (1): 95–109.

Winkler, W. (2005) 'Das Wunder von Bern', Goethe-Institut Guest Lecture, Manchester Metropolitan University, 3 November.

Wood, M. (2000) *In Search of England: Journeys into the English Past*, Berkeley, CA: University of California Press.

Wortmann, S. (dir.) (2003) *Das Wunder von Bern*, film, Soda Pictures Ltd.

Index